THE RETURN OF
JESUS IN EARLY
CHRISTIANITY

THE RETURN OF

JESUS IN EARLY

CHRISTIANITY

JOHN T. CARROLL

WITH

ALEXANDRA R. BROWN, CLAUDIA J. SETZER,
JEFFREY S. SIKER

HENDRICKSON
PUBLISHERS

© 2000 Hendrickson Publishers, Inc.
P. O. Box 3473
Peabody, Massachusetts 01961–3473

Printed in the United States of America

First Printing — October 2000

Scripture quotations from the New Revised Standard Version of the Bible are copyright © 1989 by the Division of Christian Education of the National Council of the Churches of Christ in the United States of America and are used by permission.

Library of Congress Cataloging-in-Publication Data

Carroll, John T., 1954–
    The return of Jesus in early Christianity / John T. Carroll;
  with Alexandra R. Brown, Claudia J. Setzer, and Jeffrey S. Siker.
    Includes bibliographical references and index.
    ISBN 1-56563-341-5
    1. Eschatology—Biblical teaching. 2. Second Advent—Biblical
  teaching. I. Title.
  BS680.E8 C37 2000
  236′.9—dc21   00-035091

CONTENTS

PREFACE

With the arrival of the year 2000, fascination with apocalyptic themes has grown exponentially, in both religious and secular arenas. There are some new elements in contemporary apocalyptic scenarios of the End—for example, the so-called Y2K or millennium bug that heightened fears of a computer-reliant generation—but for the most part speculations about the End are replaying old, familiar tunes. This study focuses on one crucial feature of such thinking within Christian circles, namely the expectation of the parousia, or "second coming," of Jesus. Why is it that some two thousand years after his first coming, many believers still fervently expect his return? What role do hopes associated with the parousia actually play within early Christian literature? What impact have such hopes (and fears!) had throughout Christian history? What should we do with them today? With perhaps a new sense of urgency, such questions are well worth asking at the dawn of a new millennium. They are the sorts of questions that underlie this study.

I am grateful to three colleagues and friends who agreed to write chapters for this volume: Alexandra Brown (ch. 2), Jeff Siker (ch. 5), and Claudia Setzer (ch. 6). Without their willingness to contribute, this book would not have been possible. I value greatly the friendships with each of them that preceded and then survived the collaborative project.

Chapter 3 and portions of the introduction and chapter 7 are based on my inaugural lecture as Harriet Robertson Fitts Memorial Professor of New Testament at Union–PSCE. I appreciate the support of President Louis Weeks and all my faculty colleagues on this occasion. I am grateful as well for the affirmation and keen insights of my students. A special word of thanks goes to my administrative assistant, Kathy Davis, whose grace and skill enabled me to keep the dean's office running smoothly even when I was distracted with the final stages of manuscript preparation; to Bill Brown, my co-editor at *Interpretation*, who assumed added editorial duties to allow me to finish the book; and to Kathy DuVall, former managing editor of the journal, whose extraordinary talent and good humor have been a continuing inspiration, and who prepared the indexes.

This study returns to a theme I first explored in my dissertation, and reminds me once again of the immense debt I owe to my teachers, above all to David Adams, Paul Meyer, Chris Beker, and John Gammie. I am grateful for what I have learned from them, and for their unfailing encouragement. But above all I thank my family—Cindy, Andrew, and Anna; Jim and Mildred; and Paul and Lenore—for the abiding love, understanding, and support that make life a delight.

The collaborating authors all wish to thank Patrick H. Alexander, who planted the seed that led to this book, and the entire editorial team at Hendrickson Publishers for their patience and expert assistance.

J. T. C.

CONTRIBUTORS

JOHN T. CARROLL *(Ph.D., Princeton Theological Seminary)*
Dean of the Theology Faculty and Harriett Robertson
Fitts Memorial Professor of New Testament, Union
Theological Seminary and Presbyterian School of
Christian Education, Richmond, Virginia.

ALEXANDRA R. BROWN *(Ph.D., Columbia University)*
Associate Professor of Religion, Washington and Lee
University, Lexington, Virginia.

CLAUDIA J. SETZER *(Ph.D., Columbia University)*
Associate Professor of Religious Studies, Manhattan
College, Riverdale, New York.

JEFFREY S. SIKER *(Ph.D., Princeton Theological Seminary)*
Professor of Theological Studies, Loyola Marymount
University, Los Angeles, California.

ABBREVIATIONS

I. GENERAL ABBREVIATIONS

B.C.E.	Before the Common Era (B.C.)
C.E.	Common Era (A.D.)
cf.	*confer*, compare
ch(s).	chapter(s)
ed(s).	edition, editor(s), edited by
e.g.	*exempli gratia*, for example
esp.	especially
ET	English Translation
i.e.	*id est*, that is
n(n).	note(s)
n.s.	new series
LXX	Septuagint
NT	New Testament
orig.	original
OT	Old Testament
rev.	revised, revised by
trans.	translated by
vol(s).	volume(s)
v(v).	verse(s)
par.	parallel passage(s) in (an)other gospel(s)

II. ANCIENT LITERATURE

A. Biblical Books with the Apocrypha

Gen	Genesis
Exod	Exodus
Lev	Leviticus
Num	Numbers
Deut	Deuteronomy
Josh	Joshua
Judg	Judges
Ruth	Ruth
1–2 Sam	1–2 Samuel
1–2 Kgs	1–2 Kings
Job	Job
Ps(s)	Psalm(s)
Prov	Proverbs
Eccl	Ecclesiastes
Isa	Isaiah
Jer	Jeremiah
Ezek	Ezekiel
Dan	Daniel
Hos	Hosea
Joel	Joel
Amos	Amos
Mic	Micah
Zeph	Zephaniah
Zech	Zechariah
Mal	Malachi
4 Ezra	4 Ezra
1–4 Macc	1–4 Maccabees
Sir	Sirach (Ecclesiasticus)
Tob	Tobit
Wis	Wisdom of Solomon
Matt	Matthew
Mark	Mark
Luke	Luke
John	John
Acts	Acts
Rom	Romans
1–2 Cor	1–2 Corinthians

Gal	Galatians
Eph	Ephesians
Phil	Philippians
Col	Colossians
1–2 Thess	1–2 Thessalonians
1–2 Tim	1–2 Timothy
Tit	Titus
Phlm	Philemon
Heb	Hebrews
Jas	James
1–2 Pet	1–2 Peter
1–3 John	1–3 John
Jude	Jude
Rev	Revelation

B. Jewish Pseudepigrapha

1 Enoch	*1 Enoch*
2 Bar.	*2 Baruch*
Apoc. Zeph.	*Apocalypse of Zephaniah*
Jub.	*Jubilees*
Pss. Sol.	*Psalms of Solomon*
Sib. Or.	*Sibylline Oracles*
T. 12 Pat.	*Testaments of the Twelve Patriarchs*
T. Benj.	*Testament of Benjamin*
T. Job	*Testament of Job*
T. Moses	*Testament of Moses*
T. Naph.	*Testament of Naphtali*

C. Early Christian Writings

Barn.	*Epistle of Barnabas*
1 Clem.	*1 Clement*
Ep. Apos.	*Epistula Apostolorum*
Eusebius	
Hist. eccl.	*Historia ecclesiastica*
Hippolytus	
Antichr.	*De antichristo*
Comm. Dan.	*Commentary on Daniel*

Irenaeus
   Haer.   *Adversus haereses*
Jerome
   Comm. Ezek. *Commentary on Ezekiel*
   Comm. Isa.   *Commentary on Isaiah*
Justin Martyr
   1, 2 Apol.   *Apology I, II*
   Dial.   *Dialogus cum Tryphone Judaeo*
Origen
   Comm. Matt. *Commentary on Matthew*
   Cels.   *Contra Celsum*
Tertullian
   An.   *De anima*
   Marc.   *Adversus Marcionem*
Other Writings
Gos. Philip   *Gospel of Philip*
Gos. Thom.   *Gospel of Thomas*

D. Dead Sea Scrolls

CD   Cairo text of the *Damascus Document*
1QM   *War Scroll*
1QS   *Rule of the Community* or *Manual of Discipline*
          from Qumran Cave 1

E. Rabbinic Literature

b.   Babylonian Talmud
Erub.   *Erubin*
ʾ*Abot R. Nat.* ʾ*Abot de Rabbi Nathan*

F. Other Ancient Authors and Writings

Cicero
   Nat. d.   *De natura deorum*
Epictetus
   Disc.   *Moral Discourses of Epictetus*
Josephus
   Ant.   *Jewish Antiquities*
   War   *Jewish War*

Lucretius
  R. nat.   *De rerum natura*
Philo
  Abr.   *De Abrahamo*
  Mos.   *De vita Mosis*
  Mut.   *De mutatione nominum*
  Post.   *De posteritate Caini*
  Praem.   *De praemiis et poenis*
  QG   *Quaestiones et solutiones in Genesin*
  Sac.   *De sacrificiis Abelis et Cain*
Plato
  Tim.   *Timaeus*
Seneca
  Nat.   *Naturales quaestiones*

III. MODERN LITERATURE

AB	Anchor Bible
ABD	*The Anchor Bible Dictionary.* Edited by David Noel Freedman
ABRL	The Anchor Bible Reference Library
ANF	*Ante-Nicene Fathers*
ANTC	Abingdon New Testament Commentary
Bib	*Biblica*
BTB	*Biblical Theology Bulletin*
BNTC	Black's New Testament Commentary
BWA(N)T	Beiträge zur Wissenschaft vom Alten (und Neuen) Testament
BZ	*Biblische Zeitschrift*
BZNW	Beihefte zur Zeitschrift für die Neutestamentliche Wissenschaft
CBQ	*Catholic Biblical Quarterly*
CEP	Contemporary Evangelical Perspectives
ConBNT	Coniectanea biblica, New Testament
CRINT	Compendia rerum iudaicarum ad Novum Testamentum
FF	Foundations and Facets
FRLANT	Forschungen zur Religion und Literatur des Alten und Neuen Testaments
GBS	Guides to Biblical Scholarship

HBT	*Horizons in Biblical Theology*
HTR	*Harvard Theological Review*
IBC	Interpretation: A Bible Commentary for Teaching and Preaching
IBT	Interpreting Biblical Texts
Int	*Interpretation*
IRT	Issues in Religion and Theology
JBL	*Journal of Biblical Literature*
JNES	*Journal of Near Eastern Studies*
JSNT	*Journal for the Study of the New Testament*
JSNTSup	Journal for the Study of the New Testament Supplement Series
LCBI	Literary Currents in Biblical Interpretation
LCL	Loeb Classical Library
NIB	*New Interpreter's Bible*
NICNT	New International Commentary on the New Testament
NIGTC	New International Greek Testament Commentary
NovT	*Novum Testamentum*
NovTSup	Novum Testamentum, Supplements
NRSV	New Revised Standard Version
NTS	*New Testament Studies*
NTT	New Testament Theology
OBT	Overtures to Biblical Theology
PRSt	*Perspectives in Religious Studies*
RB	*Revue biblique*
RestQ	*Restoration Quarterly*
RSV	Revised Standard Version
SBLDS	Society of Biblical Literature Dissertation Series
SBLMS	Society of Biblical Literature Monograph Series
SBLSBS	Society of Biblical Literature Sources for Biblical Study
SBLSP	Society of Biblical Literature Seminar Papers
SBLSS	Society of Biblical Literature Semeia Series
SJLA	Studies in Judaism in Late Antiquity
SNTSMS	Society of New Testament Studies Monograph Series
SP	Sacra Pagina
SPOT	Studies on Personalities of the Old Testament
SSS	Special Studies Series

Str-B	H. Strack and P. Billerbeck, *Kommentar zum Neuen Testament aus Talmud und Midrasch*
TANZ	Texte und Arbeiten zum neutestamentlichen Zeitalter
TDNT	*Theological Dictionary of the New Testament.* Edited by Gerhard Kittel and Gerhard Friedrich
TI	Theological Inquiries
TPINTC	Trinity Press International New Testament Commentaries
TynBul	*Tyndale Bulletin*
USQR	*Union Seminary Quarterly Review*
VC	*Vigiliae christianae*
WBC	Word Bible Commentary
WTJ	*Westminster Theological Journal*
WUNT	Wissenschaftliche Untersuchungen zum Neuen Testament
ZNW	*Zeitschrift für die Neutestamentliche Wissenschaft*
ZSNT	Zacchaeus Studies: New Testament
ZST	*Zeitschrift für systematische Theologie*

INTRODUCTION

Eschatology has enjoyed a checkered career in the history of Christian theology. Certainly in the modern period, the belief that the world (or history) would soon end, and that the Messiah Jesus would return to deliver the faithful and judge God's enemies, has fallen into disfavor in many "enlightened" circles. Yet a remarkable synergy of forces, both religious and secular, was the catalyst for the resurgence of apocalyptic enthusiasm in the closing years of the twentieth century. Among many other factors, fear of ecological disaster, terror at the prospect of a catastrophic nuclear war, and, for some, a perceived prophetic significance in the reappearance of the state of Israel have all contributed to a heightened eschatological sensibility.

Fervent apocalyptic hope may go into hiding now and then, but study of two millennia of the church's history reveals that the intense eschatological consciousness we have witnessed at the turn of the century is not an aberration, novel though some of the details may be. Eschatology—that is, patterned beliefs, ideas, and expectations concerning the end of the world (or history)—has been a potent force in the construction of Christian theology from the very beginning.[1] Yet the forms and functions of eschatological teaching have been remarkably diverse. Confusion abounds, as anyone who attempts to teach a class on the book of Revelation knows well. At a time when interest in such questions is high, the aim of this book is to profile New Testament and other early Christian teaching about the parousia of Jesus and associated eschatological imagery. Although the study centers on the views expressed in the New Testament literature, valuable perspective is gained through consideration of the first-century Jewish context, as well as important later Christian developments.

The method of the study is primarily literary, employing close reading of the New Testament texts in their finished (canonical) form. These texts are located culturally and historically, however, and so matters of social and historical context will be considered as appropriate. The uses of history here are modest. My contributing authors and I do not presume to construct a systematic account of "the history of Christian eschatology" (an impossible task). The theological aims of the study are equally modest. No attempt is made to fashion a coherent, much less compelling, theology of last things for our day. As our analysis of the New Testament and other early Christian writings will show, the rich variety of ideas, hopes, and images resists system building.

The first chapter of the study sketches the ways in which the expectation of Jesus' parousia figures in the Synoptic Gospels (Mark, Matthew, and Luke) as well as the Acts of the Apostles. Each of these narratives, in its own way, comes to terms with an apparent delay in the promised consummation of history, yet each does so without relinquishing the conviction that Jesus will return in triumph in the near future. From the beginning,

---

[1] This is true even if we must reject exaggerated accounts of the development of Christian theology in which eschatology (particularly adaptations necessitated by the experience of parousia delay) is determinative. Perhaps the best example of such an approach is still that of M. Werner, *The Formation of Christian Dogma: An Historical Study of Its Problems* (ET; New York: Harper & Brothers, 1957). See further ch. 5 below.

eschatological hope proves to be adaptive and resilient. These stories summon reading communities to tenacious hope in the face of opposition, to bold mission activity, and to moral integrity in the time—of uncertain duration—that precedes the End.

In chapter 2, Alexandra Brown probes the teaching about the parousia in the Pauline Epistles, focusing her study on the seven letters of undisputed Pauline authorship (1 Thessalonians, 1 and 2 Corinthians, Philippians, Philemon, Galatians, and Romans). Brown holds that apocalyptic hope lies at the very heart of Paul's theology. She notes that Paul's eschatological teaching has been read "forensically," as if Paul were emphasizing the moral accountability of the person and community of faith on the "day" of judgment. Much more promising, however, is a "cosmological" reading of Paul's apocalyptic hope, which centers on the liberative activity of God for the whole of creation.

The Johannine literature claims attention in chapter 3. Three writings associated with the name "John" document the wide range of early Christian ideas about the parousia and about the future that God is fashioning. The Gospel of John presents a radical reinterpretation of conventional eschatological notions; for John the present, not the eschatological future, is the decisive moment, the time of "resurrection" life and of judgment, with a believing response to Jesus being the key. The first letter of John gives greater prominence to traditional eschatological formulations, and even contends that the Johannine community's own struggle with schism and deficient christological teaching is evidence that the end time is at hand: "antichrist" has already appeared in the guise of these schismatic teachers. With the Revelation of John, the pendulum swings even farther toward the future. The potent and evocative imagery of John's visions offers a counterintuitive reading of the world. Rome's time is short: the prophet points readers to the working out of divine justice against systems of domination and oppression; God's sovereign rule over all nations will soon become evident. The author, confident that Jesus will come soon, urges people of faith to stay the course, despite the intensifying clash between the claims of faith and the culture of the empire.

Chapter 4 turns to the "general epistles" and discovers in four quite different writings—1 Peter, James, Hebrews, and 2 Peter—significant common ground. Eschatological hope remains vitally important, even with the passing of time, and it is closely tied to the work of community formation. These authors seek to shape the moral life of the community by orienting faith toward the future coming of Jesus to deliver the faithful and judge evil. Images connected with the parousia, then, encourage persons in distress and adversity, but also lend urgency to moral appeals.

In chapter 5, Jeffrey S. Siker explores developments in Christian thinking about the parousia of Jesus during the second and third centuries. He finds evidence of a wide spectrum of eschatological views among the church's early theologians, a pattern that prevails in later centuries.

Chapter 6, by Claudia J. Setzer, situates early Christian notions of the Messiah's return in their first-century Jewish context. Examining Jewish reflections on the Old Testament figures Enoch and Elijah, as well as the "Righteous Teacher" of Qumran, casts light on the emergence of Christian beliefs that link the Messiah's resurrection and his future return.

Highlighting a few of the most interesting figures from the fourth century C.E. to the twenty-first, the final chapter addresses the continuing importance of eschatological hope, including the expectation of the second coming of Jesus. Even a cursory survey of Christian history reveals that, in part owing to the variety of New Testament images and perspectives on the End, ideas about the parousia and the consummation of history have assumed diverse forms. At the close of the chapter, I suggest reasons why Christian theology—even after twenty centuries of "parousia delay"—is irreducibly eschatological. I will contend that although biblical pictures of the glorious second coming of Jesus need not be understood literally, they must be taken seriously. God's work of creation and redemption continues in a broken world, and God's people participate in that divine project even as they await the full realization of the divine purposes for the world.

✠ ONE

THE PAROUSIA OF JESUS IN THE SYNOPTIC GOSPELS AND ACTS

Parables, meals, healings—all these are emblems of the sovereign rule of God in the public ministry of Jesus. So, according to the Synoptic Gospels, Jesus pointed his contemporaries to the realm of God, graciously inviting their participation, but also summoning them to lives of costly commitment and claiming them for God's work in the world. God's rule was not something to be awaited in the future but was even now exerting itself; forces opposed to God were on the run and God's people were experiencing liberation and empowerment for a life of radical service.

One could therefore both proclaim and practice in the present the life of the blessed future promised by God. Yet Israel's experience mirrored another reality as well. Roman domination of the Holy Land and Holy City was not touched in the least by Jesus' mighty deeds. Surely the crucifixion of Jesus—expression of the brutal, coercive power of Rome—put the lie to premature claims for the presence of God's mighty rule. And if the first followers of Jesus embody the possibilities of the new order being fashioned by God, what a fragile order it must be!

For all the signs of God's activity in Jesus' own life and words, in the end, one was still left waiting and hoping. Even the triumph of Easter left the agenda unfinished: Jesus may be installed in power by God's own side in heaven, but life on earth continues much as before. So he will come again to complete his mission, calling evil to account and gathering the faithful into God's eternal realm. This second coming, then, would differ dramatically from the first: he would come in power, in glory, and in triumph. None will escape his coming. The whole world—indeed, the whole universe—will take note.

Mark, Matthew, and Luke witness to this complex array of experiences, hopes, and adaptations of belief, yet each Gospel develops the theme in its own way. The task of this chapter will be to describe the patterns of parousia expectation in each of the Synoptics, beginning with the earliest (Mark) and concluding with Luke and its sequel (Acts).

THE GOSPEL OF MARK

The future beckons. God's mighty rule, with its promise of liberation and peace, is breaking into the world; time has nearly run its course. On this note of intense expectation, Mark's narrative begins. John the Baptizer, whom Jesus will later identify as Elijah, the end-time prophet of restoration (9:12–13), announces the coming of a stronger one who will baptize with the Holy Spirit (1:7–8). Jesus' very first words then mark the present as a time of fulfillment and decisive encounter with God. This is the gospel he proclaims in Galilee (1:14b): "The time (καιρός) is fulfilled, and God's reign has drawn near; repent, and believe in this good news" (1:15).

Jesus is that stronger one in whom the dominion of God begins to reclaim the world from the evil one's domination. Through exorcisms, he liberates those whom Satan has oppressed; the powerful enemy of God is now on the defensive (cf. 3:23–27). And the authority of the Son of humanity extends beyond these clashes with demons. He claims the divine prerogative to offer forgiveness (2:10), and expresses this authority both in acts of healing (2:1–12) and in fellowship at table (2:15–17). Not even time-honored restrictions on Sabbath conduct can keep him from mighty deeds of healing, for he, the Son of humanity, is "Lord of the Sabbath" (2:28). If we are to believe the confession of Peter and Jesus' own reply to the high priest's query, Jesus' ministry is the work of Israel's Messiah (8:29; 14:61–62). In the first "coming" of Jesus—to preach good news, summon sinners into God's household, and liberate the oppressed (1:38; 2:17; 10:45)—eyes of faith can discern the transformative work of the sovereign God.

Eyes of faith, however, are seldom in evidence, even among Jesus' closest followers: far easier to restore sight to the blind than to give spiritual discernment to the Twelve![1] That the disciples fail to grasp the "mystery of God's reign" opened up to them by Jesus (4:11) is neither surprising nor ultimately discrediting. The Messiah was not expected to encounter rejection, humiliation, and death on a cross. Death in God-forsaken disgrace, deserted by his most devoted followers—this was not to be the Messiah's vocation. The end of the story belies the confident declaration of fulfillment with which the narrative began. Evil is not so easily vanquished after all.

But of course the reader is not caught off guard by these developments. Jesus repeatedly alerts Mark's audience to his approaching fate, beginning with an implicit prophecy of his demise as early as 2:20 ("the bridegroom will be taken away"). The clues become increasingly obvious and specific after the conversation with disciples near Caesarea Philippi (8:31; 9:31; 10:32–34). Jesus is the Son of humanity precisely as one who

---

[1] The two healing scenes in which Jesus restores sight to blind men (8:22–26; 10:46–52) frame a section in which Jesus discloses his identity and destiny, but the disciples fail to comprehend either. On the negative portrayal of the disciples in Mark, see S. R. Garrett, *The Temptations of Jesus in Mark's Gospel* (Grand Rapids: Eerdmans, 1998), 69–82; R. M. Fowler, *Let the Reader Understand: Reader-Response Criticism and the Gospel of Mark* (Minneapolis: Fortress, 1991), 66–73; M. A. Tolbert, *Sowing the Gospel: Mark's World in Literary-Historical Perspective* (Minneapolis: Fortress, 1989), 176–230; V. K. Robbins, *Jesus the Teacher: A Socio-Rhetorical Interpretation of Mark* (Philadelphia: Fortress, 1984).

experiences suffering, rejection, and death; the eschatological glory fitting for the Son of humanity (e.g., Dan 7:13–14; *1 Enoch* 46) will have to wait. First comes crucifixion: ironically, this is his royal coronation.[2]

In pointing to his coming death, Jesus also anticipates his vindication by God through resurrection on the third day (8:31; 9:31; 10:34). The specificity of these predictions is matched by the mystery that enshrouds the event itself. After the Last Supper, extending these passion/resurrection predictions, Jesus speaks not only of his resurrection—after the "sheep" have been "scattered" (14:27, alluding to Zech 13:7)—but also of reunion with the disciples in Galilee (14:28). The young man at the empty tomb reminds the women disciples[3] of this promise: "But go, tell [Jesus'] disciples, and Peter, that he is going ahead of you to Galilee; there you will see him, as he told you" (16:7). Yet the narrative closes without relating any encounter with the risen Jesus. The last word of the Second Gospel is one of silence and mystery: fleeing the tomb in fear,[4] the women tell no one what they have witnessed.

The reader has good reason to believe that the promised reunion—and implied restoration of the disciples—did actually occur. After all, Jesus is a supremely reliable speaker in this gospel;[5] every verifiable prediction to this point in the story has been fulfilled.[6] And the reader is hearing the account of these

---

[2] See F. J. Matera, *Passion Narratives and Gospel Theologies: Interpreting the Synoptics through Their Passion Stories* (TI; New York: Paulist, 1986), 7–85; idem, *The Kingship of Jesus: Composition and Theology in Mark 15* (Chico, Calif.: Scholars Press, 1982); D. Senior, *The Passion of Jesus in the Gospel of Mark* (Wilmington, Del.: Glazier, 1984).

[3] The women show themselves to be authentic disciples, even if the term is not applied to them in Mark; they follow Jesus to the tomb, while the male disciples have fled.

[4] As the male disciples before them had fled the garden.

[5] Because his point of view squares with the "evaluative point of view of God," which is normative in this narrative. See J. D. Kingsbury, *The Christology of Mark's Gospel* (Philadelphia: Fortress, 1983), 47–50.

[6] Most notably Judas's betrayal, Peter's denial, and the "scattering" of the rest of the disciples; cf. D. H. Juel, *A Master of Surprise: Mark Interpreted* (Minneapolis: Fortress, 1994), 114–15.

events; the women must have ended their silence. Still, the story ends with only the tantalizing *promise* of reunion and restoration, and with one final sign of discipleship failure. The effect of this narrative "closure" is that anticipation of encounter in Galilee with the risen Lord and expectation of the parousia of Jesus converge. We are left awaiting Jesus' return to meet his restored community; since the Easter appearance goes unreported, the narrative's close points the reader ahead to the parousia. Not Easter but the still-future parousia is the time of fulfillment toward which faith strains. But what will happen when Jesus returns?

Mark's Gospel presents various images relating to the parousia, many of them concentrated in the eschatological discourse of chapter 13. This discourse, addressed privately to four disciples on the Mount of Olives opposite the temple, responds initially to the disciples' query, When will this magnificent temple's destruction, of which you have just spoken, happen? Throughout the speech, however, Jesus broadens the scope of his instruction to include the whole cosmos.

Concern with the timing not just of the temple's demise but of the End itself runs throughout Mark 13.[7] On the one hand, Jesus accents the imminence of these events, with such pictures as the Son of humanity (by implication) at the door (v. 29) and the claim that Jesus' generation will witness the End (v. 30; cf. 9:1). On the other hand, the discourse gives prominence to the motif of delay. The eschaton will not arrive immediately, but only after various events first occur. During the period leading up to the End, God's people will witness cosmic strife and earthquakes (vv. 7–8), and they will experience persecution (vv. 9, 11, 13), family strife (v. 12), and for those living in Judea, suffering

---

[7] On the interpretation of this discourse, and of Markan eschatology generally, see T. J. Geddert, *Watchwords: Mark 13 in Markan Eschatology* (JSNTSup 26; Sheffield: Sheffield Academic Press, 1989); G. R. Beasley-Murray, *Jesus and the Last Days: The Interpretation of the Olivet Discourse* (Peabody, Mass.: Hendrickson, 1993); V. Balabanski, *Eschatology in the Making: Mark, Matthew, and the Didache* (SNTSMS 97; Cambridge: Cambridge University Press, 1997), 55–100.

of unprecedented intensity (vv. 14–20). All the while, the community of disciples is charged with carrying the gospel to all nations in the time that stretches out before the End (v. 10). The parousia will *follow* this period of worldwide mission (v. 10) and unprecedented distress (vv. 24–25). Twice, Jesus also mentions deceivers who will bring confusion into the community with claims to be or to be able to identify the Messiah (vv. 5–6, 21–22). The parable at the discourse's close reinforces this theme of delay. Servants awaiting their master's return must perform their assigned tasks faithfully during his absence, because the time of the master's return is unknown (vv. 33–36). In the same way—despite all the specific information the discourse provides regarding the End and its timetable—Jesus insists that the timing of the End is known only to God (v. 32). The eschatological discourse, therefore, holds the imminence of the parousia and its delayed arrival in tensive balance. Jesus will surely come, and soon, but not immediately—and no one knows precisely when.

The parousia of Jesus will occur soon but cannot be predicted. The only posture that squares with such a belief is unwavering alertness and readiness. And this is precisely the approach Jesus commends in Mark 13. As a refrain throughout the last half of the discourse, the appeal to "be alert" or "stay awake" (vv. 23, 33, 35, 37) confronts the reader. This message is not confined to Jesus' immediate audience of Peter, James, John, and Andrew, but is emphatically addressed "to all" (v. 37). The entire community must remain ever vigilant.

Mark 13 shows considerable interest in the question, When will the parousia happen? As we have already begun to discover, however, other questions are of greater significance. What will happen when Jesus returns? And above all, what are we to do, and how are we to live, in the light of this hope? How do these images of the parousia and related end-time events work on the reader of Mark's Gospel?

In a passage laced with imagery borrowed from Old Testament prophetic oracles, Mark associates Jesus' future coming with cosmic portents affecting sun, moon, stars, and other heavenly forces (13:24–25).[8] In stark contrast to the hollow claims of messianic pretenders and other eschatological deceivers ("I am he" [13:6]; "Look! There's the Messiah!" [13:21]), the parousia will be accompanied by remarkable events no one will miss. The scale is grand and cosmic.

Three times in Mark, Jesus taps Daniel's vision of the Son of humanity (Dan 7:13–14) to portray his own future coming in glory (8:38), or with clouds and great power and glory (13:26; 14:62). As in Daniel 7, Mark assigns the parousia both negative and positive functions. Negatively, the majestic presentation of the Son of humanity renders judgment against evil; positively, it vindicates the Son of humanity (and with him, the chosen people), and it is the occasion for the gathering or constitution in power of the elect community of God's faithful.

After revealing (or rather, attempting to reveal) to the disciples his messianic destiny of suffering and rejection as the Son of humanity (8:31–33), Jesus warns the crowds as well that the call to follow him is a summons to a life of adversity and self-surrender (8:34–37). Despite the great peril and cost of discipleship, Jesus expects his followers to remain loyal. They are to hold firm in their public witness to him; otherwise, he (as the Son of humanity) will in turn repudiate them "when he comes in the glory of his Father with the holy angels" (8:38). Mark 9:1 shifts from the language of the coming of the Son of humanity to that of the coming of God's dominion. Jesus assures his audience that some of them will live to see that the reign of God has come "with power." The parousia is evidently a crucial element of the future expression of God's sovereign rule, with which it is so closely linked here. Like 13:30, then, this passage affirms the imminence of the eschatological appearing of Jesus—within a generation—and implies that it will bring vindication for the faithful, even as it calls to account those whose allegiance has wavered. The image of Jesus' final coming therefore supports this discourse's appeal for courageous, steadfast commitment to the path of discipleship.

---

[8] See Isa 13:10; 34:4; Ezek 32:7–8; Joel 2:10, 31; Amos 8:9.

Even more clearly, the parousia serves to vindicate (Jesus) and indict (his adversaries) in 14:62. Under interrogation by the high priest after his arrest, Jesus again turns to the vision of Daniel 7, this time in combination with the exaltation text of Ps 110:1. Not content to affirm his messianic status in reply to the high priest's query, Jesus embellishes: "[Y]ou will see the Son of humanity seated at the right hand of power, and coming with the clouds of heaven."[9] Jesus, the one about to be condemned to death, will soon be installed in power by God and, as an expression of that power, will return to turn the tables on his accusers. Once again, Jesus' future coming vindicates those who remain true to God in the face of suffering, and at the same time judges those who condemn him.

The end-time discourse of chapter 13 develops the positive aspect of the parousia. On the occasion of sustained and severe suffering for God's people, Jesus will come to deliver the saints. Dispatching heavenly messengers on the four winds, he gathers the chosen of God from even the most remote locations on earth. For all who persevere in faith and commitment to the ways of God, the final coming of Jesus means not condemnation but salvation. In the context of social crisis and intense suffering for one's faith, therefore, the parousia sustains hope and thereby undergirds persevering religious commitment on the part of a hard-pressed community. It may seem that deliverance will never come, but God is merciful and may be trusted to act on behalf of the faithful. Parousia hope challenges the wavering to stay the course, despite adversity, and it consoles and reassures the community still caught in the grip of oppression and suffering.

To summarize: how does expectation of Jesus' return work on Mark's reader? (1) It reinforces belief that Jesus—the apparently disconfirming evidence of the crucifixion notwithstand-

---

[9] See the discussion of this saying by D. Bock, "The Son of Man Seated at God's Right Hand and the Debate over Jesus' 'Blasphemy,' " in *Jesus of Nazareth: Lord and Christ. Essays on the Historical Jesus and New Testament Christology* (ed. J. B. Green and M. Turner; Grand Rapids: Eerdmans, 1994), 181–91.

ing—is the agent of divine salvation. (2) In association with the fearful prospect of end-time judgment, it holds the community accountable and warns how much is at stake in continuing faithful witness to the gospel. (3) It sustains hope in a community facing intense social pressures, and reassures them that hardship will soon fade and they will experience liberation for eternal life from a gracious God.

THE GOSPEL OF MATTHEW

Only in Matthew among the canonical Gospels does the word *parousia* (παρουσία) appear (see 24:3, 27, 37, 39), a detail that suggests the cardinal importance of Jesus' future coming—and of the end-time events generally—in this narrative. Yet it is not Jesus' return but above all else imagery relating to eschatological judgment that dominates the apocalyptic vision of Matthew.

Parousia and Matthew's Narrative: Literary Features

Although the structure of this narrative has been described in various ways, the contribution of Jesus' major discourses to the structure and thematic coherence of Matthew is widely recognized and can scarcely be overstated.[10] Eschatological images and themes are prominent in each of these six discourses, especially in their culminating sections.[11] The Sermon on the Mount

---

[10] For a recent discussion of the problem of Matthew's literary structure, see D. Senior, *Matthew* (IBT; Nashville: Abingdon, 1997), 24–32; cf. J. D. Kingsbury, *Matthew As Story* (2d ed.; Philadelphia: Fortress, 1988), 40–42; idem, *Matthew: Structure, Christology, Kingdom* (Philadelphia: Fortress, 1975), 1–39; D. R. A. Hare, *Matthew* (IBC; Louisville: John Knox, 1993), 1–2.

[11] A point made by D. Hagner, "Apocalyptic Motifs in the Gospel of Matthew: Continuity and Discontinuity," *HBT* 7 (1985): 63–68. Although Hagner (with most Matthean commentators) speaks of five discourses, the clear change of location and audience (just the disciples now) in 24:1 suggests that a new (sixth) discourse begins in ch. 24. On the coherence of chs. 23–25, see F. W. Burnett, *The Testament of Jesus*

(5:3–7:27) warns listeners that they must refrain from judging others, if they are to avoid being judged themselves (7:1). Hints of judgment are interspersed throughout the discourse (5:22, 29–30; 7:13), alongside the fearful prospect of exclusion from the company of those blessed by God (5:20; 7:21–23). The second discourse, in which Jesus authorizes and instructs his disciples for their mission (10:5–42), incorporates some of the material contained in Jesus' eschatological discourse in Mark 13 (see Matt 10:17–22—the rest appears in Matthew 24), and enriches it with further pictures of final judgment (10:15, 28, 33) and eschatological urgency: "… you will not come to the end of the cities of Israel before the Son of humanity comes" (10:23). So Matthew 10 places the church's mission, and the missionary context of opposition and persecution, in an eschatological frame. The parables of God's sovereign rule (13:3–50) cast the spotlight on the reality of eschatological judgment. For the present, God is patient with evil in the world, but in the end, separation of the just and the wicked is certain (vv. 36–43, 47–50). The ecclesial discourse (18:2–35) summons the community of disciples to the ideals of humility, mercy, and accountability, reinforcing these moral appeals with stern warnings of future judgment (vv. 8–9, 35). Jesus' indictment of the "scribes and Pharisees, hypocrites" (23:2–39) concludes on this note as well. For a grim history of violence against God's righteous ones, Jesus' contemporaries ("this generation") will pay the price. The Holy City and Holy Residence of God will from now on know desolation and divine absence (vv. 34–39). Naturally, the end-time discourse of chapters 24–25, with its fervent appeals for vigilance, readiness, and faithful service and its closing picture of final judgment of the nations, clinches a prominent concern of Jesus' public teaching in this gospel.[12]

Sophia: A Redaction-Critical Study of the Eschatological Discourse in Matthew (Washington, D.C.: University Press of America, 1981).

[12] For recent discussion of Matthean eschatology, see Balabanski, *Eschatology in the Making,* 24–54, 135–79; D. C. Sim, *Apocalyptic Eschatology in the Gospel of Matthew* (SNTSMS 88; Cambridge: Cambridge

It is fitting, therefore, that the risen Messiah's (and the gospel's) final words point ahead to the "close of the age" (28:20). Yet Matthew's story shows keen interest in what happens in the meantime; this is, in fact, the situation of the reader.[13] This situation presupposes the experience of delay in the completion of the divine agenda with Israel and with the world (e.g., 24:8, 14, 48; 25:1–30). And during this time of waiting, the community will encounter severe tests of its fidelity to its Lord. Even within the community of disciples, law keeping will be relaxed and love will "grow cold" (24:12). Only those who persevere in faith, those who remain faithful during this time of waiting before the Lord's return, will know the eternal blessing of heaven. Between resurrection and parousia, however, the community is not left to its own devices. It has a mission: to carry the teaching of the Messiah to all nations, making disciples everywhere (28:16–20). And in fulfilling this task, the community of disciples will be guided and empowered by the Messiah present among them (28:20, forming with 1:23 a frame around the entire story of Jesus: "God-present" in Emmanuel, 1:23; cf. 18:20; 25:40). One must be ever ready for the Messiah's second coming, but the Messiah who will come is the same one who has brought Israel's entire history to its goal (the point of the genealogy in 1:2–17), and whose death and resurrection have already inaugurated the eschatological era.[14]

University Press, 1996); B. Charette, *The Theme of Recompense in Matthew's Gospel* (JSNTSup 79; Sheffield: Sheffield Academic Press, 1992); D. E. Orton, *The Understanding Scribe: Matthew and the Apocalyptic Ideal* (JSNTSup 25; Sheffield: Sheffield Academic Press, 1989); note also the recent dissertations by J. Gibbs, " 'Let the Reader Understand': The Eschatological Discourse of Jesus in Matthew's Gospel" (Union Theological Seminary in Virginia, 1995), and K. Weber, "The Events of the End of the Age in Matthew" (Catholic University of America, 1994).

[13] See Kingsbury, *Matthew As Story*, 147–48.

[14] Especially evident in the apocalyptic signs of Matt 27:51–53. See J. T. Carroll and J. B. Green, *The Death of Jesus in Early Christianity* (Peabody, Mass.: Hendrickson, 1995), 48–49; R. E. Brown, *The Death of the Messiah: From Gethsemane to the Grave: A Commentary on the Passion*

Parousia and History:
Matthew's Apocalyptic Perspective

From the very beginning, Matthew announces that the history of God's people has reached its goal: Messiah has come! (1:16–17). For the characters we meet in Matthew's story, it would not miss the mark to borrow a line from Paul: these are the ones "upon whom the ends of the ages have come" (1 Cor 10:11). Jesus distinguishes "this age" from "the age to come" (12:32), and in allegorical explanations of two parables about God's reign speaks of the "end of the age" (13:39–40, 49). With the recurring image of the harvest—a vivid image of the end of the age—Matthew indicates that the transition to the new age (cf. 19:28) is imminent (see 3:12; 9:37–38; 13:30; cf. 13:39).

John the Baptizer associates Jesus with this eschatological harvest (3:12). Jesus, in turn, identifies John as "Elijah who is to come" (11:14)—that is, as Jesus later instructs the disciples, the Elijah who "is coming and will restore all things" has already come (17:9–13). John's suffering and violent death prefigure the suffering and death of the Son of humanity. And that latter death is the pivot on which history turns. Borrowing imagery from the prophetic scriptures (Ezek 37:7, 12–13; Zech 14:4–5; Joel 2:10), Matthew paints Jesus' death in apocalyptic colors. Darkness covers the land (27:45), and when an earthquake attends the moment of death, the tombs are opened and "many saints" are resurrected (27:51–53). While this stunning set of events, narrated only by Matthew, anticipates and does not constitute the eschatological resurrection, such a rendering of the crucifixion highlights its eschatological significance. Much more prominent in this gospel, however, is the imagery of end-time judgment. Underlying and reinforcing this temporal dualism of the ages is a strident ethical dualism.

Narratives in the Four Gospels (2 vols.; New York: Doubleday, 1994), 2:1118–34; D. Senior, *The Passion of Jesus in the Gospel of Matthew* (Wilmington, Del.: Glazier, 1985), 143–49.

Parousia and Judgment

Warnings and depictions of eschatological judgment permeate Jesus' teaching in Matthew. Fundamentally, judgment means separation of the good and the bad, the righteous and the evil that are so thoroughly intertwined in this age—even within the community of disciples. As the parable of the wheat and the weeds makes clear (13:24–30, together with the allegorical exposition in vv. 36–43), Satan is the source of the world's evil, which often masquerades as good. The community must therefore exercise careful discernment, yet it is not charged with the responsibility of rooting out evil in the present; while it is to embody the highest ideals of justice and accountability (18:15–20), its primary charge is to seek out and restore the lost (18:10–14). In fact, even God patiently allows good and evil to coexist for the time being. Only at the eschaton will evil be definitively named and condemned. The Son of humanity, who as the sower of good seed—the children of God's realm—is Satan's counterpart in the world's conflict (13:37–38), also serves as God's agent to administer judgment "at the end of the age." The Son of humanity will send his angels, and they will remove evil from the midst of the righteous (13:41). A furnace of fire awaits the wicked, while the righteous will enjoy the brilliant splendor of God's realm (vv. 42–43).

The parable about good and bad fish, for a time tossed together in the net but eventually separated on the shore (13:47–50), and the judgment scene of the sheep and the goats with which Jesus' teaching concludes (25:31–46) return to the theme of eschatological judgment as separation.[15] If we take our cue from the picture of judgment in Matthew 25, the glorious parousia of the Son of humanity sets the stage for the judgment of the nations, and there will be some surprises. Whether commended for actions of love and mercy or called to account for neglecting the needy among them, people express surprise at their good (or

---

[15] In this connection one thinks also of the abrupt expulsion of the wedding guest who lacks appropriate attire (22:11–13).

bad) fortune. In their action, or in their inaction, they had not realized that in these "little ones" they actually encountered the
King/Judge himself.[16] The element of surprise in this passage
works with the motif of the intermixture of good and bad until
their eventual separation at the End to undergird the moral appeals of Jesus in Matthew. A community shaped by such teaching will be marked by humility and will never become self-
assured and complacent before the challenges to faithfulness
that life in this age presents.

Judgment involves an ultimate separation of good and bad
for which only God, through the agency of the Son of humanity,
is the arbiter. What are the criteria for judgment? A number of
images come into play:

1. Has one performed the will of God (7:21; 12:50)?

2. What kind of fruit does one produce (3:8, 10; 7:16, 20;
   12:33)?

3. Has one acknowledged Jesus (10:32–33)?[17]

4. Does one manifest the humility of a child, who lacks social status (18:3–4; cf. 19:14)?

5. Has one extended forgiveness to others before expecting
   to be the recipient of divine mercy (6:14–15; 18:35)?

---

[16] For recent discussion of the interpretation of this parable, see J.
P. Heil, "The Double Meaning of the Narrative of Universal Judgment in
Matthew 25.31–46," *JSNT* 68 (1998): 3–14; U. Luz, "The Final Judgment
(Matt 25:31–46): An Exercise in 'History of Influence' Exegesis," in *Treasures New and Old: Contributions to Matthean Studies* (ed. D. R. Bauer
and M. A. Powell; Atlanta: Scholars Press, 1996), 271–310, esp. 304–8.
Luz makes a strong case that the Matthean community belongs to the
πάντα τὰ ἔθνη and will be judged by the same criterion (305). Such a
reading of the parable accords well with Matthew's concern with the formation of this community's moral life.

[17] Contrast the Sanhedrin's hostile reception of Jesus in 26:57–68.
Since they have refused to acknowledge him, his glorious coming (v. 64)
can only mean trouble for his accusers.

6. Has one kept the commandments and, specifically, surrendered possessions (19:16–22)—that is, does the pattern of one's life display radical obedience to God?[18]

In order to withstand the eschatological judgment, the
community is called to a life that conforms to the will of God, disclosed in the Torah and the prophets and definitively expounded
by Jesus. He has taught the will of God, and at his parousia (as
Son of humanity) he "will repay everyone for what they have
done" (16:27).[19]

The penalties for failing to perform the will of God are
harsh. Matthew develops the judgment theme with severe images of torment and exclusion. One who fails to hear and heed
the teaching of Jesus is like a house that comes to ruin (7:26–27).
Persons who should have inherited God's realm and enjoyed the
company of the patriarchs are displaced from the table and find
themselves in darkness, where they "weep and gnash their
teeth" (8:11–12)—an ominous refrain that returns with varia-
tions in 13:42, 50; 22:13; 24:51; 25:30. Cities that did not repent
after witnessing the Messiah's acts of power and compassion
will fare worse "on the day of judgment" than Sodom (11:20–24).
A fiery furnace awaits evildoers at the eschaton (13:41–42,
49–50). In a parable about a slave who receives mercy but insists
on justice in dealing with another slave, Jesus warns that when
mercy fails, justice will be swift and severe (18:23–35). An unfor-
tunate wedding guest who lacks appropriate attire is bound and
thrown into the "outer darkness" (22:11–13). A slave who takes
advantage of the master's protracted absence and abuses other
slaves will be cut in pieces and consigned to a place of torment
"with the hypocrites" (24:48–51). Members of the wedding party
who are unprepared for the bridegroom's arrival will be excluded from the wedding feast (25:1–13). A cautious and fearful

---

[18] One might point also to 5:20, which offers as a condition of entry
into God's realm the living out of a righteousness surpassing that of
scribes and Pharisees. The antitheses (5:21–48) exemplify the higher
righteousness Jesus requires of his disciples.

[19] Including careless and malicious speech (5:22; 12:36–37).

slave who fails to invest a talent entrusted to his management is—no surprise here!—cast into the outer darkness among those who weep and gnash their teeth (25:30). And those who neglect the needy among "the least" are sent to eternal punishment in the form of a perpetual fire (25:41, 46).

Even this partial list makes the point. Matthew's readers learn that they are accountable for what they say and do, and if they prove unfaithful the consequences will be dire. Membership within the community of disciples is no guarantee. As in apocalyptic texts generally, pictures of end-time judgment in Matthew undergird the moral appeals advanced in the course of the narrative.[20] The community addressed by this gospel is to exemplify the highest ideals of righteous living. Underscoring with this haunting judgment imagery how much is at stake, this narrative will not let its audience off the hook. The parousia will be for the community—as for the rest of the world—a time for accounting. And that means anticipation of the parousia has as much to do with the community's present life as with its future.

The Parousia and the Community's Present

Responding Appropriately to the Experience of Delay

Although Jesus speaks in Matthew of the near approach of the parousia for his generation (10:23; 16:27–28; 24:34; cf. 23:36), the narrative addresses an audience that has experienced a delay in the fulfillment of the promised eschatological events. The delay motif is especially prominent in the eschatological discourse (chs. 24–25), but it is already implicit in the symbolism of the parable on wheat and weeds (13:24–30). Troubled by the appearance of tares, the slaves who work the field ask their master whether they should proceed at once to uproot these weeds

---

[20] J. J. Collins (*The Apocalyptic Imagination: An Introduction to the Jewish Matrix of Christianity* [New York: Crossroad, 1984], 32) contends that apocalyptic literature, by opening up a transcendent perspective on reality, typically serves the twin functions of consolation and exhortation. Matthew sharply accents the latter.

(v. 28). The owner of the field counsels patience, however; the weeds will be allowed to grow with the wheat until the harvest (vv. 29–30). Just so, the wicked will coexist with the righteous until the close of the age. At the parousia, evil will be rooted out of God's realm; for now, judgment—and the righteous—will have to wait.

The end-time discourse (chs. 24–25) develops the theme explicitly. The disciples ask Jesus a two-part question: (1) when will the temple's destruction occur, and (2) what signs will prefigure the parousia and the end of the age (24:3)? Jesus' response begins by applying the brakes. A period of international crisis and warfare, of earthquake and famine, does not signal the End but marks the onset of the eschatological distress that precedes it (vv. 6–8). The End will arrive only after the church's mission to all nations, which will also be a time of persecution and community strife (vv. 9–14). Still, at the close of this period, the parousia of the Son of humanity will be universal, unmistakable, and immediate—to the consternation of the nations but for the deliverance of the chosen (vv. 15–35).

This juxtaposition of delay and imminence sets the stage for the urgent appeals for vigilance in 24:36–25:30. Since the precise chronology of the end-time events is unknown, readers are admonished to be continually awake and alert, if they would avoid the fate of Noah's contemporaries (vv. 36–39). For that generation, the day of the flood began with business as usual, and because they were unaware and unprepared it ended in their destruction. The arrival of the Son of humanity will happen so suddenly that workers in the same field and women grinding grain together will be separated (vv. 40–41). Like a thief, the Son of humanity will come unexpectedly (vv. 42–44).

Jesus combines the motifs of delay and unexpected arrival in two parables drawn from household life (24:45–25:13). The first parabolic narrative (24:45–51) contrasts (1) a faithful and discerning (φρόνιμος) slave, who at his master's return (as usual) is carrying out his assigned duties, and (2) an evil slave, who at the realization of his master's delay (χρονίζει) parties and beats other slaves. When the κύριος ("master" or "Lord") does come, the unfaithful slave will be severely punished. The ensuing parable turns on a contrast between discerning (again, φρόνιμοι) and foolish young women (25:1–13). When a bride-groom delays (χρονίζοντος) on his way to the wedding banquet, the five bridesmaids who come prepared with an ample supply of lamp oil are privileged to enter, while the door is shut on the five who did not consider the possibility of delay and so were un-prepared. Verse 13 drives home the point for Matthew's commu-nity of readers: "So be alert, for you do not know the day or the hour." Their Lord may well delay, and they do not know the chronology of the parousia, but if they remain vigilant they will be ready for his glorious return.

How should the community of readers respond to the expe-rience of delay? The importance of constant vigilance and readi-ness is clear from the materials we have treated so far, but so too is the summons to faithfulness. During a time of waiting, the household slave or the member of the wedding party is to per-form the task allotted to him or her. The parable of the talents further develops this theme: a wealthy master's lengthy delay tests the faithful service of three slaves (25:14–30). Only those slaves who take the risk of investing their master's money and produce a profit receive commendation and reward. The one slave who, immobilized by fear, simply buries the talent en-trusted to him is branded "evil" and consigned to the outer dark-ness. The Matthean community will not doubt that they too must produce a return on the wealth—including above all the mes-sage of God's reign and the teaching of Jesus—that has been en-trusted to them.

If the culminating parabolic scene in the chapter—the judg-ment of the nations (25:31–46)—is to be read as a universal judg-ment scene that includes the disciples among "all the nations,"[21] then this passage, too, reinforces the connection between escha-tological judgment at the parousia and the community's faithful performance of the will of God. In this case, it is the active ex-pression of love and mercy toward the needy "least ones" that

---

[21] So, e.g., Heil, "Double Meaning."

makes all the difference. During the time that stretches out before the Lord's return, the community must extend hospitality and compassionate care to those in need.[22]

Present Crisis and Threats to Community:
Solidarity and Faithfulness

Faithfully serving God will not come easily during the time that stretches out between the Messiah's resurrection and his parousia. Jesus warns that dissension within the church and conflict with outsiders will seriously threaten community solidarity and fidelity. The ecclesial discourse (ch. 18) pictures a community in which grievances may go unresolved, requiring the expulsion of some members (vv. 15–17).[23] And the eschatological discourse (chs. 24–25) anticipates a period of such intense and frequent persecution that many within the community will turn against their brothers and sisters in faith. Matthew's church will know acts of betrayal, the confusing claims of false

---

[22] For some scholars, the needy "least ones" with whom the king identifies are the disciples—or, more specifically, the community's missionaries. The message would therefore be that the rest of the world will be judged on the basis of their treatment of the disciples (missionaries). The passage, on this view, consoles a community undergoing adversity in the course of its mission. See, most recently, Hare, *Matthew*, 288–92; G. Stanton, *A Gospel for a New People* (Edinburgh: T&T Clark, 1992), 207–32; D. J. Harrington, *The Gospel of Matthew* (SP 1; Collegeville, Minn.: Liturgical Press, 1991), 357–60. Nevertheless, the parenetic thrust of the end-time discourse as a whole, with the continuity between its picture of final judgment as separation and earlier examples of such judgment extending to the community of disciples, supports the argument that the disciples are judged here along with the rest of the nations. Unlike the rest of the nations that fail to bear fruit, however, they can prove to be a nation (ἔθνος) that produces fruit (21:43).

[23] Given the roles played by "Gentiles and toll collectors" in Matthew, ironically, those expelled—now as outsiders ("a Gentile and a toll collector," v. 17)—become the target of the community's mercy and mission. Sim (*Apocalyptic Eschatology*) sharply exaggerates the anti-Gentile animus of Matthew. His treatment of Matthean eschatology emphasizes the element of group solidarity and social control (esp. 235–41).

prophets, and the dissolution of communal norms (ἀνομία [*anomia*], "lawlessness," 24:9–12). Jesus effectively captures the social crisis that will beset Matthew's church with this disturbing image: "[T]he love of many will grow cold" (24:12).

These haunting images near the close of Jesus' public teaching reinforce the picture that the mission discourse (ch. 10) had already painted of the disciples' mission as "sheep [sent] into the midst of wolves" (v. 16). Interrogation and physical abuse before synagogue and town council (vv. 17–20), family division and betrayal (v. 21), widespread animosity and rejection (vv. 22–23)—this is the character of the disciples' mission on behalf of a messiah who was likewise rejected as an agent of evil (vv. 24–25). If the Matthean church is to remain true to its calling as it awaits deliverance at the triumphant return of its Lord, it has its work cut out for it.

The Church in Mission to Israel and to the Nations

"But the one who endures to the end will be saved" (10:22; the promise reappears in 24:13): the perseverance of which Jesus speaks includes persistence in mission activity in the face of opposition and persecution. In the course of his own ministry among the lost in Israel, Jesus initially directs his followers to heal and proclaim God's reign among the "lost sheep of the house of Israel," bypassing Gentile and Samaritan alike (10:5–6; cf. 15:24). This mission among the towns of Israel—in the face of adversity and persecution—would not be completed before the parousia of the Son of humanity (10:23).

Yet in the narrative's impressive culminating scene, the risen Jesus broadens—indeed, universalizes—the scope of the disciples' mission. Now they are sent to "all nations" to make disciples, to baptize, and to teach (28:19–20a).[24] They do so confident that they are not on their own; the presence of the risen

---

[24] Some understand πάντα τὰ ἔθνη to mean "all Gentiles," excluding Jews (e.g., the scholars mentioned in n. 22 above). It seems much more likely that, as in the earlier judgment scene (25:32), the expression means "all nations," including Gentiles and Jews.

Lord sustains them for as long as their mission may last, until the close of the age (28:20b). Even though this last scene in the narrative appears to mute the earlier expectation of an imminent parousia before the close of the mission to Israel (10:23), the last words of the gospel—"until the close of the age"—reinforce the message that despite the passage of time and the obvious reality of a delay in Jesus' return, Matthew's community conducts its mission to Israel and to the world in the shadow of the End.

Effects of Parousia Imagery in Matthew: One Reader's Reflection

The parousia of Jesus is closely tied to the pivotal Matthean theme of eschatological judgment. With these images of the future toward which the community strains, the teaching of Jesus in this gospel clearly aims to motivate readers to lead lives that express obedience, justice, and mercy. One must hear and then put into practice the wise teachings of the Messiah Jesus. Confronted over and over again by glimpses of the contrasting eschatological destinies that await the just and the wicked, readers get the point that much is at stake in the community's response to the treasure that has been entrusted to it.

A reader today will likely struggle with the imagery the narrative employs, and will come to acknowledge its limitations even while affirming the fundamental values of justice and mercy Matthew seeks to promote. Be merciful, or face eternal torment! Act generously and compassionately toward others, or you will be cut off from the company of heaven! How effectively do threats like this support the appeal to show mercy? If Matthew's first readers were not troubled with such questions, they do give many a modern reader pause. And yet we may readily affirm Matthew's insistence on the divine commitment to justice— with all that means for our own commitment to justice. It matters how we live, how we respond to divine grace. The gospel is only heard—really heard—when it springs to life in acts of love and mercy and faithful service. If threats of punishment fall on resistant ears today, Matthew also lures us toward its moral vision with more subtle and positive charms. Above all, there is the reality of divine graciousness, as modeled in Jesus' own life among toll collectors and sinners, pressing outward beyond the lost sheep in Israel's house and extending even to Gentiles. Having experienced undeserved mercy, one cannot but be impelled to extend mercy also to others. And then comes the surprising discovery: in serving others out of love one is in fact serving the sovereign God before whom nations, history, and time itself bow in reverence (25:31–46).

THE GOSPEL OF LUKE

Matthew and, to a lesser degree, Mark both enable readers to come to terms with the experience of delay. Despite the delay in God's deliverance of the faithful and in Jesus' promised return, hope directed toward these eschatological events is reaffirmed. They will happen in the near future, and the community must live faithfully and vigilantly in preparation for the End. Luke's Gospel charts a similar course, addressing with even greater clarity the problem of delayed fulfillment. At the same time, Luke throws the spotlight on the presence of salvation in the public ministry of Jesus and—already by anticipation in the gospel and by narration in its sequel, Acts—on the extension of God's saving work to all people.

Jesus Embodies Salvation for the People of God

From its opening lines, the Gospel of Luke celebrates the fulfillment of God's saving purposes. This narrative, according to the preface, concerns "the things that have been fulfilled among us" (1:1), and the story begins by recalling ancient promises of deliverance and blessing for Israel. These promises, given ages before to Abraham (1:55, 73), to David (1:32), and to all the people through the prophets (1:55, 70–72)—promises long deferred and seemingly long forgotten—will now be honored by God. John will ready the nation for the deliverance the Messiah will bring, and Jesus will embody divine salvation for the people, though in ways that surprise, astonish, and even provoke many within Israel.

The air is charged with expectancy as the story opens. Bards heavenly and human sing of the hope that the era of fulfillment has arrived. The angel Gabriel takes the voice away from an aging priest named Zechariah when he greets with incredulity the prophecy that he would have a son destined to take up Elijah's mantle (1:17–20). Gabriel then amazes a more trusting Mary with the news that she will give birth to a king who will sit on David's throne forever (1:31–33). Displaying greater discernment than her husband, Elizabeth acclaims as "Lord" the child Mary carries, and praises her believing reception of the word of promise (1:43, 45). This is Mary's cue, and she responds with a song of praise (1:46–55) that rings with echoes of Hannah's prayer (1 Sam 2:1–10). God's honoring of the young peasant girl signals a sweeping program of reversal that will succor Israel by disenfranchising the powerful and empowering the powerless.[25] At the birth and naming of John, even Zechariah finds his voice (1:68–79) and joins the chorus singing praise to God, who has acted to bring salvation to Israel—liberation from enemies by the hand of a deliverer from David's line (1:69, 71, 74), but also, with a nod to the adult John's message, forgiveness of sins (1:77).[26] When an angelic herald directs a band of shepherds to

---

[25] The aorist tenses throughout Mary's song point with prophetic confidence to the accomplishment of events that are actually still in prospect. Yet, as exemplified already in an act of benevolence toward Mary, God's work of salvation has actually begun.

[26] R. C. Tannehill (e.g., "Israel in Luke–Acts: A Tragic Story," *JBL* 104 [1985]: 69–85) contends that these promises of salvation for Israel— notably, deliverance from enemies—have a tragic character in Luke's narrative, which in the end shatters such hopes. In my view, the meaning of Israel's salvation is redefined as the accent shifts to the theme of repentance and forgiveness and the horizon extends to embrace Gentiles. The apparent shattering of hopes (e.g., 24:21) points to the need for a new perspective on Israel's salvation. On Luke's development of the theme of salvation, see J. B. Green, *The Theology of the Gospel of Luke* (NTT; Cambridge: Cambridge University Press, 1995), 22–101; cf. idem, *The Gospel of Luke* (NICNT; Grand Rapids: Eerdmans, 1997); idem, " 'Salvation to the End of the Earth' (Acts 13:47): God as Saviour in the Acts of the Apostles," in *Witness to the Gospel: The Theology of Acts*

the newborn Savior, who is Messiah and Lord (2:10–11), this announcement recapitulates for the reader the bold claims and promises expressed by inspired speakers in chapter 1.

Israel's salvation is finally on the horizon; the era of fulfillment has dawned. As the story unfolds, however, blessing will not be confined to the Jewish people. Ironically, the prophetic voice that first anticipates the incorporation of Gentiles into Israel's salvation[27] belongs to a pious old man who has spent a lifetime awaiting "the consolation of Israel" (2:25), and the scene for this disclosure is the temple at Jerusalem (2:25–35). Simeon, holding the infant Jesus in his arms, has indeed glimpsed the salvation from God (v. 30) that means glory for Israel (v. 32b). Yet revelation will illumine also the Gentiles (v. 32a), and since some within Israel will resist the agent of divine deliverance, this child will cause "the fall . . . of many in Israel" (vv. 34–35). Simeon's oracle about the "fall and rising of many" recalls the Magnificat's picture of the divine program of reversal, which elevates the lowly and demotes the mighty (1:51–53). This pattern of reversal dominates the narrative of Jesus' ministry: rich and poor, powerful and powerless, righteous and sinner exchange places. When they encounter Israel's Savior, some fall and others are raised up. And resistance begins at Jesus' very first stop, when before a hometown crowd he links his own care for the marginalized (4:18–21) to the favor God had extended to Gentiles through the prophets Elijah and Elisha (4:25–27).

The opening words of John the Baptizer pick up the theme of Gentile inclusion within the salvation promised by God. Quoting Isaiah, John draws all humanity ("all flesh") into the arena of God's salvation (3:4–6, citing Isa 40:3–5).[28] Even though Jesus addresses his ministry almost entirely to the Jewish people,

---

(ed. I. H. Marshall and D. Peterson; Grand Rapids: Eerdmans, 1998), 83–106.

[27] Cf. also the hint given by the genealogy, which traces Jesus' roots all the way back to Adam (3:23–38).

[28] Only Luke extends the Baptizer's quotation from Isaiah 40 to include the line "all flesh will see God's salvation."

these signals of Gentile participation in Israel's salvation early in the narrative are reinforced explicitly in Jesus' response to the centurion's faith (7:1–10) and implicitly in the healing of the Gerasene demoniac (8:26–39).[29] Jesus' final words in the gospel then show the disciples that Scripture impels them to take the message of repentance and forgiveness to all nations (24:46–47). Returning to the birth narrative, one then realizes that the juxtaposition of Augustus as the emperor of "all the world" (the census in 2:1) and the newborn Jesus as the "Savior" (2:11) intimates that the salvation he brings extends not only to Israel but also to the whole world.

With the births of John and Jesus, salvation from God has burst into Israel's history; this is the era of fulfillment of ancient promises to the people. Nevertheless, the work of forming a people who will participate in that salvation continues through the narrative of Acts and beyond it, until the parousia. The same pattern of present fulfillment coupled with future completion is suggested by two other images, the Holy Spirit and the reign of God. One of the indicators that the heralds of salvation in Luke 1–2 are reliable speakers who give voice to the purposes of God is the frequent ascription of their speech to the inspiration of God's Spirit. The Spirit prompts the words of Elizabeth (1:41), Zechariah (1:67), and Simeon (2:25, 27). Moreover, John (1:15), Mary (1:35), and Jesus (1:35; 3:16, 22; 4:1, 14, 18; 10:21) are all associated with the activity of God's Spirit. In fact, the narrator emphatically portrays the beginning of Jesus' ministry under the powerful impulse of the Holy Spirit (baptism, 3:22; testing in the wilderness, 4:1; first teaching in Galilee, 4:14, 18). If the dramatic presence of the Spirit points to the arrival of the eschatological era— as Luke evidently reads Joel (Acts 2:16–21)—the story Luke tells concerns the final movement in God's symphony with Israel.[30]

---

[29] Jesus' positive remarks about Samaritans (10:30–37; 17:11–19) also anticipate the inclusion of Samaritans in the mission in Acts (8:4–25).

[30] For further discussion of Luke's eschatological perspective, see J. T. Carroll, *Response to the End of History: Eschatology and Situation in*

The motif of God's reign points in the same direction.[31] To discerning eyes, God's sovereign rule is in evidence in Jesus' activity. The exorcisms he performs demonstrate the vanquishing of evil and the powerful presence of God's realm (11:14–23): "If by the finger of God I cast out demons, then God's rule has come to you" (v. 20). Pharisees curious about the warning signs of the coming reign of God hear a similar message. Why should they be on the lookout for observable signs? The rule of God is already in their midst (ἐντὸς ὑμῶν, 17:21).[32] And when the penitent evildoer crucified with Jesus asks to be remembered in Jesus' (future) realm, he replies with the promise of paradise that very day (23:42–43). God's rule is already operative in Jesus' acts of mercy and power. Yet the agenda remains unfinished. Jesus may have witnessed Satan's fall from heaven (10:18)—emblematic of the evil one's defeat—but the prince of evil returns to orchestrate Jesus' death (22:3).[33] And the obvious fact of Roman oppression justifies the disciples' post-Easter query, "Is this the time when you will restore dominion to Israel?" (Acts 1:6). During the mission of the church "to the ends of the earth" (Acts 1:8), the exalted Jesus "sits at the right hand" of God, while his enemies are being subdued (Luke 20:42–43 and Acts 2:33–35, citing Ps 110:1; cf. Acts 7:55). God's sovereign rule has not yet been established in its fullness; it remains a matter of hope.

A Resistant Generation and the Offer of Repentance

Ancient promises fulfilled, a savior born for Israel and for the world, God's Spirit unleashed with end-time power, demonic forces routed, God's mighty rule pressing into history and re-

---

Luke–Acts (SBLDS 92; Atlanta: Scholars Press, 1988); J. B. Chance, *Jerusalem, the Temple, and the New Age in Luke–Acts* (Macon, Ga.: Mercer University Press, 1988); cf. J. Nolland, "Salvation-History and Eschatology," in Marshall and Peterson, *Witness to the Gospel*, 63–81.

[31] On the reign of God in Luke, see Carroll, *Response*, 80–87.

[32] On the interpretation of this text, see Carroll, *Response*, 79–80.

[33] On this text, see S. R. Garrett, *The Demise of the Devil: Magic and the Demonic in Luke's Writings* (Minneapolis: Fortress, 1989), 46–57.

drawing the maps of human society—all these images so prominent in the narrative advance the claim that Jesus' ministry
brings salvation to the people of God. Yet Jesus' contemporaries
("this generation") do not fully embrace the salvation he offers.
He summons a resistant generation to repentance, but the win-
dow of opportunity is of limited duration.

Jesus claims that the exorcisms he performs demonstrate
the approach of God's realm, which liberates persons oppressed
by evil powers. This claim is prompted, though, by his critics'
charge that his exorcisms betray an allegiance to the prince of
evil (11:15). With the haunting image of seven unclean spirits
taking the place of one that had been banished, the narrative—
Jesus—warns that in a world like ours even the gift of exorcism
can fail to set one free (11:24–26). The forces antagonistic to God
are potent indeed. Jesus goes on (11:29–32) to indict a sign-seek-
ing generation that demands convincing proof of divine com-
missioning but is unwilling either to listen (as the queen of the
South listened to Solomon) or to repent (as Nineveh repented in
response to Jonah's preaching). Such a generation is ripe for
judgment; in fact, it will be held accountable not only for its own
evil but for that of previous generations that had also martyred
God's righteous prophets (11:47–51).

Even the crowds that flock to Jesus to hear his teaching are
faulted for their failure to discern the significance of the time in
which they live. They are able to predict the weather on the basis
of their observation of the sky, but they are clueless when it
comes to the moment of eschatological decision that greets them
in the activity of Jesus (12:54–56). When Jesus later asserts the
presence of God's sovereign rule in the midst of his audience, he
is addressing Pharisees (17:20–21), whose resistance to Jesus'
ministry throughout the narrative suggests that they are unable
to perceive that divine activity.[34] Their final appearance in the

---

[34] See Carroll, *Response,* 76–80; idem, "Luke's Portrayal of the
Pharisees," *CBQ* 50 (1988): 604–21; J. A. Darr, *On Character Building:
The Reader and the Rhetoric of Characterization in Luke–Acts* (Louis-
ville: Westminster John Knox, 1992) 85–126.

narrative—demanding that Jesus silence the shouts of acclamation from crowds of his disciples as they enter Jerusalem—confirms this impression (19:39). Once again, Luke does not fault the Pharisees alone. Jesus has just told a parable to dampen the fervent eschatological expectation of the people—"they thought the reign of God would appear at once" (19:11)—that accompanied the approach to Jerusalem, and immediately followed his declaration of salvation "today" at the home of Zacchaeus (v. 9). This parable merges two plots: (1) a master calls servants to account for the service they have rendered in his absence; and (2) a king-designate deals with repudiation by his own citizens (19:12–27). Like this man who would be king, Jesus too will be rejected by his people and will be acclaimed king in a distant land (heaven), not in Jerusalem. He will return (at the parousia) to call his servants to account for the service they have performed while he has been away (exalted at the right hand of God). The parable of the pounds and throne claimant paints a vivid—and tragic—picture of the hostile reception Jesus receives from his contemporaries.

The Passion Narrative enacts this rejection that Jesus has expressed metaphorically in the parable. Despite their attraction to Jesus and their genuine interest in his teaching—an interest that posed a serious obstacle to the religious authorities who were plotting his demise (e.g., 19:47–48; 20:19; 22:2) —the Jewish public in Jerusalem in the end reject him and join their leaders in demanding his death (23:18–25).[35] This pattern of resistance and rejection is not the whole story, of course. There are many who embrace Jesus' offer of salvation—notably, the sick, sinners, and toll collectors. They gladly come to the feast other invited guests decline to attend (cf. 13:24–30; 14:15–24). Nevertheless, in the Lukan narrative, the generation of Jesus stands in need of repentance. The apostles in Acts will have ample reason to invite their listeners to repent (e.g., see Acts 2:38; 3:19; 5:31).

---

[35] A portrayal of the people reinforced by the speeches of Peter and Paul in Acts (2:36–38; 3:13–15, 17, 19; 5:30–31; 10:39; 13:27–29). See Carroll and Green, *Death of Jesus,* 77–79.

And repentance is a central theme in the Gospel (Luke 3:8; 5:32; 7:36–50; 15:7, 10, 17; 16:27–31; 19:1–10).

The call to repentance continues to ring out, but only for a time. Luke places the parable of the barren fig tree (13:6–9) as the culmination of a series of eschatological instructions that appeal for watchfulness (12:35–48), warn of divided households (vv. 49–53), challenge listeners to read the times the way they read the weather (vv. 54–56), and urgently commend initiatives of reconciliation and repentance so that listeners may avoid destructive judgment (12:57–13:5). In the parable an unfruitful tree on the verge of destruction receives a temporary reprieve when the gardener pleads with the owner of the land for one more year. This allegorical commentary on Israel's present circumstance suggests that while God may be patient, extending the opportunity for repentance and forgiveness through Jesus (and later through the apostles), God's wrathful judgment against the unjust and unfaithful will not be deflected much longer. The expansiveness of Jesus' mercy toward sinners does not nullify John's earlier call to repent in the face of imminent destruction, underscored with the vivid image of an ax poised to strike at the tree's roots (3:7–9, 17). The people receive one more chance to align themselves with the purposes of God—in Jesus' ministry and the mission of the apostles after Easter—but dare not presume upon the mercy of God.

The crucifixion scene dramatically portrays the opportunity and the peril that attend the call to repent. The religious leaders, soldiers, and one crucified criminal treat Jesus with contempt to the bitter end (23:35–37, 39). He saved others but cannot save himself. Nor, in the face of such implacable hostility, can he save them. Or can he? Luke introduces this unrelieved ridicule by recording Jesus' request that God forgive those who were killing him (23:34).[36] The apostolic invitation to repentance and a second chance in Acts will extend even to them.

---

[36] On the authenticity of this verse, see Carroll and Green, *Death of Jesus,* 71 n. 40.

Alongside the adamant refusal of some characters to re-pent, the crucifixion scene also pictures the blessing that awaits the penitent. The Jewish public mourn as Jesus goes to his death (among them the "daughters of Jerusalem," 23:27–28), express remorse as they return home afterwards (23:48), and do not join the mockers who heap verbal abuse upon Jesus (23:35). In large numbers, they will respond to the apostles' summons to repen-tance by joining this new community (e.g., Acts 2:37–42). More immediately and more dramatically, the penitent criminal who defends Jesus' honor and asks to be remembered in Jesus' future kingdom—an act of repentance, though the word is not used—receives assurance that he will enter the domain of the righteous that very day (23:43). At the point of death himself, he seizes the opportunity for deliverance; under the pressure of true repen-tance, the kingdom script is rewritten and paradise welcomes a sinner "today."

Delay and Persevering Faith: Eschatological Instruction

The prominence of such motifs as salvation, the Holy Spirit, repentance, and God's reign gives the Lukan narrative a strongly eschatological tenor. The present fulfillment and future comple-tion of end-time hopes are nicely balanced. In fact, Luke pres-ents eschatological instruction with care and considerable fi-nesse. Readers find proper orientation to the end time particu-larly in the discourses of Jesus, especially in 12:35–48; 17:20–18:8; 21:5–36. The problem posed by delay in the parousia of Jesus is all the more acute within the narrative because of its many signals that the present is the era of fulfillment, the time of salvation, the inauguration of God's eschatological reign. In Luke's Gospel Jesus addresses this concern directly and clearly.

Within a larger narrative unit in which Jesus is teaching the disciples (12:22–53), he commends the virtues of vigilance and faithfulness during the time preceding their master's return (vv. 35–48). Slaves waiting for their master to return from a wed-ding banquet—all night if necessary—will be rewarded if they stay awake and ready to open the door for him (vv. 35–38). How-ever long the wait, they must constantly be ready for immediate action (v. 35). The next parabolic image on prevention of burglary (vv. 39–40) emphasizes the element of uncertainty that is already implicit in the preceding verses. Verse 40 makes the crucial point: the coming of the Son of humanity will be no more predictable than a burglar's arrival, and one must therefore be ready at all times for Jesus' return.

Peter's question about the intended audience for this parabolic teaching (v. 41: "for us or for all?") then sets up a further parabolic narrative on slaves and their household tasks (vv. 42–48). Jesus poses a question of his own: Who will be entrusted the responsibility of supervising and caring for the household slaves? Jesus contrasts a trustworthy, discerning household manager and an abusive, intoxicated slave. What is the difference between these two slaves? One was performing his assigned duties at the time of his master's return (v. 43), while the other lived as if the delay in his master's return would be indefinite (v. 45). Their rewards are commensurate with the quality of their service. So far the reply to Peter's question has been indirect, as the parable portrays certain slaves charged with household management and the care of other slaves. Verses 47–48 then develop the theme. Of two slaves who fail to carry out their master's wishes, one who acts in ignorance will receive lighter punishment than one who willfully disregards the master. Jesus concludes with the observation that persons to whom more has been entrusted will be expected to produce more. The images throughout this passage suggest that some members of the community will be assigned greater responsibility. More will be expected of them. Yet all are to perform the tasks given them, and all are to be alert and ready at any time. So the answer to Peter's question—"for us or for all?"—is yes.

Luke 12:35–48 joins the motifs of the Lord's delayed return and his arrival at an unexpected hour. This pattern marks the extensive eschatological discourses in 17:22–18:8 and 21:5–36 as well. Luke introduces the first of these discourses with the exchange between Jesus and Pharisees on the signs of God's reign (17:20–21). Those who cannot perceive its operation in the present should not expect to see signs announcing its arrival in the

future. Verse 22, addressed to the disciples, signals a shift in perspective; now Jesus brings into the foreground the future and a
protracted period of waiting for the parousia. Twice he refers to
the days (plural) of the Son of humanity (vv. 22, 26), in analogy
to the days of Noah and Lot (vv. 26, 28). The parousia of Jesus
will come on "his day" (v. 24; cf. vv. 30–31), but only after a
lengthy period that includes the suffering and rejection of the
Son of humanity (v. 25). The path to glory passes through rejection and adversity.

Verses 26–29 set up two analogies:

(1) As in the days of Noah (v. 26a),
    so in the days of the Son of humanity (v. 26b)—
        while they were eating, drinking, and marrying . . . destruc-
        tion for all (v. 27).
(2) As in the days of Lot (v. 28a),
        while they were eating and drinking, buying and selling,
        planting and building . . . destruction for all (vv. 28b–29)—
    likewise on the day the Son of humanity is revealed (v. 30).

The eschatological crisis will resemble these catastrophes
seared in Israel's memory. Disaster swept away an entire generation (the flood) and an entire city (Sodom). Why? There is no
mention of the wickedness of the victims; rather, their absorp-
tion in the routine activities of life left them unprepared for the
destruction that struck so suddenly. Luke's audience is left to
conclude that the parousia will in the same way threaten the security of those who are preoccupied with life's routine affairs
and so are caught off guard. Once again, the experience of delay
and surprise at the unexpected onset of the End are both at play.
Corresponding to the emphatic "destroyed them all" that culmi-
nates the Noah and Lot elements (vv. 27, 29), a haunting image
closes chapter 17: "Where the corpse is, there the vultures will
gather" (v. 37). For those who are not prepared for the parousia,
its sudden occurrence means disaster.

The lesson is clear: one must always be prepared. This discourse also spells out the manner in which the Son of humanity
will appear. The parousia is not a matter of a specific location,
nor will it be an ambiguous event. It will be as unmistakable and

as universally (and suddenly) evident as a lightning flash that illumines the whole sky. In part, this depiction of the parousia gives a second answer to the Pharisees' query in v. 20. This connection is suggested by the way Luke stitches vv. 22–37 to vv. 20–21 through the repetition of "Look, here!" and "Look, there!" (though in inverse order). One need not seek out empirical signs of the coming of God's reign because it is already operative, though undetected by Jesus' listeners, and because there will be no missing and no mistaking—and therefore no escaping—the parousia with which God's realm comes to earth in its fullness.

Jesus' eschatological discourse to the disciples concludes on a practical note. The parable about a widow who perseveres until an unsympathetic judge grants her justice (18:2–5), together with the narrative frame Luke supplies (18:1, 6–8), brings eschatological instruction home to the community's life of faith and prayer. The narrator predisposes readers to hear in the parable an appeal for persevering prayer (v. 1). The woman models persistence that overcomes every obstacle to justice, including a judge who "has no fear of God and no respect for human beings"—even a widow (v. 4). Verses 6–8 employ a lesser-to-greater argument to convey the parable's message. If a corrupt judge will finally intervene to deliver justice, how much more can Luke's readers trust God to vindicate them—and without delay! Yet both the plot of the parable and the picture of the faithful crying out "day and night" (v. 7) counter any naïve expectation that God will immediately act to deliver the community of readers. Their prayers must continue through every ordeal, and their faith must endure. That such persevering faith will be a genuine achievement is clear from the disturbing rhetorical question with which the discourse ends: "Nevertheless, when the Son of humanity comes, will he find faith on earth?" In the difficult time that stretches out before the parousia, faith will be put to the test.

Prompted by the temple setting, in 21:5–36 Jesus links his future parousia to the traumas of history: the Roman siege against Jerusalem and the destruction of the temple in 70 C.E.

Despite the obvious indicators of disaster within this speech—
war, earthquake, famine, plague, and Jerusalem's desolation—
this discourse develops the parousia itself in more positive
terms. The discourse in 17:21–18:8 issues warnings against
being unprepared for the unexpected arrival of the Son of humanity (so building on the imagery of 12:35–48). There the tone
is ominous. Chapter 21 does not minimize the strife and suffering the end-time events will bring, but strikes a more reassuring
balance between menacing threat and the promise of deliverance. While summoning readers to enduring faithfulness and at
the same time inspiring steadfast hope, Jesus' temple discourse
also clearly describes the course of events that will lead from the
time of the speech through the Jewish rebellion and on to the deliverance of the faithful at the parousia.[37]

As in Mark and Matthew, the speech responds to a question of the disciples, but the setting and audience are markedly
different in Luke. The discourse is part of Jesus' public teaching within the temple, rather than private instruction set on the
Mount of Olives. Not a select group of disciples (Mark) or the
disciples in private (Matthew), but the disciples "in the hearing
of all the people" (Luke 20:45) receive this instruction. The eschatological discourse forms part of a larger narrative unit
(20:45–21:38) that is framed by references to "all the people" as
auditors of Jesus (20:45; 21:38).

When Jesus prophesies the temple's destruction, the disciples inquire when this event will occur and what signs will
precede it (21:7). The reply to this question about the temple
runs through v. 24. Jesus characterizes the era of strife and crisis
that will precede the siege against Jerusalem and its devastation
(vv. 8–19), and then depicts the fall of Jerusalem as an act of
judgment in fulfillment of scriptural prophecy (vv. 20–24). During this turbulent period leading up to the temple's destruction,
some will claim that the time (καιρός) is near, but they should
not be followed (v. 8). This is not the time of the End but the time

---

[37] For a redaction-critical analysis of Luke 21:5–36, see Carroll, *Response*, 103–19.

that precedes the End. This is a time of persecution and family schism, but also an opportunity for bearing witness in the assurance of divine empowerment and protection (vv. 12–19). Readers of Luke's second volume encounter example after example of this pattern.

In the last part of the speech Jesus presses beyond the desolation of Jerusalem to picture the eschatological events proper: the coming (again!) of God's realm, the parousia of the Son of humanity, and his activity as judge of humanity (vv. 25–36). Sometime after the fall of Jerusalem, when the era of Gentile domination has run its course, cosmic portents will signal the return of Jesus (the Son of humanity) in glory and power (vv. 24–28). There will be no mistaking—and no missing—these events. But fearsome as these phenomena may be, this is a time for consolation; the parousia means liberation ("redemption") for the faithful (v. 28).

From the temporal perspective of Jesus and his disciples within the story, the End appears to be delayed, requiring patient endurance. But in the later situation of Luke's community of readers, the temple's destruction is already a painful memory, and the period of witness and crisis prophesied by Jesus in the first half of the discourse now lies in the past. For such an audience, the parousia looms on the horizon, just as a tree in leaf signals the approach of summer (vv. 29–31).[38] There will be no escaping the end-time events, which will overtake all humanity (v. 35). The faithful, however, will at long last be delivered; therefore they are to pray to escape eschatological judgment—that is, to stand blameless before their heavenly judge (the Son of humanity, v. 36). Jesus issues one final appeal for unceasing vigilance: "Be alert at all times" (v. 36). The discourse closes with an explicit statement of the aims of this speech, and of Jesus' eschatological instruction throughout the gospel—to enable listeners to persevere in their faithful service of God and to emerge unscathed from

---

[38] For a sustained argument for this view of Lukan eschatology, see Carroll, *Response.*

final judgment. For them, the parousia will be an answer to prayer (cf. 18:6–8).

In the meantime, readers are called to keep faith and hope alive. Although the present is the era of Jerusalem's desolation, the expression "until the times of the Gentiles are fulfilled" (21:24) takes on new meaning, as the mission to the ends of the earth draws more and more Gentiles into the people of God (in Acts). Luke's God is the God of surprising reversals; history in the hands of such a God is laced with irony. And the deepest irony of all is the heavenly reign of the one who was rejected by the nation and crucified. He has been vindicated by God and installed in the seat of power, where he waits "from now on" (22:69) while his enemies on earth are vanquished (20:42–43). Meanwhile, his "name" and the dynamic presence of the Holy Spirit continue to direct and empower his followers until he returns to complete the work of salvation he has already begun.

THE ACTS OF THE APOSTLES

The language and imagery of eschatological hope become much less prominent in the Acts of the Apostles. The ending of the book—Paul preaching without hindrance from his mission headquarters under house arrest in Rome—opens onto an extended period of witness, particularly among Gentiles (28:17–31). There is no mention of the parousia of Jesus after chapter 3, although his role as eschatological judge does form the climax of Paul's appeal to his sophisticated audience in Athens (17:31). For the most part, the narrative betrays little concern with the return of Jesus in the future, highlighting instead the expansive mission of the church in the present. Luke celebrates the triumphant spread of the word despite every obstacle.

Acts begins, however, by diverting the attention of the apostles, and the reader, from the ascending Jesus to the returning Jesus: he will come back in the same way in which they see him now departing (1:9–11). Eschatological images remain important in the foundational mission speeches of chapters 2 and 3. While the challenges and successes of the church's early decades dominate the narrative, these opening chapters point forward to the future events that will bring Israel's story to closure.

The book of Acts begins, as the Gospel of Luke ends, with an ascension scene (Luke 24:50–53; Acts 1:9–11).[39] Both accounts are oriented toward the future, but while the end of Luke anticipates the empowerment of the disciples for their mission to the world, the Acts account points beyond the ascension to the parousia. Jesus' eschatological return will mirror his departure, according to the two men in white (vv. 10–11).[40] So why should the apostles stand staring into heaven? This rhetorical question posed by the two men—in concert with Jesus' answer to the query introducing this unit (v. 6: will Jesus now restore dominion to Israel?)—redirects attention from the future (parousia) to the present task entrusted to the apostles. The timetable of the End is God's business and not their concern (v. 7). Rather, they are to bear witness for him in Jerusalem, in Judea and Samaria, and to the whole world. During the period that stretches from ascension to parousia, while Jesus resides in heaven, the community of the faithful does not simply wait for his return. Energized by the Spirit he grants (2:33), they take the word of repentance and forgiveness to the ends of the earth. The proleptic mention of the parousia as Jesus ascends to heaven, therefore, instills in the apostles the confident hope that will free them for the mission that lies before them.

Immediately after the Pentecost descent of the Spirit, the mission commences. Peter finds himself speaking to a crowd of Judean and Jerusalem Jews representing many countries of origin. Appropriately, he builds his case for Jesus the Messiah by means of a dense web of Scripture quotations.[41] It is striking that

---

[39] Although the chronology differs: in Luke the ascension occurs on Easter day, while Acts places the event forty days later.

[40] E.g., each event is associated with a cloud (Luke 21:27; Acts 1:9), as is the transfiguration christophany (Luke 9:34–35).

[41] See Carroll, *Response,* 128–37; idem, "The Uses of Scripture in Acts," *SBLSP 1990* (ed. D. J. Lull; Atlanta: Scholars Press, 1990), 520–21; D. Juel, "Social Dimensions of Exegesis: The Use of Psalm 16 in Acts 2," *CBQ* 43 (1981): 543–56.

the first prophetic text cited, Joel 3:1–5 LXX (Acts 2:17–21), marks the Pentecost intervention of the Spirit as an explicitly eschato-logical phenomenon. God will pour out the Spirit "in the last days," a Lukan enrichment of the Joel passage. The Spirit will make visionaries of young and old alike, and will turn men and women into prophets. These scriptural prophecies are realized as the narrative progresses. With imagery reminiscent of Luke 21:25–27 (cf. 17:24, 29–30), however, vv. 19–20 anticipate the cosmic upheaval just before the parousia; this remains a matter of hope for the future even at the end of the narrative. This first step in the discourse closes by affirming the offer of salvation for all who call upon the name of the Lord (v. 21, citing Joel 3:5).

The balance of the sermon (2:22–36) proves that the Lord in whose name salvation resides is none other than the crucified and resurrected Jesus. He was put to death by the very persons Peter is addressing (vv. 23, 36), but God vindicated him by raising him from the dead (v. 24), thereby fulfilling the scriptural promise that the "holy one" whom David called Lord would not be abandoned to death but would be raised up to the right hand of God (vv. 25–35, quoting Pss 16:8–11; 110:1). From this position of honor and power in heaven, the risen Jesus has sent the Holy Spirit, whose effects prompted Peter to speak in the first place. In the exchange between Peter and his listeners that follows the speech, the offer of salvation for all (through repentance and forgiveness) is rehearsed one more time. The mission to the ends of the earth has begun, and the access to salvation that featured so prominently in Luke's narrative of Jesus' ministry continues in the preaching of the apostles. Acts ends on this same note: despite the mixed reception with which a Jewish audience in Rome greets Paul's message, he predicts with his last words in the story that Gentiles will hear (i.e., heed) "this salvation from God" (28:28). And as the curtain falls he is still preaching the message of Jesus and God's reign to all who will listen (vv. 30–31). This is the situation of Luke's community of readers. In the final chapter of Israel's history that has been inaugurated by Jesus' ministry, and by his resurrection, ascension, and pouring out of God's Spirit, the mission to all nations—in the shadow of the com-ing parousia—is in their hands.

Peter's second mission sermon continues to play the eschatological tune (3:12–26). The discourse is triggered by the healing of a lame man at the temple gate. The echoes of Isa 35:6 ("the lame shall leap") already suggest that the healing fulfills eschatological prophecy.[42] Peter, explaining the significance of the event to the amazed crowd that has gathered, further develops the eschatological import of what is happening. He begins to deflect credit for the healing miracle from himself (and John) to the "God of our ancestors" who has honored Jesus (3:12–13). But before explicitly attributing the healing to Jesus ("through faith in this name," v. 16), Peter pins responsibility for the death of God's "holy and righteous one" on his auditors (vv. 13–15). The effective rhetorical shaping of this part of the speech employs a chiastic form:

a God has glorified the servant Jesus,
　　b whom you handed over and rejected before Pilate (who
　　　had decided to release him).
　　b′ You rejected the righteous one in exchange for a murderer;
　　　you killed the author of life,
a′ whom God raised from the dead (and we are witnesses).

This narration sets up the point of the speech: the appeal to the listeners to repent. They opposed God's righteous one out of ignorance (v. 17; cf. Luke 23:34), but now have the opportunity to receive forgiveness (v. 19).

This appeal for repentance is embedded in a passage thick with eschatological imagery (vv. 17–26). Peter characterizes the Messiah's death as divinely purposed in fulfillment of scriptural

---

[42] On the interpretation of this healing, see D. Hamm, "Acts 3:1–10: The Healing of the Temple Beggar as Lukan Theology," *Bib* 67 (1986): 305–19; idem, "Acts 3:12–26: Peter's Speech and the Healing of the Man Born Lame," *PRSt* 11 (1984): 199–217. On the speeches of Acts as a whole, see M. L. Soards, *The Speeches in Acts: Their Content, Context, and Concerns* (Louisville: Westminster John Knox, 1994); cf. H. F. Bayer, "The Preaching of Peter in Acts," in Marshall and Peterson, *Witness to the Gospel*, 257–74.

prophecy (v. 18). He then announces as the goal and benefit of repentance the experience of "times of refreshing"—namely, the sending (again) of the Messiah Jesus (v. 20). Although he resides in heaven for the present, he will return when the time of the "restoring of all things," as declared by God through the prophets, has arrived.[43] This universal restoration encompasses the reconstruction of David's "house" through the Messiah's resurrection and the forming of a renewed people of God that incorporates Gentiles (15:14–18),[44] but presses beyond the mission Luke narrates to embrace the whole world. Thus as Paul later affirms before the cultured Athenians, God is the creator of all that is; all nations fall under God's sovereignty, "all people everywhere" must heed the summons to repent, and they will be held accountable by the righteous cosmic judge whom God has raised from the dead (17:24–31; cf. 14:15–16).

After mentioning God's universal restoration project, which is now underway but will be completed only in the eschatological future, Peter shows what is at stake for his listeners: their participation in God's covenant people (vv. 22–26). Just as Moses promised, God has raised up a prophet like Moses—raised up, that is, from the dead—whom the people must hear and heed if they are to remain within the people of God (vv. 22–23, citing Deut 18:15–20 and borrowing a phrase from Lev 23:29). Returning one more time to the theme of prophetic promises fulfilled (v. 24), Peter concludes the speech on a positive note. The aim of the divine activity he has been describing is to extend to "all families of the earth" the covenantal blessings promised so long ago to Abraham (vv. 25–26). To have a share in that divine blessing, the audience must turn away from evil—that is, repent. So the sermon underscores its rhetorical goal one final time.

After the rich eschatological materials in Acts 1–3, the story unfolds, for the most part, with the parousia nowhere in view.

---

[43] On the translation and interpretation of this difficult text, see Carroll, *Response,* 142–48; L. T. Johnson, *Acts* (SP 5; Collegeville, Minn.: Liturgical Press, 1992), 68–74.

[44] As James puts it, drawing upon Amos 9:11–12.

Yet if we take our cue from the eschatological teaching Jesus provided in the gospel, this is not a surprise. The apostles, and later, with their endorsement, Philip and Paul and others, are taking the invitation to God's salvation to the farthest reaches of the earth. This is the church's business in the period—of uncertain duration—before the parousia brings history to closure. Although the parousia is not a prominent motif in Acts, enough has been said at the commencement of the apostles' mission to the nations to remind the community of readers where they are in this grand story. The parousia will come, and may come in the very near future. But what matters in the meantime is that they faithfully and persistently carry out the mission that God has entrusted to them.

✦ TWO

PAUL AND THE PAROUSIA

by Alexandra R. Brown

The parousia of Christ is often conceived by readers of Paul's letters as the end point of a simple historical continuum moving from the past events of the crucifixion of Jesus and his resurrection to a future event, his return in glory and the accompanying general resurrection of all the dead to judgment. Such a reading is, indeed, supported by Paul's description of the coming of Christ "in the clouds" to those (including Paul) "who are left until the coming of the Lord" (1 Thess 4:13–18). Surely, there is forward motion in Paul's end-time theology; the world awaits the future coming of the Lord even as it celebrates and participates in his first coming. The present points to the future by which it will be completed.[1]

---

[1] Helmut Koester begins to complicate this picture when he notes that in 1 Thessalonians, which he sees as a utopian document pitted against Roman imperial eschatology, " 'the children of the day' or 'the children of light' in their 'work of faith, labor of love, and patience of hope' (1 Thess 1:3) are the architects of the new eschatological community in which the *future is becoming a present reality*" (italics mine). See H. Koester, "Imperial Ideology and Paul's Eschatology in 1 Thessalonians," in *Paul and Empire: Religion and Power in*

But a differently focused reading of the full corpus of Paul's letters—including the apparently noneschatological passages—reveals a concurrent and rather more complicated trajectory that takes its direction from Paul's uniquely apocalyptic vision, namely, one that moves from the divine future to the human present. Here we are led beyond the commonplace of the "already-not yet" tension everywhere present in Paul—the kingdom of God is both already present (e.g., 1 Cor 4:20; Rom 14:17) and yet to be fully manifested (1 Thess 2:12; 1 Cor 6:9–10; 15:24, 50; Gal 5:21)—as we attend to the ways in which the future reign of God is envisioned by Paul to be on the move towards the present, where it has already in Christ inaugurated cosmic warfare.[2] What he seems to anticipate at the return of Christ, his writings indicate, is the final overtaking of the "present evil age" (Gal 1:4) by the future and final triumph of God. Having already won cosmic victory through the death and resurrection of Jesus Christ, God will, at Christ's return, make that victory manifest to the whole creation, defeating the enemies of God and bringing their tyranny to an end. When all things are brought under subjection to God, then, at last, "God may be everything to everyone" (1 Cor 15:28). Although the present is a time of "struggle for the extension of God's rectifying justice into the whole world," that rectification is, in Paul's view, moving steadily toward and embracing human beings who are now "genuine actors in the struggle of history."[3]

Roman Imperial Society (ed. R. Horsley; Harrisburg, Pa.: Trinity Press International, 1997), 163, 166.

[2] For the argument that Paul envisions the "victorious march of God's gospel into the world (1:13–3:5)," see J. L. Martyn, *Galatians* (AB 33A; New York: Doubleday, 1997), 103. A similar theme is identified by J. Marcus in the Gospel of Mark, where "entering the *basileia* is not an autonomous human action that transfers the disciple into another world, but rather an incorporation of him into God's powerful invasion of *this* world" ("Entering into the Kingly Power of God," *JBL* 107 [1988]: 674).

[3] J. L. Martyn, "Leo Baeck's Reading of Paul," in *Theological Issues in the Letters of Paul* (Nashville: Abingdon, 1997), 63. To illustrate the struggle, Martyn cites 2 Cor 11:29 and 2 Cor 6:4–5. "The real cosmos, then, is not a harmony, but the scene of struggle. The arena in which we

The sequence of events in this message of liberation Paul preaches is given most explicitly in 1 Corinthians 15: first Christ's death and resurrection, and then his return, which will be accompanied by the general resurrection of believers, the defeat of the enemies, and the final subjection of all to God's rule. It is a critical feature of Paul's eschatological thinking, however, that what is coming (i.e., the final victory of God) is not arising now out of conditions of the present—as in some formulations Paul may have known (e.g., the eschatological dualism of the Essenes) by which, for example, law observance is a condition for the Lord's coming—but comes toward the present from the already sovereign reign of God. Spatial images serve us somewhat more adequately here.[4] The realm of God, already taking hold wherever the liberating gospel of that realm is heard, is steadily growing and will ultimately encompass the whole creation.[5]

For Paul there is a crucial difference between the two directions (mundane present to divine future versus divine future to mundane present) that distinguishes his apocalyptic theology from other eschatological expressions known to him and that explains where the parousia fits in his theological vision. For him, the hope whose fulfillment is promised—God's liberation of

---

now find ourselves is hotly contested territory. Individual battles are sometimes won and sometimes lost. . . . Finally, however, the results of individual battles do not constitute the ultimate issue. For, truly perceived, this apocalyptic war is a war whose outcome is not in question" (J. L. Martyn, "From Paul to Flannery O'Connor with the Power of Grace," in *Theological Issues,* 283).

[4]V. P. Furnish notes that in Paul's eschatology "the priority and sovereignty of God's power are expressed not only in the spatially conceived mythology of God's dwelling in 'heaven' (e.g., Rom 1:18; 1 Cor 15:47; Phil 2:10; 1 Thess 1:10) but also in the temporally conceived mythology of God's future triumph over all hostile powers (e.g., 1 Cor 15:20ff.). . . . this future is totally *God's* future, and it does not progress or develop from the past (which is man's)" (*Theology and Ethics in Paul* [Nashville: Abingdon, 1968], 214–15).

[5]For discussion of related ideas in the Gospel of Mark, see J. Marcus, "Kingly Power of God," 663–75.

the enslaved cosmos—has already, in effect, been cosmically accomplished in the events of the first advent, the cross and resurrection of Jesus. And yet the future parousia remains the locus of
human hope in the present; it is the promise of final liberation
from hostile powers that continue, despite their *actual* defeat at
the cross, to hold sway over human affairs. Lacking a firm expectation of the future parousia, believers are liable to the loss of
hope, courage, and conviction that threatens the embattled existence of those "upon whom the ends of the ages have come"
(1 Cor 10:11). This threat is most obvious in 1 Thessalonians,
where loss of hope (and notably *not* loss of faith or love: 3:6, 10)
is a primary issue. Here Paul, like a wise counselor, comforts and
exhorts his disheartened audience, by first validating (in recount-
ing his share in) their experience of suffering and struggle
against Satan's hindrance (2:17–20), and then drawing them with
their deceased loved ones into the image of the Lord's future
coming (4:13–5:10), a sequence designed to assure them of their
own future as a reunited community and ultimate victory over
death in the eschatological resurrection.[6] What is emphasized
here for the sake of a grieving community is the same animating
insight that drives Paul's letters generally, the insight that God's
power liberates human beings from the grasp of hostile forces.

The situation in 1 Thessalonians calls for an explicit picturing of end-time deliverance for believers in a way that is not repeated elsewhere in the letters (although in 1 Corinthians another situation elicits a somewhat similar pictorial rendering of
eschatological events). For this reason, a waning of Paul's interest in the parousia, or at least in its imminence, from early to late
in the letters is sometimes argued.[7] But the letters taken together

---

[6] In Koester's view, the issue discussed here is not a religious question ("Will there be a resurrection of the dead?") but a communal question ("Will the dead be united with us in order to meet the Lord when he
arrives?"). See Koester, "Imperial Ideology," 160. See also J. Holleman,
*Resurrection and Parousia: A Traditio-Historical Study of Paul's Escha-
tology in 1 Corinthians* (Leiden: Brill, 1996), 125.

[7] See J. C. Beker, *The Triumph of God: The Essence of Paul's
Thought* (trans. L. Stuckenbruck; Minneapolis: Fortress, 1990), 31. J.

and read with attention to Paul's pervasive apocalyptic perspective demonstrate that the parousia hope, whether imminent or distant, is fundamental to his theological vision, inextricable from his gospel, and pastorally operative even where it is not explicitly narrated.[8]

This theme is a variation, it will be recognized, on the theories of scholars who see Paul primarily as an apocalyptic thinker, notably E. Käsemann, J. L. Martyn, and J. C. Beker. Certainly the prominence of parousia-related language and ideas in Paul's letters builds a case for his apocalyptic orientation. Here, however, I will focus on the place of the parousia per se in Paul's writings by examining both how his apocalyptic perspective informs his shaping of parousia traditions and how these traditions in turn inform his practice in specific pastoral situations.

The first part briefly outlines the principal vocabulary and concepts associated with eschatological and apocalyptic ideas in Paul's writings. Part two then turns to the question, How did Paul arrive at the eschatological schema that posits the parousia as the locus of Christian hope in God's liberating power? Is it his own creation, forged in the heat of community conflict and crisis, or is it a piece of pre-Pauline Christian tradition that he shapes to his own purpose? In either case, are the units of the eschatological narrative derived from his Jewish eschatological expectations, or is Paul's scenario more adequately understood as an innovative response to information newly available to him from the Jesus tradition, or from his own apocalyptic encounter with Christ (Gal 1:12)? Part three shows how the parousia hope functions as the linchpin of Paul's pastoral response in situations of crisis in the early church.

Plevnik also holds that there is little evidence of a shift between 1 Thess 4:13–18 and 1 Cor 15:50–56 (in regard to the nearness of the parousia). What changes, rather, is the circumstance in which Paul articulates his parousia teaching (*Paul and the Parousia: An Exegetical and Theological Investigation* [Peabody, Mass.: Hendrickson, 1997], 279).

[8] For additional argument to this effect, see Plevnik, *Paul and the Parousia,* 275. Plevnik points to parousia expectation in 1 Thess 4:13–5:11; 1 Cor 1:8; 15:23–28, 50–56; 2 Cor 4:14; Phil 3:20–21; 4:5; Rom

THE TEXTS AND THE TERMS FOR THE COMING OF CHRIST AT THE END TIME

Explicit References to the Parousia, End Time, or Coming of Christ

Two passages in Paul's authentic letters[9] describe in extensive pictorial terms the eschatological appearance of Christ and its implications for believers: 1 Thess 4:13–5:10 and 1 Cor 15:22–28, 50–55. In addition, 2 Cor 5:1–10 briefly discusses the Christian hope of resurrection in a context which, by mentioning the judgment seat of Christ, implies the eschatological coming of Christ but does not mention the resurrection of Christ. The term parousia is used in association with Christ in 1 Thess 2:19; 3:13; 4:15 and 1 Cor 15:23 (and in the disputed 2 Thessalonians at 2:1, 8, 9). Elsewhere Paul refers to the end-time appearance of Christ without using the word parousia but rather by employing expressions already known in Jewish eschatological thought, e.g., the "day of the Lord" and the "day of Christ."

13:11–12. He cites similar conclusions by P. Hoffmann, *Die Toten in Christus: Eine religionsgeschichtliche und exegetische Untersuchung zur paulinischen Eschatologie* (Münster: Aschendorff, 1966), 326–29. In addition to the letters mentioned by Plevnik and Hoffmann, Galatians should be added, as will be argued in the present chapter.

[9] Here I will focus on the seven letters of undisputed authorship: 1 Thessalonians, 1 and 2 Corinthians, Philippians, Philemon, Galatians, and Romans. I will not consider 2 Thessalonians in this essay. It is generally accepted that the other deutero-Paulines (Colossians, Ephesians, and the Pastoral Epistles) reflect a more realized eschatology by which believers are, for example, "already raised up with Christ and seated with him in the heavenly places" (Eph 2:5–6). In this later development, the emphasis on an end-time parousia is, obviously, diminished. J. J. Collins observes that realized eschatology was not unknown in Jewish apocalyptic traditions: "the members of the Dead Sea sect believed that a turning point of history had come with the rise of their movement and that they were already living with the angels" (*The Apocalyptic Imagination: An Introduction to Jewish Apocalyptic Literature* [2d ed.; Grand Rapids: Eerdmans, 1998], 268).

Paul's Use of the Term *parousia*
and Other Related Terms

The term *parousia* (παρουσία) occurs frequently in Paul's writings, but slightly more often in a mundane sense to designate ordinary comings (such as his own to a particular place) than as a term referring to the Lord's coming.[10] There is no clear evidence in pre-Christian apocalyptic literature for the word's technical use to describe a coming eschatological figure.[11] Donfried and Koester have argued separately for the Hellenistic imperial context of Paul's parousia terminology. In 1 Thessalonians, it is argued, *parousia* is used in conscious opposition to imperial court language regarding the parousia (imperial visit) of an emperor, king, or dignitary. The political context is especially evident when the term is combined, as it is in 1 Thessalonians, with other politically resonant language such as ἀπάντησις, a term which describes the meeting of a dignitary about to visit a city, and κύριος (lord), a term applied to emperors from the time of Augustus on. Hence, Donfried argues that in the Hellenistic context of 1 Thessalonians, the term *parousia* takes on decidedly political overtones.[12] He finds corroborating evidence in Acts 17, where Paul and his associates are accused in Thessalonica of "acting against the decrees of Caesar" (Acts

---

[10] Paul uses the term six times for his own or his associates' coming (2 Cor 7:6, 7; 10:10; Phil 1:26; 2:12; 1 Cor 16:17) and five times for the coming of the Lord (Plevnik, *Paul and the Parousia*, 4).

[11] Koester ("Imperial Ideology," 158 n. 1) notes the "frustrated attempt of A. Oepke in the *TDNT* entry 'Parousia, pareimi' to establish such evidence" (*TDNT* 5: 861–65). For a helpful summary of the terms used in the LXX and other Jewish sources, see Plevnik, *Paul and the Parousia*, 5–6.

[12] See K. Donfried, "The Imperial Cults and Political Conflict in 1 Thessalonians," in Horsley, *Paul and Empire*, 217. He cites several sources for the technical uses of these terms. Among them, for parousia, G. Milligan, in *St. Paul's Epistles to the Thessalonians* (New York: Macmillan, n.d.); for ἀπάντησις, E. Best, *The First and Second Epistles to the Thessalonians* (BNTC; Peabody, Mass.: Hendrickson, 1972), 199; for κύριος, A. Deissmann, *Light from the Ancient East* (1927; repr. Peabody, Mass.: Hendrickson, 1995), 351–58.

17:7). Krentz, holding similarly that *parousia* enters Christian language in 1 Thessalonians by way of Hellenistic political usage, shows that the term is used more frequently in the politically charged 1 Thessalonians than elsewhere in the New Testament to describe Jesus' return (2:19; 3:13; 4:15; 5:23).[13]

There are pitfalls, however, in interpreting the parousia in relation to Hellenistic political concepts without adequate attention to Paul's apocalyptic perspective. E. Peterson's argument, for example, that Paul derives his meaning of "meeting" Christ in the air from the Hellenistic concept of ἀπάντησις—the meeting of the emperor by citizens who make their way toward him—is attractive on the surface but founders on the matter of agency.[14] For as J. Dupont argues in his critique of Peterson, the agency of the meeting (ἀπάντησις) and its direction in Paul is exactly the *opposite* of the Hellenistic imperial convention. In 1 Thess 4:17 the faithful are acted *upon:* they are taken up (ἁρπαγησόμεθα) by God and Christ, and do not make their way *toward* Christ (or God). While Paul may know such a technical imperial usage, he does not rely on its technical Hellenistic sense here unless he does so in a deliberate reversal of its usual meaning.[15]

Dupont finds a closer conceptual parallel to Paul's eschatological meeting language in the Septuagint rendering of the meeting of the people Israel with God in the Sinai theophany (Exod 19:10–18). There the meeting (συνάντησις) is initiated by God, and the faithful are brought to God (Exod 19:17). The fact that other apocalyptic writers make use of the Sinai theophany (e.g., *1 Enoch* 1:3–9) would seem to support Dupont's idea. We

---

[13] E. Krentz, "Great Expectations, Great Choices," in *The Christian Century* 113 (31, 30 October 1996): 1033.

[14] E. Peterson, "Die Einholung des Kyrios (1 Thess IV, 17)," *ZST* 7 (1930): 682–702, as cited in Plevnik, *Paul and the Parousia*, 6–10.

[15] Some scholars question Peterson's assessment of ἀπάντησις as a technical term. Like *parousia*, it is a term used frequently with nontechnical meaning. See J. Dupont, ΣΥΝ ΧΡΙΣΤΩΙ: *L'union avec le Christ suivant saint Paul* (Louvain: Nauwelaerts; Paris: Desclée de Brouwer, 1952), 168, cited in Plevnik, *Paul and the Parousia*, 8 n. 22, who gives an expansive treatment of the scholarly exchange (7–10).

are further instructed by J. J. Collins, who sees in *1 Enoch* 2–5 a certain relativizing of the Sinai theophany. By placing the newly revealed apocalyptic knowledge under the authority of Enoch, who predates Moses, the author of *1 Enoch* moves beyond conventional uses of the Sinai tradition.[16] Paul similarly relativizes traditional theophanic conventions about Sinai (as Jewish apocalyptic visionaries before him had done) to make way for the new revelatory data of the Christian gospel.[17] As is typical in Paul's use of traditional or conventional language of any kind, here he is able to use subversively the linguistic fields surrounding both Hellenistic parousia and Jewish divine meeting traditions to create a new language fit for his apocalyptic vision.

The "Day," the "Day of the Lord," and the "Day of Christ"

Often Paul associates the eschatological coming of Christ rather traditionally with language concerning that "day" (Rom 2:16; 13:12; 1 Cor 3:13; 1 Thess 5:4) or, more expansively, with the "day of the Lord" (1 Thess 5:2), the "day of Christ Jesus" (Phil 1:6), the "day of Christ" (Phil 1:10; 2:16), the "day of wrath" (Rom 2:5), or the "day of salvation" (twice in 2 Cor 6:2). Occasionally the day of the Lord as a judgment day is implied (1 Cor 1:7–8; 4:1–5; 2 Cor 5:10; Rom 2:5–7; 14:10). This usage is closely related to similar language in both prophetic and apocalyptic Judaism.[18]

---

[16] Cf. 4 Ezra and *2 Baruch,* in which there is a more direct association of the visionaries' messages with Mosaic law. Collins does not mean to suggest that in *1 Enoch* Sinai is at variance with the laws of nature promoted in this document, "but the ultimate authority is older than Moses and applies not only to Israel but to all humanity" (*Apocalyptic Imagination,* 49).

[17] This effect is most obvious, of course, in Galatians (3:19–20). See Plevnik, *Paul and the Parousia,* 10.

[18] The biblical expression "latter (or last) days" typically connotes a future time that will precede, coincide with, or follow a decisive divine reckoning. Associated terms are "day of the Lord," "day of judgment," or simply "the [that] day." The earliest uses of the term in Hebrew concern the coming temporal victories and defeats of Israel and the nations. Used in this sense, the term is closely related to the "day of the Lord," a common theme in the prophets that refers to the judgment of God's enemies in battle (Num 24:14). The Deuteronomist sees the latter days as a time

ἀποκάλυψις and ἀποκαλύπτω

Finally, Paul sometimes uses the noun ἀποκάλυψις and the verb ἀποκαλύπτω to refer to explicitly eschatological events (Rom 2:5; 8:19; 1 Cor 1:7). He also uses both noun and verb in less explicitly eschatological, but nonetheless strongly apocalyptic settings. The noun is used, for example, when Paul describes his own encounter with Christ by way of ἀποκάλυψις (Gal 1:12), when he gives his reason for going up to Jerusalem after his first revelation ("I went up by ἀποκάλυψις," Gal 2:2), and as a way of referring to the gospel ("the ἀποκάλυψις of the mystery," Rom 16:25).[19] The verb ἀποκαλύπτω likewise appears in eschatological settings—as in 1 Cor 3:13, where "the Day will reveal (ἀποκαλύπτω) each person's work," and Rom 8:18, where Paul writes of the "glory that will be revealed to us." And it is found also in noneschatological (but nevertheless apocalyptic) settings—as in 1 Cor 2:9–10, where "What no eye has seen . . . God has revealed (ἀποκαλύπτω) through the Spirit," and Gal 1:16, where God "revealed (ἀποκαλύπτω) his Son."[20]

---

of tribulation and exile for Israel when "evil shall befall" (Deut 4:30; 31:29). Similarly, Jeremiah cites the latter days when Israel will understand the wrath of the Lord (Jer 23:20; 30:24; cf. Ezek 38:16). But the latter days may also be a time of restoration for nations previously punished (Jer 48:47; 49:39) or for Israel, who will return to seek the Lord (Hos 3:5). For Isaiah and Micah, the latter days will bring the restoration of Jerusalem, when God's rule will be universally recognized (Isa 2:2; Mic 4:1). Job awaits the restoration of justice at the latter (day) when his redeemer shall stand upon the earth (Job 19:25–27). Jewish apocalyptic and Christian writers typically associate the latter days (or "last times") with cosmic events: the coming tribulation, last judgment, and salvation (4 Ezra 6:34; 8:63; 10:59; cf. 1QM 1, 11; 2 Bar. 24:1; 51). In Daniel, the events of the latter days are mysteries, to be revealed from heaven (Dan 2:28; 10:14). The text of this note is an excerpt (with minor modifications) from A. R. Brown, "Latter Days," Eerdmans Bible Dictionary (ed. A. C. Myers; Grand Rapids: Eerdmans, forthcoming).

[19] See also 1 Cor 14:6, 26 and 2 Cor 12:1, 7 for noun forms.

[20] See also Gal 3:23 and Phil 3:15. J. L. Martyn, commenting on the dynamism inherent in Paul's notion of apocalyptic invasion, shows that in Gal 3:19–4:7 Paul uses the terms "to be revealed," "to come," and "to

φανερόω and Related Terms

In a few instances the verb φανερόω, "to make manifest," occurs in contexts that make it roughly synonymous with ἀποκαλύπτω. Hence, "the righteousness of God has been manifested apart from the law" (Rom 3:21), and the "mystery that was kept secret for long ages is now manifested" (Rom 16:25–26). When the Lord comes "he will make manifest the purposes of the heart" (1 Cor 4:5), and "we must all appear [be made manifest] before the judgment seat of Christ" (2 Cor 5:10). Other uses of the terms are less obviously linked with apocalyptic concepts or terminology (Rom 1:19; 2 Cor 2:14; 3:3; 4:10; 7:12; 11:6).[21]

κτίσις and καινὴ κτίσις as Eschatological Categories
in 2 Corinthians

Three instances of "creation" (κτίσις) language in Paul are important indicators of the scope of his apocalyptic vision. In Romans 8, the creation that is "subjected in hope . . . will be set free from its bondage to decay and obtain the glorious liberty of the children of God" (vv. 19–23). But in 2 Corinthians and Galatians the "new creation" (καινὴ κτίσις) is said to be already present in the believer. In 2 Cor 5:17 we read, "If anyone is in Christ, there is a new creation; the old has passed away, behold, the new has come." And in Gal 6:15 Paul declares, "For neither circumcision nor uncircumcision counts for anything, but a new creation." Here it is as if the new creation is an established stronghold as God's realm advances. "Now is the day of salvation" (2 Cor 6:2).

Implicit References to the Parousia, End Time, or Coming of Christ

In addition to the explicit language of end-time coming, judgment, or revelation, Paul employs certain strategies, not al-

---

be sent" interchangeably. "Paul sees that the coming of Christ is the invasion of Christ" ("From Paul to Flannery O'Connor," 282).

[21] The frequency of the term in 2 Corinthians may signal the polemical context of that letter.

ways obvious in his vocabulary alone, that point to end-time apocalyptic realities—that is, in his theological vision, to the liberating triumph of God now in motion toward human beings. Into this category would fall the language of meeting (ἀπάντησις in 1 Thess 4:17) if Paul has consciously transposed the term from its political usage in Thessalonica to make the opposite point, namely, that God is on the march to meet (indeed, to take up) human beings. Elsewhere, we find Paul interrupting conventional expectations of logic and even grammar in order to point to the "new creation" already taking hold. Hence, in 1 Cor 1:18–25 the cross appears foolish but is actually the power (δύναμις) of God, and what is conventionally wise is actually folly. By attending to such strategies of inversion and subversion in Paul's rhetoric, Martyn demonstrates that Galatians, long considered the least apocalyptic of Paul's writings, is perhaps Paul's most thoroughly apocalyptic letter.[22] Here we are guided not only by vocabulary (language of "apocalypse") but also by deeply embedded epistemological shifts. To "get" these shifts is to participate in the new creation they describe and, in Paul's "theo-logic," to be grasped already by the liberating power that will finally triumph at the last day.[23]

TRADITION HISTORY OF THE RESURRECTION-PAROUSIA SEQUENCE

It is not self-evident how Paul arrived at the eschatological scenario embedded in his apocalyptic teaching. In certain partic-

---

[22] Martyn notices, for example, that in what happens to conventionally paired opposites in the letter (male and female, Jew and Greek, slave and free)—namely, their dissolution—the "fundamental building blocks of the cosmos are denied any real existence," a denial whose effect is to announce the death of the cosmos those opposites once defined (J. L. Martyn, "Apocalyptic Antinomies in Paul's Letter to the Galatians," *NTS* 31 [1985]: 414).

[23] On the potential of Paul's preaching of the cross to stimulate perceptual shift by means of epistemological crisis, see A. R. Brown, *The Cross and Human Transformation: Paul's Apocalyptic Word in 1 Corin-*

ulars, precedents are to be found in Jewish thought, especially in Jewish apocalyptic and martyrological ideas, but, as Holleman argues, nowhere before Paul do we find his combination of resurrection and parousia ideas: (1) the resurrection of the Messiah as the beginning of the general resurrection; (2) the parousia of the Messiah as the moment of the future general resurrection; and (3) the resurrection of believers as a participation in Jesus' resurrection.[24] Was there precedent in Jewish eschatology for the linking of a resurrected divine agent to the general eschatological resurrection, or of a returned messiah to the same event? Was there an earlier conception of general resurrection via participation in a martyr's resurrection? Or is the combination of eschatological ideas in 1 Corinthians Paul's own invention?

Jewish Eschatological Traditions

It is often noted that Christian ideas about end-time events have parallels in Jewish eschatological writings, such as Daniel, *1 Enoch* (especially the latest stratum of this work, the Similitudes of Enoch), *2 Baruch,* and 4 Ezra.

General Eschatological Resurrection

It is a commonplace in New Testament studies that some Jews living at the time of Jesus believed in the resurrection of the dead.[25] But we know from surveying biblical sources that such belief came relatively late in Judaism. According to G. W. E. Nickelsburg, the assertion that "physical death does not nullify God's justice or abrogate the covenantal relationship for individ-

---

thians (Minneapolis: Fortress, 1995); also J. L. Martyn, "Epistemology at the Turn of the Ages: 2 Corinthians 5:16," in *Christian History and Interpretation: Studies Presented to John Knox* (ed. W. R. Farmer et al.; Cambridge: Cambridge University Press, 1967), 269–87.

[24] Holleman, *Resurrection and Parousia.*

[25] On Pharisaic belief in resurrection, see Josephus, *War* 2.163. But note the warning of E. P. Sanders that perhaps it was not *only* Pharisees who so believed (*Paul and Palestinian Judaism* [Philadelphia: Fortress, 1983], 151 n. 19).

uals" represents a "breakthrough" in Jewish thought whose earliest clear expression may be the postexilic (end of the Persian period) Isaianic apocalypse (Isaiah 24–27):[26]

> Your dead shall live,
>   their corpses shall rise.
> O dwellers in the dust,
>   awake and sing for joy!
>   (Isa 26:19)

A second postexilic (and apocalyptic) text also envisions a resurrection of the dead:

> At that time Michael, the great prince, the protector of your people, shall arise. There shall be a time of anguish, such as has never occurred since nations first came into existence. But at that time your people shall be delivered, everyone who is found written in the book. Many of those who sleep in the dust of the earth shall awake, some to everlasting life, and some to shame and everlasting contempt. (Dan 12:1–2)

The emergence in this literature of the belief in resurrection is linked, significantly, with the beginnings of apocalyptic thought in Israel and with the notion that God's final justice for individual (martyred) righteous ones, as well as for corporate Israel, will not be thwarted despite apparent defeat by the nations. Several different ideas about the nature of this resurrection can be found in Jewish literature. Some sources picture a bodily resurrection (Isa 26:19; 2 Macc 7:22–29; 14:46), while others envision a resurrection of the soul or the soul's removal to a new body on the day of resurrection (Josephus, *War* 2.163; 3.374).[27] In some subsequent literature the model of Isaiah 24–27 is followed and only the righteous dead are raised (e.g., *1 Enoch* 6–36; 83–90; *Pss. Sol.* 3; *2 Bar.* 30); in other sources, both righteous and unrighteous are raised, each receiving their just reward (*T. Benj.* 10:6–8; 4 Ezra 7:31–35; *Sib. Or.* 4; cf. John 5:28–29; Acts 24:15).

---

[26] Nickelsburg, "Resurrection," *ABD* 5:685.

[27] Regarding the Pharisees, Josephus states: "Every soul, they maintain, is imperishable, but the soul of the good alone passes into another body while the souls of the wicked suffer eternal punishment" (*War* 2.163).

The ideas of resurrection and final judgment are found combined also in Dan 12:2; *1 Enoch* 51; *Biblical Antiquities* 3:10; and *Sib. Or.* 4:181–83.[28]

From these traditions regarding resurrection in Second Temple Judaism, it is easy to imagine the emergence of early Christian expectations of the eschatological resurrection that, in their own formulation of the end-time scenario, foresaw the double selection of good and bad to *bodily* resurrection and subsequent judgment. This must be, in part, the picture Paul had in mind (1 Thess 4:16–18; 1 Corinthians 15). But in an apparent innovation on Jewish precedents, he has linked the resurrection of the righteous martyr—who comes also as judge—to the general resurrection.

Jesus' Resurrection as the Beginning of the General Resurrection

In 1 Corinthians, Paul refers to Christ as the "first-fruits (ἀπαρχή) of them that sleep," meaning the first to have arisen in the expected eschatological resurrection (15:20, 23). There is reason to suspect, according to Holleman, that this is Paul's own invention, and that other New Testament texts that express the idea are dependent on Paul (Col 1:18; Rev 1:5; Acts 26:23).[29] The nearest parallel in Judaism may be the connection of the general resurrection with an eschatological agent. In several documents (Dan 12:2–3; *2 Bar.* 30:1; *1 Enoch* 51; 4 Ezra 7:26–44), as Holleman points out, "the future resurrection is not only connected with the final judgment, but also with the activities of the eschatological intermediary."[30]

For Jewish parallels to the idea of *Jesus'* resurrection, Holleman turns to traditions regarding the raising of righteous individuals, an often cited example being the resurrection of the martyrs in 2 Maccabees (late second century B.C.E.). Again the

---

[28] Holleman, *Resurrection and Parousia,* 93 n. 1.

[29] Ibid., 137.

[30] Ibid., 127. It is significant that in none of these instances is the eschatological agent identified as a resurrected martyr.

scene involves the unjust treatment of Israel by a foreign power (Antiochus IV Epiphanes). Although the seven brothers who are the heroes of 2 Maccabees suffer torture and martyrdom, they will be restored to life by God (2 Macc 7:22–23, 27–29).[31] Their mother faithfully proclaims the miraculous restoration beforehand:

> "I do not know how you came into being in my womb. It was not I who gave you life and breath, not I who set in order the elements within each of you. Therefore the Creator of the world, who shaped the beginning of humankind and devised the origin of all things, will in his mercy give life and breath back to you again, since you now forget yourselves for the sake of his laws." (2 Macc 7:22–23)

The Maccabean martyrs are expected to rise into heaven soon after death, and there receive heavenly vindication. Holleman finds this resurrected-vindicated martyr tradition to be the most likely background for the belief in the resurrection of Jesus.[32] But again, it is a tradition isolated from other eschatological motifs in Judaism, connected with neither the general resurrection tradition nor the traditions of eschatological agents associated with the end time. Indeed, as J. D. G. Dunn observes, before Christianity there seems to have been "no clearly expressed idea of the vindicated righteous returning in triumph to earth or of their vindication being displayed on earth."[33]

---

[31] Cf. 2 Macc 7:9: "[T]he King of the Universe will raise us up [ἀνίστημι]." Note the parallel vocabulary for Jesus' rising in 1 Thess 4:14 (ἀνίστημι).

[32] Holleman, *Resurrection and Parousia,* 148, 204. A. Segal makes the connection to Jesus' death as a martyr: "The expectation that Jesus might survive death on the cross is understandable in the context of his death as a martyr. As the Book of Daniel shows, whoever else may have deserved immortality, martyrs pre-eminently were granted the privilege of immortality, because they died sanctifying God's name" (*Rebecca's Children: Judaism and Christianity in the Roman World* [Cambridge, Mass.: Harvard University Press, 1986], 64).

[33] In Dunn's view the idea must be traced to the postresurrection days if not to Jesus' own parables and interpretation of the Son of Man vision in Daniel (J. D. G. Dunn, *The Theology of Paul the Apostle* [Grand Rapids: Eerdmans, 1998], 295).

The Combining of Eschatological Resurrection and the
Parousia of Jesus

Elsewhere in this volume, Claudia Setzer shows that "the
longing for redemption, sometimes coupled with the expected
appearance of a particular messianic figure, percolates through
Jewish history."[34] Some developments in Jewish thought, we
have seen, prepared the way for the early Christian expectation
of Jesus' parousia by promoting, through accounts of various
apocalyptic visionaries (such as Daniel and Enoch), the expectation of God's future justice-dealing action through some sort of
intermediary.[35] The frequent allusions to Daniel in Mark's Gospel and, more broadly, the (controversial) use of "Son of humanity (Man)" terminology in the gospel tradition show that the
early Christians knew and adapted Jewish ideas about eschatological intermediaries.[36] J. J. Collins observes that the earthly
Davidic Messiah (e.g., *Pss. Sol.* 17:21), and not an apocalyptic figure as in Daniel or the Enoch literature (*1 Enoch* 37–71; *2 Bar.*
39:7–40:4), was the primary messianic mode among Jews in the
first century. Nevertheless, early Christians may well have had
in mind the apocalyptic figures described in this postexilic apocalyptic literature, figures whose divine mission seemed analo-
gous to that of the resurrected and returning Jesus.[37]

---

[34] See chapter 6.

[35] D. Allison points out in this connection that Mal 4:5–6 expressed
the hope that Elijah would return for a ministry of reconciliation (*Jesus
of Nazareth: Millenarian Prophet* [Minneapolis: Fortress, 1998], 129).
Note also the comment of Dunn: "The thought of Elijah's reappearance
on earth was already well established. And already Enoch was probably
linked with Elijah in this role. But that was less surprising. After all, neither Enoch nor Elijah had died. Instead, they had been translated to
heaven. . . ." (*Theology of Paul the Apostle*, 295).

[36] J. J. Collins suggests that the identification of the "Son of Man"
with the Messiah in *1 Enoch* 48:10 paves the way for understanding the
Messiah as a supernatural figure. Similarly, he notes the possible supernatural connotations of the emphasis in the Similitudes of Enoch on
having "faith in" the Son of Man (*Apocalyptic Imagination*, 192).

[37] Holleman holds that the "Son of Man" undergoes a significant
shift from Daniel to *1 Enoch*—from a collective figure (Israel) to an

Paul's Schematization of Eschatological Traditions

While these traditions offer fruitful parallels to Christian resurrection and parousia developments, they do not explain either the content or the sequence of Paul's *combination* of messianic resurrection, general eschatological resurrection, and parousia expectations. Holleman argues that the combination is Paul's own creation in 1 Corinthians, developed in reaction to the Corinthians' dualistic anthropology and to the consequent denial of the general resurrection at the end of time. First Corinthians 15:2–23, he thinks, is the first joining of the parousia with two different resurrection traditions—martyrological and eschatological—and the first joining of these concepts with the idea that the general resurrection will take place via participation in Christ's resurrection. Lying behind Paul's scenario in 1 Corinthians 15, according to Holleman, is the idea that the martyr's resurrection began the general resurrection which will itself be completed at the parousia.[38]

The formulation in 1 Thessalonians is a simpler rehearsal of preexisting and already linked traditions, namely, the tradition of general resurrection (likely in place even in Jesus' time among his followers) and the tradition of Jesus' parousia (likely formulated very soon after Jesus' death). In 1 Thessalonians, these two linked traditions are given special emphasis due to the crisis—defined in the letter as hopelessness—encountered by the Thessalonians upon the deaths (by persecution?) of loved ones.[39] In 1 Corinthians, a different situation calls for expansion of this earlier linking of (general) resurrection and parousia tra-

---

individual figure—and that this shift is happening at the time of formative Christianity. Early Christians combined the messianic consciousness of Jesus (and their own expectations) with the Son of Man tradition, which was not originally associated with messianic tradition. This combination is pre-Pauline, Holleman thinks. Paul bases his own concept of the parousia upon Son of Man tradition even though he does not use the term "Son of Man" (*Resurrection and Parousia,* 113).

[38] Ibid., 204–206.

[39] Ibid., 123. For the view that Thessalonians were dying under persecution, see Donfried, "Imperial Cults," 219–20.

ditions, but in both cases the development of parousia theology comes in response to community needs.[40] The remainder of this chapter will consider the ways in which the apocalyptic setting of Paul's theology causes him to shape the parousia teaching he addresses to his churches and to their particular problems.

PASTORAL DIMENSIONS OF PAUL'S PAROUSIA THEOLOGY

In his book *The Analogical Imagination,* theologian David Tracy remarks on the "corrective challenge" brought by New Testament apocalyptic thought to early Catholicism and to the church today. Tracy cites apocalyptic as "the genre evoked in times of crisis" that recognizes "rejection and conflict in history" and as "the genre most frequently employed to articulate the sense of expectancy for the *parousia*." In his analysis of the corrective powers of the apocalyptic genre, Tracy captures, I think, key pastoral elements of Paul's parousia teaching in the specific and varied circumstances of his letters, namely, its corrective force against fear and despair on the one hand (e.g., in 1 Thessalonians), and against complacency on the other (e.g., in 1 Corinthians). Apocalyptic should be invoked, he argues,

> as a challenge, for example, to any purely "private" understanding of the Christian event by forcing a recognition of the genuinely public, the political and historical character of all Christian self-understanding; as a challenge to all the privileged to remember the privileged status of the oppressed, the poor, the suffering in the scriptures; as a challenge to the living not to forget the true hope disclosed in these texts of a future from God for all the dead; as a challenge to all wisdom and all principles of order to remember the reality of the pathos of active suffering untransformable by all thought ordering cosmos and ethos; as a challenge to face the reality of the really new, the novum, and the future breaking in and confronting every present, exploding every complacency. . . .[41]

---

[40] Holleman, *Resurrection and Parousia,* 204.

[41] D. Tracy, *The Analogical Imagination: Christian Theology and the Culture of Pluralism* (New York: Crossroad, 1981), 265–66.

In early Catholicism by contrast, and especially in its major genre of doctrinal confessions, Tracy notes, the "tension" inherent in apocalyptic "seems relaxed, though not spent; the sects, the charismatic communities have become an ordered institution of the 'great church'; the act of proclamation and its disclosure of the sheer 'that it happens now' has largely yielded to the content of its confession."[42] For Tracy this is no cause for alarm, for he goes on to argue that just as apocalyptic is a corrective challenge to "any tendency in early Catholicism to slacken eschatological intensity for real history, for the *novum* and the future, any relaxing of the power of the negative and the not-yet in all other genres," so too, early Catholicism brings its own corrective:

> Early Catholicism serves as the corrective of any temptation to shirk the ordinary, including the ordinary and necessary human need to find some clarity and explicitness for certain shared beliefs as doctrines to allow for the human need to find order in thought and some structure in community.[43]

On Tracy's trajectory, then, we move finally into the world of the deutero-Paulines with the characteristic softening of parousia expectations that accompanied the development of the institutional patterns typical of early Catholicism.[44] This is, of course, a natural consequence of a canonical reading of Paul alongside the deutero-Paulines and the rest of the New Testament texts. But with Paul's undisputed letters we are not yet there. His advice to churches—already structured, of course, and to that degree "institutions" themselves, to be sure, but still more "charismatic" than "institutional"—is still fueled by the expectation of God's apocalyptic final and future triumph over the dominating powers of sin and death.

---

[42] Ibid.

[43] Ibid., 268.

[44] In Colossians and Ephesians the church is no longer one of an aggregate of Christian communities spread across the ancient world, but has become an absolute entity, *the* church (e.g., Col 1:18). It is "the household of God, built upon the foundation of the apostles and prophets, with Jesus Christ as the cornerstone" (Eph 2:19–20).

In 1 Thess 4:13–5:10 and 1 Cor 15:22–28, 50–55, Paul's explicit expositions of the parousia bring the challenge of his apocalyptic theology to particular human situations. In 1 Thessalonians, the parousia presents the challenge, in Tracy's words, "not to forget the true hope of a future from God for all the dead," and in 1 Corinthians both the challenge "to remember the public, the political and historical character of all Christian self-understanding" (e.g., 1 Corinthians 11, 12, 14) and the challenge presented by cross and parousia to "all wisdom and all principles of order" (e.g., 1:18–31) are issued. In Galatians, where there is no explicit mention of the parousia, Paul's call to face the reality of the "really new, the *novum*" (the "new creation" of Gal 6:15) and in that reality to see the death of the old cosmos with its dominating powers is nevertheless a striking testimony to the *hope* of parousia. That this challenge depends upon the culminating event of the parousia no less in Galatians, where it is not mentioned, than in 1 Thessalonians and 1 Corinthians, where it is explicit, becomes clear as the ongoing struggle between flesh and Spirit comes to light. That struggle has an end that Paul eagerly awaits, "for through the Spirit, by faith, we wait for the hope of rectification" (Gal 5:5). And that future triumph is the hope of all who, although snatched out of the grasp of the "present evil age," continue to struggle against its desperate pull toward reenslavement.

1 Thessalonians 4:13–5:10 and the Parousia Hope

We have already alluded to the problem Paul encountered at Thessalonica: the deaths of some in the community have caused the congregants to lose hope (4:13–18). It is impossible to recover from the letter exactly what the problem was. It is doubtful, however, that by 49 or 50 C.E. no one has yet died in this congregation and that the question of the resurrection of believers is just now being broached. What seems more likely is that the already numerous deaths of believers have left some wondering about the delay of the parousia and somehow, too, about the relation of the dead to the living at the last day. This, at least, is where Paul seems to focus his comments and not, as in 1 Corinthians, on defending bodily resurrection per se.[45]

The two principal eschatological themes in the parousia teaching in 1 Thessalonians are the assurance of the parousia of Christ and the assurance that the eschatological resurrection will accompany the parousia, with special emphasis on the chronological relationship of the raising of the dead in Christ to the raising of those who are alive at his coming: the dead will be raised first and then the living caught up together with them (1 Thess 4:16–17). Clearly, Paul's aim is to encourage a congregation whose hope needs restoring and at the same time to exhort them to holy behavior. How, then, does the parousia language in particular work to achieve this end in the congregation?

Some commentators stress that the parousia encourages both scrutiny regarding one's own moral disposition and continued work in the world. In this view, the Christians are called to reflect on the parousia as the motive to "lead a life worthy of God," that is, to holy behavior (5:1–11). Moreover, they are themselves exhorted to "admonish idlers, encourage the fainthearted, help the weak . . . always seek to do good to one another and to all" (5:14–15). And this is in view of the final blessing, "May the God of peace sanctify you wholly; and may your spirit and soul and body be kept sound and blameless at the coming of our Lord, Jesus Christ" (5:23).[46] In this way of reading the letter, parousia language appears to function primarily as moral ex-

---

[45] J. Plevnik finds in Paul's response to Thessalonians anxious about the deceased faithful further evidence against Hellenistic usage of parousia language. "The real problem in the Thessalonian community concerns the taking up. The apostle taught them that at the Lord's coming, they will all be taken up. The unspoken assumption was that they will be alive at the Lord's coming" and "that one had to be alive in order to be taken up. . . . The taking-up motif here makes it unlikely that the apostle thinks of the parousia as the *Einholung*—the bringing in—of the Lord, modeled on the Hellenistic [parousia]. . . . The faithful do not go up; they are lifted by the power of God" (*Paul and the Parousia*, 97). Cf. Koester's view on this problem (n. 6 above).

[46] What Paul envisions here is uncertain. D. Allison lists Paul among those apocalyptic visionaries who envisage an interim state be-

hortation. And pastoral implications follow: the call to holy living leads to cohesion with the group ethos and consequent relief from anxiety. The parousia, whose time cannot be predicted, keeps hearers vigilant and focused on their accountability on the day of judgment.

The choices made here about how to interpret apocalyptic themes in the letter and the reading of 1 Thessalonians that ensues bear certain resemblances to what M. C. DeBoer has called "forensic apocalyptic eschatology."[47] The stress falls on the moral accountability of the individual and on the last judgment as a time of reckoning moral responsibility. In this reading, the theological centrality of Paul's parousia teaching is related to the priority parousia hope gives to ethical action as a function of human responsibility. Among the Pauline scholars who stress Paul's apocalyptic orientation, J. C. Beker has given perhaps the most attention to the place of the parousia per se in the larger theological picture. He also places the most emphasis on human responsibility:

> The time between the cross/resurrection and the end is a time for commitment, mission, endurance, and obedience. Those who are disobedient to the gospel will be judged and destroyed in the last judgment, for they continue to behave as though the powers defeated by Jesus Christ are still in charge. Thus Paul balances the notion of a universal salvation with an emphasis on the responsibility and obedience of those who have heard his gospel.[48]

Reading the same parousia imagery in 1 Thessalonians 4–5 through different apocalyptic lenses, however, we see another picture come into view. If the emphasis is now placed on the apocalyptic agency of God, who "destined us not for wrath, but for the possession of salvation through our Lord Jesus Christ" (5:9), and on the agency of "God's son from heaven, whom he

---

tween death and resurrection as in 2 Macc 7:9; *1 Enoch* 22; 60:8; 62:15; 4 Ezra 7:32, 76–101). See Allison, *Jesus of Nazareth*, 141 n. 166.

[47]M. C. DeBoer, "Paul and Jewish Apocalyptic Eschatology," in *Apocalyptic and the New Testament: Essays in Honor of J. Louis Martyn* (ed. J. Marcus and M. L. Soards; Sheffield: JSOT Press, 1989), 169–90.

[48]Beker, *Triumph of God*, 26.

raised from the dead, the one who delivers us from the wrath to come" (1:10), we are hard pressed to identify the autonomous human agents who might, by lacking moral vigilance at this hour, choose to avoid the salvation for which they are destined. Parousia language in this reading functions not so much to deliver moral admonition as to bring the grieving Thessalonians once again into the liberated zone of hope from their slippage into the worldly powers of despair. And this is a hope without threat of judgment, for it is a hope precisely for *deliverance* from the powers of sin and death.

The choices made here about how to interpret the apocalyptic motifs in the letter and the reading that arises from those choices resemble DeBoer's alternative apocalyptic model, which he characterizes as "cosmological apocalyptic eschatology." This model of apocalyptic sees the problem faced by human beings as cosmic in scale. Anti-God forces have led human beings into slavery. But God will not long tolerate the captivity of God's creation and will liberate at the parousia the entire creation from its evil captors.[49] Now the emphasis falls not on the accountability of individuals, but on the corporate reality announced as a proleptic victory meant to encourage the hopeless: "You are not in darkness. You are all children of light and children of the day; we are not of night or of the darkness!" (1 Thess 5:5). In this reading the parousia functions within Paul's larger apocalyptic gospel as the hope of God's final and universal victory over the cosmic powers of sin and death, so that no one is left in their grasp at the last day. There is no emphasis on the disobedient in the community and no stress on their judgment at the parousia, because the God who has already made them "children of light" will, at the end, subject all things to God's self, and will be all in all (1 Cor 15:28).[50]

---

[49] This definition is cited in Martyn, "Glossary," *Theological Issues,* 298–99.

[50] In his adaptation of DeBoer's categories, J. L. Martyn characterizes cosmological apocalyptic eschatology in this way: "Anti-God powers have managed to commence their rule over the world, leading human beings into idolatry and thus into slavery, producing a wrong sit-

1 Corinthians 15 and the Parousia Hope

The two eschatological schemas that appear in the interpretation of 1 Thessalonians are present also in interpretations of 1 Corinthians, where Paul takes on a very different sort of problem. In 1 Corinthians 15, as Holleman has suggested, it is likely that Paul combines the resurrection of Jesus and his parousia with the general resurrection to counteract the Corinthians' dualistic anthropology. In their way of thinking, which may have originated in Hellenistic Jewish traditions concerned with the exegesis of Genesis, the world was divided into spiritual and nonspiritual classes of people. The self-appointed "spiritual" people, those addressed by Paul here, apparently espoused a doctrine of asomatic immortality for the elect and thereby denied the resurrection of the body.[51] Instead they may have expected to pass directly from bodily existence into spiritual existence, unified with Christ as the First Adam, the heavenly man who bears the incorruptible image of God.[52] Death was a transition into spiritual bliss for them, and not an enemy to be defeated by God's rectifying power.

It may be against such a view that Paul develops his defense of *bodily* resurrection, grounding that defense in the bodily crucifixion and resurrection of Christ and linking it, on the one

---

uation that was not intended by him. For in his own time, God will inaugurate a victorious and liberating apocalyptic war against these evil powers, delivering his elect from their evil grasp and thus making right that which has gone wrong because of the powers' malignant machinations" ("Glossary," in *Theological Issues*, 298).

[51] Citing G. Sellin (*Der Streit um die Auferstehung der Toten: Eine religionsgeschichtliche und exegetische Untersuchung von 1 Korinther 15* [FRLANT 138; Göttingen: Vandenhoeck & Ruprecht, 1986], 30–31), Holleman concludes that for these "spiritual" persons "a resurrection is not only impossible since it concerns the body, it is also unnecessary because immortality is reached by receiving the Spirit" (*Resurrection and Parousia*, 37).

[52] For the Jewish exegetical traditions that might support such a doctrine, see B. Pearson, *The Pneumatikos-Psychikos Terminology in 1 Corinthians* (Missoula, Mont.: Scholars Press, 1973), 17–24.

hand, to a future event, the parousia, and on the other, to a participation in Christ's own resurrection. One pastoral effect of the linkage he produces in 15:22–28 is to undergird the integration of body and spirit toward which he has pressed throughout the letter. Because it is the body that will be raised (albeit transformed into a "spiritual body"), the life one lives in one's body and toward other bodies has ultimate relevance. For the bodies of those who are called already participate in the crucifixion of Christ, the event by which they are called into active duty under God's new commandment, the singular law of Christ (1 Cor 10:24; 11:29; Gal 5:14; 6:2). Moreover, the battle being fought against the cosmic powers—including the final enemy, death—in the present has as its goal the future liberation of the whole world at the parousia. As Paul envisions the sequence, participation in Christ has its focus now in his crucifixion and the battle which that event commenced. But in the resurrection of Christ, already accomplished, stands the hope of everyone who now participates in his death: as he was raised, so too will all be raised at the time of his coming, the final triumph of God.

It is imperative, as Paul reads the Corinthian situation, to accent the *future and bodily* nature of the general resurrection. Otherwise the Corinthian proclivity is to absent oneself—through spiritual resurrection now, on analogy with Jesus' resurrection in the past—from the earthly struggle necessitated by the clashing of the law of love with the powers and principalities of the world.

For Paul, then, death is a cosmic power whose defeat is assured by Jesus' resurrection but completed by the general resurrection, conceived as a communal participation in Jesus' resurrection. All are being drawn, through the ongoing effects of Jesus' resurrection, toward bodily resurrection at the End. At the parousia, and only then, all will enter fully into the realm of God, whose power will be manifest in the defeat of the last enemy, death. The parousia in 1 Corinthians undergirds the integration of body and spirit upon which Paul's pastoral advice depends throughout the letter.

The forensic reading does not come easily to the cosmological fifteenth chapter of 1 Corinthians. Even where it would appear to be the operative view, e.g., "If Christ has not been raised, your faith is futile and you are still in your sins" (1 Cor 15:17), it appears that Paul is speaking tongue-in-cheek, reducing the argument of his opponents *ad absurdum*. The resurrection of Christ has indeed, in his view, freed humanity from the powers of sin and death. To reject Christ's resurrection is to reject God's liberation of the whole creation, already begun in Christ but yet to be fulfilled at the parousia (cf. Rom 8:21).

One way of reading the chapter forensically would be to see the resurrection body as the locus of judgment on the "day of the Lord Jesus Christ" (1 Cor 5:5). Indeed, Paul has earlier written to the Corinthian congregants "not to associate with anyone who bears the name of brother or sister who is guilty of immorality or greed" (5:9–11). And, as we have seen, he has clear interest elsewhere in the parousia as the day of judgment. But the most explicit portrayal of judgment in the letter once again seems to mix the forensic and the cosmological. In 1 Cor 3:12–15 the metaphor of building with superior or inferior materials describes the relation of one's work to one's judgment. On the "day" the fire will disclose each person's work. And yet the penalties are not meted out to the individuals themselves, but rather, to their work: "If any man's work is burned up, he will suffer loss, *though he himself will be saved,* but only as through fire."

Again, in 1 Cor 6:9–10, some find a certain signal of damning judgment against the immoral.

> Do you not know that wrongdoers will not inherit the kingdom of God? Do not be deceived! Fornicators, idolaters, adulterers, male prostitutes, sodomites, thieves, the greedy, drunkards, revilers, robbers—none of these will inherit the kingdom of God.

But the following lines return the hearer to the reality of God's victory over the corrupting influences.

> And this is what some of you used to be. But you were washed; you were sanctified, you were justified in the name of the Lord Jesus and in the Spirit of our God (6:11).

Considering the remarkable cosmological promise of 1 Cor 15:21–28, it is difficult to read the rest of the letter, even its judgment scenes, through forensic lenses:

For as by a man came death, by a man has come also the resurrection of the dead. For as in Adam *all* die, so also in Christ shall *all* be made alive. But each in his own order: Christ the first fruits, then at his coming those who belong to Christ. Then comes the end, when he delivers the kingdom to God the Father after destroying every rule and every authority and power. For he must reign until he has put all his enemies under his feet. The last enemy to be destroyed is death. For "God has put all things in subjection under his feet." . . . When all things are subjected to him, then the Son himself will be subjected to him who put all things under him, that God may be everything to everyone (RSV).[53]

CONCLUSION

Forensic and cosmological apocalyptic readings of Paul both find the parousia indispensable for his theology. And both views produce coherent pastoral theologies when applied to the situations presented in the letters. One way of solving the dilemma this presents is to see, with DeBoer, that in Jewish apocalyptic texts before Paul "the two tracks can, like those of a railway, run side by side, crisscross, or overlap in various ways, *even in the same work.*"[54] The overlap and crisscrossing in Paul's own thought would then explain the contrasting trends in interpretation. Paul, in this view, is not consistent enough in his own eschatological outlook to dictate one or the other point of view exclusively.

Another way to read the evidence, however, is indicated in DeBoer's account of the overlapping tracks. In one example, Romans 1–8, a text in which he finds both perspectives relatively

---

[53] J. C. Beker does find in 1 Corinthians 15 an emphasis on ethical responsibility: "In an environment that threatened to collapse eschatology into Christology and to celebrate life in Christ as the epiphany of the divine presence on earth, so that historical life is absorbed into Christ mysticism, Paul emphasizes the 'not yet' of the Christian life and stresses the need for ethical responsibility in the light of both the Christ-event and the last judgment" (*Paul the Apostle: The Triumph of God in Life and Thought* [Philadelphia: Fortress, 1980], 345).

[54] DeBoer, "Paul and Jewish Apocalyptic Eschatology," 177 (emphasis mine).

isolated from each other, the appearance of the two tracks side by side—the cosmological track (obvious in 6:1–8:38) and the forensic track (8:1, 33–34)—is explained by the situation behind the letter. Paul's "conversation partners" in Rome had adopted the forensic model, "notably its understanding of the role and function of the Law."[55] When Paul sets justification of faith over against observance of the law, and when he makes faith a function of God's invasion, not human decision, he is setting his own cosmological view over against the forensic view of his opponents. To read the whole in forensic perspective, according to this view, is to radically misinterpret the nature of faith as God's own agent sent to liberate human beings from the deadly powers of sin and death, powers in whose grip the law itself now lies.[56]

A similar situation of parallel eschatologies at war is displayed, DeBoer argues, in Galatians, where Paul counters the Jewish-Christian teachers' forensic understanding of the saving significance of law observance with his own cosmological view of law's participation with cosmic powers in the bondage of the human being. The weight of the evidence, which in this chapter has been drawn from Paul's apocalyptic vocabulary and strategy throughout the letters, would seem to support DeBoer's argument.

To understand Paul's parousia teaching, I have suggested, is to recognize its place in his innovative apocalyptic theology, which addresses above all else—and in every pastoral situation—the urgent matter of liberation. Using spatial imagery, Paul points to the parousia of Christ as the culmination of the cosmic struggle when "every rule, authority, and power" is put under subjection to Christ and, ultimately, under subjection to God who will at last be "all in all" (1 Cor 15:28). The eschatological theme is clearly related, for Paul, to the effects of the first coming of Christ (and especially his crucifixion) as the moment of liberation from enslavement under law, or "the elemental spirits of the universe," and sin (Gal 3:23; 4:5; Rom 3:19–20; 7:7–12). Upon those so enslaved, however, the "ends of the ages have come"

---

[55] Ibid., 183.
[56] Ibid., 184.

(1 Cor 10:11); faith has been "apocalypsed" and the captives have been liberated (Gal 3:23–25). These are, already, the conditions of the "new creation" (2 Cor 5:17); the old cosmos has come to its end in the cross of Christ (Gal 6:14–15).

And yet the very resistance of his hearers to the announcement of cosmic liberation, stimulated by the apparent persistence of worldly powers, causes Paul to hold the parousia ever before his hearers. The burden of Paul's preaching is, again and again, to address the news of liberation to communities that seem bent on living as if the liberation has not happened (Galatians), or as if it is completely realized for the spiritual elite so that the neighbor has disappeared from view (1 Corinthians), or as if the message of liberation were fatally flawed by the delay of the end time or by ambiguities about the status of the dead before the general resurrection (1 Thessalonians). In these circumstances, Paul crafts his parousia teaching to respond to needs of particular communities to cope with the hiddenness of the cosmic victory.

The crafting of that teaching, as we have seen, reflects the influence of apocalyptic and martyrological traditions (as these were filtered through Paul's Hellenistic milieu), on the one hand, and earlier Christian convictions about Jesus as Messiah, on the other. But the product—the linking of Jesus' resurrection and parousia with the general resurrection and the defeat of powers inimical to God at the last day—is Paul's own dynamic rendering of the news that is good news only if the cosmic powers are finally defeated for all. Taking his bearings from the conviction that God's victory is already accomplished in the cross of Christ, he presents the parousia—the coming culmination of God's victory over sin and death—as the certainty that challenges every misconstrual of the liberation accomplished by God in Christ.

THREE

THE PAROUSIA OF JESUS IN THE JOHANNINE LITERATURE

The New Testament writings associated with the name of John present a broad spectrum of views on the parousia of Jesus. In the Gospel according to John, the public ministry of Jesus represents his eschatological coming; hopes and expectations connected with his future parousia are drawn into one's present encounter with the incarnate Word. The First Letter of John assigns traditional eschatological images a much more prominent place, while preserving the Johannine Gospel's insistence that Jesus is the definitive disclosure of God to the world. John's Apocalypse, the book of Revelation, again and again points to Jesus' parousia in the near future; by casting the spotlight on his imminent return to vanquish God's enemies and judge evil, Revelation reassures the faithful that God will honor all who persevere in faith during times of crisis.

GOSPEL ACCORDING TO JOHN

Readers of John encounter familiar eschatological images, notably the Messiah who is "coming into the world," the Son of humanity cast in the role of eschatological judge, eternal life, resurrection of the dead, and the sending of the Spirit of God. Yet this gospel develops each motif in a distinctive way, drawing hopes associated with the end time into the present of Jesus' public ministry and the life of the believing community. Traditional hopes tied to the parousia of Jesus undergo radical reinterpretation in John.[1]

Jesus: Sent from Above

On four different occasions within the narrative, characters give voice to an expectation of the Messiah's appearance. From the outset, John the Baptizer deflects interest from himself as a potential messianic figure (1:20) to Jesus, who is the Lamb of God (1:29, 36) and the Son of God (1:34). Later, when Jesus has become embroiled in heated conflict with many in his audience, the crowd becomes polarized as it considers the possibility that he may be the Messiah. Aware of the enmity of the religious leaders toward Jesus, but struck by the boldness of his public teaching, some people speculate whether he may be the Messiah—yet the fact that they know "where he comes from" speaks against any such claim, for "when the Messiah comes, nobody knows where he is from" (7:26–27). Others in the crowd counter that the signs Jesus has performed are legitimate messianic credentials (7:31). Of course, rejection of Jesus' messiahship because of his Galilean origins (cf. 7:41–42) exposes the audience as victims of irony; they really are clueless as to his origins (8:14; 9:29).[2] He has been sent "from above," or "from heaven," or "from God [the Father]." The Messiah who will come into the world has come already.

The Samaritan woman speaks at Jacob's well of the Messiah who "is coming" and will declare "everything" (4:25). Jesus

---

[1] See J. T. Carroll, "Present and Future in Fourth Gospel 'Eschatology,'" *BTB* 19 (1989): 63–69.

[2] Cf. John 6:41–42, where the audience disputes Jesus' claim to have come "from heaven" because they know who his parents are.

redirects her messianic expectation from the future to the present: "I am [he]" (4:26), and as she reflects on their exchange, Jesus' powers of discernment suggest to her his messianic identity (4:29–30). And just before the raising of her brother Lazarus, Martha responds to Jesus' claim to be the "resurrection and the life"—the source of eternal life for all who have faith—by affirming that he is the Messiah "who is coming into the world" (11:27).

Clearly, the messianic status of Jesus is a central concern of the Johannine narrative—and, given the setting of polemic and controversy in which it appears in the gospel, of John's social world as well.[3] If Jews in John's community looked to the Messiah's future coming as agent of God's deliverance, John could point to the past as the locus of the eschatological coming of the Messiah. Yet even more important than Jesus' messianic identity in the story is the image of his having been "sent by the Father."[4]

Jesus discloses the character and activity of God; he has been commissioned and dispatched from heaven for this work of revelation on which salvation hinges, as a survey of the Johannine "sending" texts shows. Jesus was "sent" not to condemn the world created by God, but to bring salvation (3:16–17).[5] As one who provides free and unlimited access to the Spirit, and as a Son whom God loves and to whom God has entrusted all

---

[3] See the classic studies by J. L. Martyn, *History and Theology in the Fourth Gospel* (2d ed.; Nashville: Abingdon, 1979); and W. A. Meeks, "The Man from Heaven in Johannine Sectarianism," *JBL* 91 (1972): 44–72.

[4] A recent probe of Johannine Christology that emphasizes Jesus' role as *agent* of God is that of P. N. Anderson, *The Christology of the Fourth Gospel* (WUNT 78; Tübingen: J. C. B. Mohr [Paul Siebeck], 1996).

[5] As P. W. Meyer points out, the sending formula always appears in the active voice when applied to Jesus in the Fourth Gospel: "[God] who sent him," not "[Jesus] who was sent." Meyer comments: "The language of 'sending' is *theo*logical language that undergirds Christology but refuses to be absorbed into it" (" 'The Father': The Presentation of God in the Fourth Gospel," in *Exploring the Gospel of John: In Honor of D. Moody Smith* [ed. R. A. Culpepper and C. C. Black; Louisville: Westminster John Knox, 1996], 264).

things, Jesus was sent to speak the very words of God (3:34; cf. 12:49; 14:24). He also accomplishes the work of God; in fact, this is all the nourishment he needs (4:34). His single-minded commitment to the will of the one who sent him also comes to expression in his exercise of judgment: God has granted to him the authority to judge, but he judges in a way that points back to the purpose and discernment of God (5:30). Therefore, the actions of Jesus (his "works") amount to testimony from God on his behalf (5:36–38; cf. 8:18; 9:4). What is required of those who experience his works is *belief;* this is itself the work of God (6:29). Those who believe will not be lost, even if it means that Jesus must raise them up on the last day (6:39, 44). The life of the God who sent him now fills everyone who "eats" this living bread from heaven, and this life is eternal (6:57–58; cf. 17:3).

Jesus teaches what God has sent him to teach, and speaks in a way that honors God (7:16, 18). Even if Jesus' critics lack true knowledge of God, he cannot but know the God who sent him (7:28–29). Anticipating his departure from this world, Jesus tells temple police ordered to arrest him that he will soon return to the one who sent him (7:33; cf. 16:5). In the course of a sharp exchange over paternity—who may legitimately appeal to Abraham as father?—Jesus returns to a familiar theme, ascribing his words and actions to the God who is true and gives testimony for him (8:26, 29). He is God's agent, and does not represent his own interests (8:42). He cannot be fairly accused of blasphemy, therefore: far from making himself out to be God, he shows himself to be God's Son by doing the works of his Father who sanctified him and sent him (10:32–33, 36).[6] To believe in him means, then, to believe in God who sent him, and whom he represents to the world (12:44–45). To accept him is to accept God, and since he now sends his disciples, this welcome must now be extended also to them (13:20; cf. 17:18; 20:21). In a world such as ours, however, many will despise both Jesus and his friends, and this hatred betrays lack of knowledge of the God who sent him

---

[6] This puts the lie to the later charge (before Pilate) that Jesus deserves to die because he "made himself out to be the Son of God" (19:7).

(15:18–21). Nevertheless, the disciples believe that Jesus was sent by God (17:8, 25); their witness and their unity are to persuade the world that this is true (17:21, 23).

Even though this brief survey represents only one strand from the dense web that is John's Christology, this extraordinary set of claims—all stemming from Jesus' discourses—exposes the nerve center of this gospel's presentation of Jesus. Eternal life is available in the present to all who respond in faith to Jesus' disclosure of the divine word and will. One might paint a similar picture out of other materials with which the sending Christology is intertwined, notably the descent-ascent pattern and language of Jesus' "coming" from God into the world.

Jesus is sent into the world from God; that is, he has come down "from above," "from heaven" (6:33, 38, 50–51, 58; 8:23).[7] Though not "from this world" (8:23; 17:16), he does enter it in order to offer eternal life to all who believe. Once his work is completed, he returns to the world above. Within this pattern of descent and ascent, Jesus' death becomes his departure to return to the Father.[8] The Son of humanity epithet for Jesus also typically serves this descent-ascent motif (3:14; 6:62; 8:28; 12:23, 34; 13:31). Jesus has come as the Son of humanity—come, in fact, to exercise judgment, a fitting eschatological role for this figure (5:27). But once again the cross transforms the image of Jesus' ascent or exaltation, for the "lifting up" or "glorification" of the Son of humanity is, paradoxically, his crucifixion. This is the long-delayed "hour," the hour of glory for which the reader has waited from the Cana wedding onward.[9] In laying down his life for the world, Jesus completes the task he came to do.

The eschatological sending into the world of the Messiah who is God's Son (and Son of humanity) has already occurred. In

---

[7] See Meeks, "Man from Heaven."

[8] See G. C. Nicholson, *Death as Departure: The Johannine Descent-Ascent Schema* (SBLDS 63; Chico, Calif.: Scholars Press, 1983).

[9] In contrast to the stress in the Synoptics on the *future* glory of the Son of humanity at his parousia (e.g., Mark 13:26). For the motif of the "hour" of Jesus, see John 2:4; 7:6–8, 30; 8:20; 12:23; 13:1.

a real sense, the eschaton is present in the incarnate one, and eternal life is available even now to those who assent to his revelation of divine truth. The presentation of the themes of judgment and resurrection (life) reinforces this shift toward the present as primary locus for eschatological salvation.

The Presence of the Eschaton: Eternal Life Now

In John 4 many Samaritans emerge from their encounter with Jesus convinced that he is the "Savior of the world" (v. 42). Their point of view is closely aligned with that of the narrator. Jesus embodies God's salvation for the world; access to the abundant life God offers is opened up even now. Yet this life comes only to those who have faith; those who remain closed to the revelation (that is, who refuse the Revealer) are left in the domain of darkness and death.[10]

Judgment

The end-time drama in apocalyptic literature highlights the motif of judgment. The nations, or the wicked, will be summoned before the seat of judgment and there held accountable for the evil they have done.[11] This "day of judgment" is characteristically an eschatological event awaited in the future. The Johannine reinterpretation of this theme is stunning. The decisive end-time judgment is shifted to the present encounter with Jesus, who reveals God to the world. Those who embrace the Revealer's message—and that means they embrace the Revealer himself—no longer face judgment (i.e., condemnation), while

---

[10] This fundamental soteriological pattern in John's Gospel is captured especially well by R. Bultmann, *The Gospel of John: A Commentary* (Philadelphia: Westminster, 1971), e.g., 154–57. On the world's encounter with Jesus as the decisive eschatological moment of κρίσις, in which humanity divides in response to God's revelation, see J. Blank, *Krisis: Untersuchungen zur johanneischen Christologie und Eschatologie* (Freiburg: Lambertus, 1964).

[11] For example, see the vivid judgment scenes in Matt 25:31–46; *1 Enoch* 61–63.

those who reject him are even now surrendered to divine judgment. After Jesus' departure to the world above, the Paraclete continues to confront humanity with this fateful decision.

The judgment theme assumes what appears to be paradoxical form in John's Gospel. On the one hand, Jesus declares that he does not judge; he came into the world not to judge but to save (3:17; 12:47). But on the other hand, he claims that the divine prerogative of exercising judgment has been given to him (in his role as Son of humanity), and he pronounces true judgment (5:22, 27; 8:16). How is the tension between these two views to be understood? John 8:15–16 suggests an answer. Jesus' audience of critics judges, but it does so κατὰ τὴν σάρκα ("according to the flesh"), that is, by human discernment apart from divine truth (8:15). This passage is permeated with forensic language (especially "testimony" and "judgment"). Jesus is, in fact, on trial.[12] Unlike his judges (i.e., his critics and accusers), Jesus does not judge. And yet if he does judge, he is truthful, because this is not Jesus' private discernment but the judgment of God, with which Jesus is in perfect accord. *Jesus* does not judge, for *God* judges with him.

A second answer surfaces at the close of Jesus' public teaching in the gospel, when he returns to the theme of judgment. Despite his last and most impressive sign—the raising of Lazarus—the tide of belief elicited by these signs has turned back, and unbelief persists (12:36b–43). In response (12:44–50), Jesus plays a familiar tune: acceptance of him is actually acceptance of God who sent him (vv. 44–46). He then repeats the "I do not judge" claim (v. 47a), insisting once again that the purpose of his coming is salvation rather than condemnation (v. 47b). Verse 48 spells out clearly the way judgment works. It is not Jesus but the word he has declared that judges persons who reject him. But since Jesus' word in fact delivers the message given to him by God (vv. 49–50), this second approach to the tension between

---

[12] Since John does not narrate a "trial" of Jesus in the passion narrative, the repeated interrogations of Jesus throughout chs. 3–12 take its place. See J. T. Carroll and J. B. Green, *The Death of Jesus in Early Christianity* (Peabody, Mass.: Hendrickson, 1995), 84.

judgment and no judgment turns out to be a variation on the first. Those who reject Jesus' message, in effect, pronounce judgment upon themselves, for they are turning away from the God who authorizes Jesus' word and work. Therefore, the decisive judgment against a world closed to divine revelation occurs not in the eschatological future but in the present when the confrontation with divine truth occurs.

Life

The same pattern emerges when we consider the images of life and resurrection. The alternative to judgment is eternal life, which comes to those who accept Jesus' word and work. The Johannine prologue (1:1–18) already presents Jesus as the Word, who is the source of both life and light (v. 4), the one in whom all must believe if they are to belong to God's family (vv. 12–13). John, in his role as witness to the light, came for the purpose of eliciting such faith (v. 7).

The encounter between Jesus and Nicodemus richly develops the prologue imagery of light and darkness; believing and birth into God's family; and resistance to belief, characterized as a refusal to "receive" the testimony of Jesus and his followers (3:1–21). This "teacher of Israel" (v. 10) is unable to comprehend Jesus' teaching about rebirth from above (ἄνωθεν)—no surprise, since he comes to Jesus "during the night" (v. 2),[13] prompted by the impressive signs performed by Jesus in Jerusalem. The narrator has just alerted readers that faith inspired by signs is not to be trusted, because Jesus himself knows better (2:23–25). Jesus shows Nicodemus—or rather, through Nicodemus's misunderstanding, shows the reader—that to perceive or to enter God's realm, one must experience a spiritual rebirth that only the Spirit of God can accomplish (3:3, 5, 8).

Language of God's reign, remarkable by its absence elsewhere in the Fourth Gospel, quickly gives way to images more at

---

[13] The symbolic potential of "night" is exploited in John 9:4 and especially 13:30 (Judas!).

home in the Johannine linguistic world. Jesus speaks of the necessity of the "lifting up" (ὑψωθῆναι) of the Son of humanity, "that everyone who believes in him may have eternal life" (vv. 14–15). The redemptive, life-giving effect of the lifting up of Jesus was prefigured by Moses' raising the bronze serpent on a pole in the wilderness, so that "all who are bitten, when they see it, may live" (Num 21:8–9). Jesus, too, will be "lifted up" on a pole—the cross (cf. 12:31–33). And this physical elevation of Jesus' body from the earth symbolizes his exaltation by God, who honors the Son's faithfulness to the point of surrendering his life for the sake of the world (e.g., 10:17; 12:23, 28). As Jesus proceeds to explain, God's gift of the Son was intended to evoke faith that enables one to receive eternal life; God's sending of the Son offered salvation to the world (3:16–17).[14]

John's Gospel replays this chord uniting belief and eternal life over and over again. It becomes increasingly clear that the life that opens up for those with faith is not something reserved for the future but already becomes a reality in the present. The Samaritan woman at Jacob's well hears of "living water" provided by Jesus: "[W]hoever drinks of the water that I will give will never thirst again, but the water I will give will become for that person a spring [or well] flowing into eternal life" (4:14). Challenged by opponents after a Sabbath healing of a paralyzed man, Jesus claims to possess divine authorization to give life (5:21, 26); therefore, "the one who hears my word and believes the One who sent me has eternal life and . . . has crossed over from death to life" (5:24). In the aftermath of the feeding of a large crowd, Jesus provokes an initially sympathetic audience with the audacious claim to be "living bread" that came down from heaven, providing eternal nourishment for those who be-

---

[14] It is immaterial whether Jesus is still speaking in 3:16 or whether the narrator has taken over. The character Jesus already expresses the narrator's "voice," which in turn represents the believing perspective of the Johannine community. The oscillation between singular and plural forms ("I" and "we," "you" [sing.] and "you" [pl.] in vv. 7, 11–12) suggests that Jesus and Nicodemus articulate the belief and resistance of John's community and its Jewish contemporaries.

lieve, those who will eat (6:35, 48, 50–51). "The one who devours this bread will live forever" (6:58), the one who believes has eternal life (6:47).

The raising of Lazarus enacts the point dramatically. This final sign discloses that Jesus is "the resurrection and the life" (11:25). He corrects Martha's believing—but only partially discerning—affirmation that her brother "will be raised up in the resurrection on the last day" (11:24). No, resurrection life is available right now: "[T]he one who believes in me even in dying will live; and everyone who lives and believes in me will never die" (11:25–26). The Fourth Gospel celebrates the "eternal life" that comes to all who accept God's self-disclosure in the person, word, and work of Jesus. And this is not life in prospect, but genuine, abundant life experienced in the present. The narrative affirms the presence of the eschaton in the midst of the believing community. Nevertheless, chapters 5 and 6 also contain language of a future resurrection. Despite such a sharp accent on the eschatological present, the future does not entirely vanish in John's Gospel.

Jesus' Future Coming and Abiding Faith

Even in a narrative so dominated by "realized eschatology," the reader encounters elements pointing to persisting eschatological hope. To be sure, Jesus has received from God, the author of resurrection life, the authority to give life to persons with faith and to judge those who persist in unbelief (5:19–24). Yet in the next step of the argument, the image of a future resurrection gains in prominence:

> [A]n hour is coming when all who are in the tombs will hear [the Son of humanity's] voice, and they will come out—those who have done good to a resurrection of life, but those who have done evil to a resurrection of judgment. (5:28b–29)

Verse 25 anticipates this image of an hour that "is coming," but in typically Johannine fashion draws that future hour into the present moment: "[A]n hour is coming *and now is* when the dead will hear the voice of the Son of God and those who hear will live." Nevertheless, the fact that the repetition of the line in verse 28 drops the phrase "now is" shows that the Johannine Jesus does not dispense with expectation of a future resurrection. Resurrection is not reduced to present experience. For those who have lived well, eschatological resurrection will open up eternal life, while judgment will greet evildoers (cf. Dan 12:2).[15]

The doing of good or evil as a criterion for one's eschatological fortunes is striking; John invariably presents believing reception of divine revelation through Jesus as the key to life. An earlier mention of evil deeds in connection with judgment (3:16–21) suggests the inner logic here. Those who do evil inevitably also turn away from the light, because the light (Jesus as revealer of truth) will expose them for what they are (vv. 19–20). On the other hand, those who do good are persons whose "actions have been done in God" (v. 21), and who are therefore persons of faith. The Fourth Gospel is not entirely innocent of moral appeals; Jesus commands the disciples to "love one another" (13:34–35; 15:12–17), and pictures their life in terms of "bearing fruit," "keeping [his] commandments," and "abiding in [his] love" (15:1–11). Each of these images, however, features the disciple's intimate relationship with Jesus himself. Doing good ("abiding in love") is the outer face of abiding faith in God's Son. Genuine faith in him, expressed in a life of love, must continue throughout life, and will be honored in the eschatological resurrection. Responding to later developments within the Johannine community, the First Letter of John will richly embellish these moral appeals.

---

[15] Against redaction and interpolation theories that assign present-oriented and future-oriented eschatology in John to different stages in the Johannine tradition, N. A. Dahl argues that "references to the future resurrection do not correct but rather support sayings about the presence of life and judgment," as an "eschatological verification of Jesus' promise" (" 'Do Not Wonder!' John 5:28–29 and Johannine Eschatology Once More," in *The Conversation Continues: Studies in Paul and John in Honor of J. Louis Martyn* [ed. R. T. Fortna and B. R. Gaventa; Nashville: Abingdon, 1994], 328).

The tension between future ("is coming") and present
("now is") surfaces again in the bread of life discourse (ch. 6).
Now the general picture of a future resurrection is given sharp,
precise focus, as Jesus speaks of resurrection "on the last day."
To skeptical and increasingly hostile ears, he presents himself as
"living bread" that has come down from heaven to offer life to
the world. Here John trumps the manna traditions associated
with Moses in Jewish memory,[16] for Jesus nourishes with bread
that has lasting effect. In verses 35–40 Jesus makes the characteristic Johannine move, advancing from the image of bread to
the inseparable motifs of belief and eternal life.[17] Yet Jesus affirms not just the gift of eternal life for those who believe but the
preservation of that life beyond death. Four times we meet the
refrain "I will raise it up on the last day" (vv. 39, 40, 44, 54). Persons who receive Jesus and the revelation he brings do so because God has drawn them to that faith (vv. 37, 39, 44, 65).
Within the discourse this claim explains the chilling effect of the
scene; all but the Twelve turn away from Jesus by the time he
has finished speaking—and one of them "a devil"! Only those
whom God truly "gives" to the Son have authentic faith that persists. The point of the resurrection image, then, is that Jesus will
honor abiding faith by preserving the life of believers even beyond death.

In a gospel that casts the spotlight on the presence of the
eschaton in Jesus, two realities evoke the image of a future, eschatological resurrection: the experienced reality of death
within the community of faith, and the reality of faith that does
not persist. If genuine faith is faith that "abides," then the escha-

---

[16] See Anderson, *Christology.*

[17] The motif of belief is already introduced in vv. 29–30 in association with the imagery of "work" and "sign." Jesus asserts that the work
of God is believing in the one sent by God. The audience grasps that
Jesus is calling for belief in himself, and asks for a sign—after having experienced the feeding of the large crowd! The motif of eternal life first
appears in the discourse in v. 27: Jesus directs his audience toward concern with food that has staying power—"unto eternal life."

tological resurrection—to life or judgment—serves to confirm the integrity of belief.

"Abiding Faith"

Will faith that draws one into abundant and eternal life endure? Will the disciple remain in productive relationship with the source of life? Eschatology cautions and warns: events of the end time—or better, *the* event of the end time—confirm the genuineness and persistence of faith. This is by no means a trivial concern in John's narrative, where faith seems to come with such difficulty and go with such ease. As we have already seen, a crowd that had just witnessed (and benefited from) the feeding "sign" and sought Jesus out with the intent of acclaiming him king encounters his radical claim to be the true bread from heaven and turns away from faith (6:1–59). Yet even his disciples find his teaching disturbing and offensive, and many walk away (6:60, 66). A similar pattern marks the aftermath of the raising of Lazarus. For many, the immediate outcome of this sign is faith (11:45), but for others conspiracy to have Jesus executed (11:46–53). And the crowd responds to Jesus' subsequent teaching in Jerusalem with unbelief (12:37).

Small wonder, then, that Jesus should address the theme of persevering faith in his farewell discourses, in which he prepares the remaining disciples for his imminent departure. Jesus seizes upon the image of a vine and its branches. As branches live only while attached to the vine, so the disciples have life only when connected to him, the source of their life (15:1–11). Their faith must last, and it must be fruitful (15:12–17), and this must occur in a world that is implacably hostile to them (15:18–27). In such a world, their ability to demonstrate abiding discipleship through their love as a community of friends (13:34–35; 15:10, 12–17; 17:26) and through their unity (17:11, 22–23) will undergo severe strain. In fact, as 1 John shows, their faith will be inadequate to the challenge. As one might expect, the author of that letter, responding to the bitter experience of community schism, gives increased prominence to specific moral appeals and explicit eschatological affirmations.

"I Will Come Again"

The farewell discourses present the image of Jesus' future "coming again" (πάλιν ἔρχομαι)[18] to encourage and console the disciples (14:3). Both the language of Jesus' coming and its pastoral function of encouragement appear to replicate the patterns of parousia expectation in the Synoptic Gospels. Appearances, however, are usually deceiving in the Fourth Gospel, and such is the case here. Jesus, though with the disciples a "little while" longer, is departing to a place where they will be unable to come (13:33). Responding to Simon Peter's uncomprehending bravado with the chilling prediction of his threefold denial (13:36–38), Jesus proceeds to reassure Peter and his comrades. He bids them persevere in their faith and find comfort in the knowledge that the divine home holds rooms specially prepared for them by Jesus himself (14:1–2). He will soon go to prepare those rooms, and then he will come again and will receive the disciples so that their fellowship with him may continue unbroken (14:3).This is the crucial point of the discourse. But what future coming of Jesus to the disciples is being promised? Is it the parousia—in which case the expectation of John approaches that of the other gospels? Or is it the resurrection appearances?[19] Moreover, since the departure of Jesus coincides with the coming of the

---

[18] The verb here is in the present tense, but with obvious future nuance: "I am going to come again." (Note that the verb paired with ἔρχομαι in 14:3 is in the future tense: "I will receive [παραλήμψομαι] you to myself.") It is characteristic of John to picture Jesus' future coming in terms of his present activity. But which future coming is in view, the resurrection or the parousia? R. Schnackenburg suggests that the expression "I am coming again [πάλιν ἔρχομαι]" in 14:13 (echoed in 14:18), relying on a traditional formulation, is reminiscent of the parousia, yet it no longer refers to the parousia but to the "saving present since Jesus' resurrection" (*The Gospel according to St John* [3 vols.; New York: Crossroad, 1968–82], 2:430).

[19] For a recent discussion of the interpretive options, see J. Neugebauer, *Die eschatologischen Aussagen in den johanneischen Abschiedsreden: Eine Untersuchung zu Johannes 13–17* (BWANT 140; Stuttgart: Kohlhammer, 1995).

Paraclete, and since the risen Jesus "breathes" the Spirit upon them (20:22), the coming of Jesus and that of the Spirit are inextricably tied.

Jesus repeats the pledge that he will come to the disciples: "I am coming [ἔρχομαι] to you" (14:18), a promise he recalls in 14:28. Then chapter 16 develops the "little while" image from 13:33. There will be a brief period when the disciples will be unable to see Jesus, "and again a little while" and they will see him (16:16). In these passages, both the language of Jesus' return to his disciples and the characterization of the time of their separation as a "little while" point to the Easter appearances as the "coming" and "seeing" of which Jesus speaks.

The farewell discourses make clear that the faith of Jesus' "friends" must abide—and therefore imagery of eschatological judgment retains a place in the Johannine symbolic universe—not only because the community must come to terms with the reality of death, and not only because they must withstand every pressure toward apostasy, but also because they must find their way without Jesus, that is, without his physical presence. And they must do so in a hostile environment. The promised coming of "another Paraclete" (14:16) lies at the heart of the rhetoric of consolation that governs these final words of Jesus to his own. The narrative's design frustrates any attempt to provide a single, unequivocal answer to the question, Which coming (and whose)? Does the recurring pattern of disciple misunderstanding throughout this section (touching on both the "little while" and the "going and coming" imagery) reflect confusion in the Johannine community over precisely eschatological questions?

The promise of a coming to the disciples finds fulfillment in the Easter appearances, which restore joy to the grieving disciples (cf. 16:22 and 20:20), and also in the "parousia" of the Spirit in the community's experience. Although an eschatological coming of Jesus is not excluded by the farewell discourses, it does not figure significantly (if at all) in the message of consolation offered here. In the farewell discourses, true to Johannine form, comfort is delivered through the vehicle of an eschatological view strongly oriented toward the present. From the vantage of John's community, the decisive parousia of Jesus lies in the past.

The closing scene of the narrative does anticipate the end-time parousia. Jesus has just restored Peter to discipleship and predicted his martyrdom (21:15–19). What of the beloved disciple with whom Peter is invariably paired (to Peter's disadvantage) in chapters 13–21? Jesus answers a curious Peter: "If I want him [the beloved disciple] to remain until I come [ἕως ἔρχομαι], what is that to you?" (21:22). Lest the reader be confused by rumors that this disciple would not die, the narrator hastens to clarify, "Jesus did not tell him, 'He is not going to die,' but 'If I want him to remain until I come'" (21:23). This exchange presupposes a delay in Jesus' return and considerable confusion in the community over the experience of death in the meantime. Moreover, unlike the rest of the Fourth Gospel, it refers clearly, though in passing, to an eschatological coming of Jesus. This solitary explicit reference to the end-time parousia in John aligns the passage with 1 John. The theory of multiple editions of the Fourth Gospel, with chapter 21 stemming from a later edition,[20] suggests the explanation that the turn toward the future in this "appendix" to John reflects later struggles in the community's history, struggles that also shaped the Epistle.

FIRST LETTER OF JOHN

Where the Fourth Gospel sharply accents the eschatological significance of the present, 1 John shifts the balance toward the future. The present life of the community, marred by a painful schism that betrays deficient christological understanding and failure to love on the part of many, is important, to be sure. Yet as the present experience of an embattled group of believers casts doubt on the authenticity of the faith of some, the letter reflects increased concern with end-time events that will confirm or impugn the integrity of belief. Such images as the (future)

---

[20] See, e.g., R. E. Brown, *The Gospel according to John* (AB 29–29A; 2 vols.; Garden City, N.Y.: Doubleday, 1966–70), 2:1077–82.

parousia of Jesus, the day of judgment, and even the appearance of antichrist draw readers' attention to the ultimate outcome of the community's present crisis.

Eternal Life and the Integrity of the Community's Faith

The recipients of this letter[21] receive assurance that they are God's children, birthed from God (1 John 3:1–2; 5:1, 4; cf. John 1:12–13). They have been transferred from the sphere of darkness to that of light (1:5–7; 2:8, 10; cf. John 1:4–5; 8:12; 9:5), from death to life (3:14; cf. John 3:15–16; 5:24). By virtue of their belief in Jesus as the Christ "come in the flesh" (4:2), as the "Son of God" (4:15; 5:1, 10–13), they enjoy permanent fellowship with God; they "have life"—eternal life. But there is no room for false assurance. Just as many "who had believed" were scandalized by Jesus' "living bread" discourse and walked away (John 6), apostasy from faith is a real possibility in the Johannine community. No, it is fact. Some have left the fold. For such persons, the author of 1 John minces no words. Those who deny that Jesus is the Christ deny God ("the Father") as well (2:22–23). Those who do not confess Jesus [Christ come in the flesh] do not belong to God (4:3). Their true identity is that of "antichrist" (2:22; 4:3). They do not "have life" (5:12). While these strictures would certainly apply to outsiders who had never embraced the community's faith, the real target appears to be former members who have left the Johannine group. The "many antichrists" of whom the author speaks in 2:18—antichrists who by denying the Son deny the Father—were once part of the community (2:19).

---

[21] Although 1 John lacks the formal markers of a letter, it is a "written" communication (e.g., 1:4; 2:1, 7, 12) and appears to be a response to a specific occasion, as with other New Testament letters. On the genre of 1 John, see C. C. Black, "First, Second, and Third John," *NIB* 12.370–71; J. Lieu, *The Theology of the Johannine Epistles* (NTT; Cambridge: Cambridge University Press, 1991), 2–4; D. M. Smith, *First, Second, and Third John* (IBC; Louisville: John Knox, 1991), 8–9; G. Strecker, *The Johannine Letters: A Commentary on 1, 2, and 3 John* (Hermeneia; Minneapolis: Fortress, 1996), 3. Strecker terms 1 John a "homily in the form of a letter."

The readers of 1 John are reassured, despite the recent strife in the community of believers, that the promise of eternal life remains in force for them (2:25), but only if their faith abides (2:24). They are assured that their sins have been forgiven (2:1–2, 12), but they must not persist in sin, as if they were children of the evil one (3:4–10).[22] They have vanquished the evil one (2:13–14), but only because they have strength derived from the presence of the divine word within them (v. 14). They have overcome the world, a world under the sway of evil, but only through the constancy of their faith in the Son of God (5:4–5, 19). They await Jesus' parousia with confidence, but only because they abide in him, and so belong to God's family (2:28–3:3).[23] They may live without fear of condemnation on the day of judgment, but only because they embody the divine love in which they continue to abide (4:13–21). Eschatological images and motifs in the letter not only encourage but also admonish, and they forge a strong link between the persistence of genuine belief and the moral life of the community.

Eternal Life and the Moral Life

It is no accident that 1 John is permeated by moral appeals that center on the author's "new" articulation of an ancient commandment (2:7–8): love of one's brother and sister. The once solid social boundaries separating the Johannine community from an antagonistic world have deteriorated, and the social co-

---

[22] The prominence 1 John gives to atonement imagery represents an intriguing departure from the Fourth Gospel, despite the presentation of Jesus as the paschal lamb "who takes away the world's sin" (John 1:29). For discussion of atonement themes in the letter, see R. E. Brown, *The Epistles of John* (AB 30; Garden City, N.Y.: Doubleday, 1982), 217–22, 238–42; Strecker, *Johannine Letters,* 29–33; Smith, *First, Second, and Third John,* 43–45.

[23] Although the third person pronouns in 1 John 2:28–3:3 are ambiguous (some may be taken as referring to God rather than Jesus), I read the passage as presenting the parousia of Jesus. See Black, "First, Second, and Third John," 409; Brown, *Epistles of John,* 382, 384, 394.

hesion that was once the hallmark of the group has grown weaker and weaker. Love and unity have proven elusive. It is these communal values that the author reinforces with fervent and often poignant moral appeals.

What is the proof that one is born of God, if not a moral character defined by that affiliation rather than by sin (3:9–10; 5:18)? While none can claim to be sinless (1:8), it is also true that sin—which is the work of the evil one—calls into question one's status as child of God (3:4–10; 5:18).[24] Those who continue in faith have been delivered from darkness and death and are assured eternal life, but what is the evidence that faith abides? Again and again the author points to the moral life as evidence of the genuineness of faith. Those who walk in the light God supplies maintain fellowship with others in the Johannine group (1:6–7). If they instead hate their brother or sister in the community, they remain in darkness, no matter how loud their claims to be walking in the light (2:9–11). Love marks one as a person of faith who has entered the domain of life, but those who hate remain in the sphere of death (3:14–15). All who truly love God will also love brother and sister in the community; otherwise, one's claim to be a lover of God is exposed as a lie (4:20).

For the most part, love is defined in quite general terms, and primarily in opposition to hate. Yet 1 John does emphatically point to Jesus as the model of the love to which the community is summoned. Love is willing to sacrifice life itself for the sake of other community members, emulating Jesus' self-surrender (3:16–17). Those who "know him" and "abide in him" must live as he lived (2:3–6). Love is not a matter of speech but of action,

---

[24] Evidently the author of 1 John is less interested in logical consistency than are many modern readers. For a treatment of this apparent paradox, see Lieu, *Theology of Johannine Epistles*, 58–65; Black, "First, Second, and Third John," 414–16; Brown, *Epistles of John*, 411–16, 430–31; Strecker, *Johannine Letters*, 101–6. Strecker (104) suggests: " 'Being incapable of sin' represents the eschatological reality" by which "the community has lived from its beginning." The "earthly reality," however, is that "sin remains a threatening force that must be repeatedly overcome, until the end of the world."

as witnessed by compassionate response to the need of another in the community (3:17–18).

Love of the other confirms that one "abides in him [God's Son]," and that connection to the source of life is the ground for confidence at the parousia of Jesus (2:28). Love of the other demonstrates that one lives out of the divine love and truly loves God, and therefore gives confidence for the day of judgment (4:17). It is revealing that these two explicit end-time images are so closely tied to the author's appeal for a community defined by love for one another.[25] But not all embody this love. In fact, the bitter experience of the community, with deficient christological understanding embodied in attacks on community solidarity, is a sign for readers that the eschatological era has begun.

"It Is the Last Hour": The Arrival of Antichrist

"Children, it is the last hour" (2:18). What is the warrant for such a bold claim? The author taps the traditional expectation "that antichrist is coming," but bends it to his own rhetorical purpose. "Many antichrists have come," and therefore the final era has dawned. We do not meet here the menacing, suprahuman figure of lawlessness and terror familiar to us from 2 Thessalonians 2, or from centuries of apocalyptic speculation.[26] Rather, the label "antichrist" fits former members of the Johannine group who, by deserting the community, have shown

---

[25] As W. A. Meeks contends, the love command in John and 1 John directs the "internal life of the Johannine sect," and "it is this mutual love within the community that is set over against the world's hatred" ("The Ethics of the Fourth Evangelist," in Culpepper and Black, *Exploring the Gospel of John*, 324). Cf. Lieu, *Theology of Johannine Epistles*, 42, 53, 68–69; Black, "First, Second, and Third John," 376–77.

[26] See B. McGinn, *Antichrist: Two Thousand Years of the Human Fascination with Evil* (San Francisco: Harper, 1994); R. Rosconi, "Antichrist and Antichrists," in *Apocalypticism in Western History and Culture,* vol. 2 of *The Encyclopedia of Apocalypticism* (ed. B. McGinn; New York: Continuum, 1998), 287–325; Strecker, *Johannine Letters,* 236–41; and, on the earlier historical development of related traditions, L. J. L. Peerbolte, *The Antecedents of Antichrist: A Traditio-Historical*

that they deny Jesus as the Christ, and therefore deny both Father and Son (2:19, 22–23). The author returns to this theme in chapter 4, where it is refusal to confess Jesus as [come] "from God" that brands one an antichrist (4:3). A further nuance is added in 2 John 7, which speaks of deceivers who "do not confess Jesus Christ coming *in the flesh*" as the antichrist.[27]

By affixing the label "antichrist," 1 John highlights the danger posed by a christological perspective that does not give full weight to the incarnation of the divine word in human flesh—presumably an early Docetic view anticipating later developments in some variants of Christian Gnosticism.[28] Disputes within the Johannine community should not be considered trivial. Those who have maintained their allegiance to the author's group are given a clear picture of what is at stake. At the same time, the deployment of the antichrist metaphor situates the reader in the time of the End. It has already begun. By drawing the eschaton into the community's present experience, 1 John makes contact with the dominant eschatological orientation of the Fourth Gospel. Yet the explicit appropriation of end-time imagery such as "last hour" and "antichrist" (in addition to "day of judgment" and "parousia") represents a genuine advance beyond the gospel.[29]

Study of the Earliest Christian Views on Eschatological Opponents (Leiden: Brill, 1996).

[27] The participle in 2 John 7 (ἐρχόμενον) is present tense, in contrast to the perfect tense in 1 John 4:2. This distinction in tenses is invested with immense significance in the historical reconstruction advanced by Strecker. He insists that the present participle in 2 John 7 must be understood as present or future, and in fact refers to the parousia, not the incarnation (*Johannine Letters*, 233–36). Second John reflects a strongly chiliastic view (expecting a messianic reign on earth) that must be earlier than the posture of the Fourth Gospel or 1 John—a position later tempered in 1 John. This one detail in 2 John simply will not carry the weight Strecker places on it in his reconstruction. Cf. Black, "First, Second, and Third John," 452 n. 187.

[28] See Smith, *First, Second, and Third John*, 130–32; Strecker, *Johannine Letters*, 69–76.

[29] Lieu (*Theology of Johannine Epistles*, 87–90) discerns an emphasis on "realized eschatology" in 1 John, while acknowledging the letter's

At bottom, the rhetorical aims of eschatological language in 1 John involve persuasion. The author would convince community members to stay, to maintain their identification with the group, and to do so by holding to its christological confession and committing themselves to love for one another.

In 1 John, faith conquers evil and overcomes the world ruled by evil—witnessed even in the community's own internal life. Abiding faith enables one to approach the coming eschatological judgment with confidence. The letter's use of the military metaphor of conquest (with the verb νικάω) represents a natural extension of the Fourth Gospel. In that narrative, Jesus consoles the disciples with the knowledge that, although they will undergo intense persecution, he has "overcome [νενίκηκα] the world" (16:33). The conquest metaphor plays a crucial role in the book of Revelation, where it is applied to the work of both Jesus and the Christian community, but only in a radically paradoxical formulation: one "conquers" through faithful witness to God to the point of martyrdom (12:11). The reader of John's Apocalypse also finds that the eschatological future assumes a central significance. Expectation of an imminent parousia and detailed scenarios of the closure events of human history claim the reader's attention from first to last.

REVELATION OF JOHN

The book of Revelation, composed by a John who identifies himself as a prophet and characterizes his work as prophetic communication (1:3; 22:9, 10), lends urgency and dramatic power to expectation of Jesus' parousia.[30] This event plays an

---

use of the language of "future eschatology." "Faced with schism and perhaps with hostility, John does not take refuge from the present in the hopes of the future" (90). Brown (*Epistles of John*, 99–100) sees a "balance" between realized and future eschatology, as the author revived an earlier view (the future emphasis).

[30] Although my discussion of Johannine literature places Revelation in the same family as the Gospel and Letters of John, I make no

important role in the larger eschatological scenario that unfolds in the visions John reports. But we will discover that the seer's disclosure of the future serves rhetorical aims that target the present life of the communities to which John entrusts this prophetic revelation.

The One Who Conquers

Farrer spoke of the "rebirth of images" in the book of Revelation.[31] No image undergoes more astonishing rebirth than the military metaphor of conquest. Each of the seven messages addressed to the churches of Asia (through their angelic mediators) extends a divine promise to "the one who conquers" (ὁ νικῶν):

the privilege of eating from the tree of life in the paradise of God (2:7);

protection from the second death (2:11);

hidden manna, and a white stone with a secret name (2:17);

authority and rule over the nations, and the morning star (2:26–28);

white clothing, a name placed in the book of life, and acknowledgment before God (3:5);

placement as a pillar in the temple, bearing the name of God, the Holy City, and Jesus (3:12);

a share in divine rule—a seat on Jesus' throne (3:21).

---

claim that this John is to be identified with the author of any of these other texts, nor even that he is to be placed in the same community. On questions of authorship, and for comparison of Revelation to the other Johannine writings, see A. Yarbro Collins, *Crisis and Catharsis: The Power of the Apocalypse* (Philadelphia: Westminster, 1984), 25–53; E. Schüssler Fiorenza, *The Book of Revelation: Justice and Judgment* (Philadelphia: Fortress, 1985), 85–113; J. Roloff, *The Revelation of John: A Continental Commentary* (trans. J. E. Alsup; Minneapolis: Fortress, 1993), 11–12.

[31] A. Farrer, *A Rebirth of Images: The Making of St. John's Apocalypse* (Boston: Beacon, 1949).

God's conquering army is promised both earthly (even cosmic) dominion and eternal blessing and nourishment as people bearing the very name of God. John adds to this impressive list when he returns to the image again in the book's final vision. One who conquers will inherit "these things," presumably the blessings of participation in the eschatological city, "new Jerusalem," as a "son or daughter of God" (21:7).

Who is "the one who conquers," and how is victory attained? According to the admonition conveyed to the Christians in Thyatira, the victors are those who persevere "to the end" (ἄχρι τέλους) in keeping the works of the exalted Christ (2:26). What works? It is significant that the image of conqueror is the culminating element in each of the seven messages. The meaning of faithful performance of the works of Jesus therefore can be read in the mix of praise and blame that forms the "body" of each message.

Three times Christians of Asia are commended for their "patient endurance," or perseverance (ὑπομονή) in faith despite antagonism around them and false teaching within their communities (2:2–3, 19; 3:10). The exhortation to Smyrna is direct and unambiguous: "Be faithful to the point of death, and I will give you the crown of life" (2:10b). This appeal-with-promise immediately follows the prophecy that the Christians of Smyrna soon will experience intense—though temporary—adversity in the form of persecution (2:9–10a). John's readers are urged to win victory in the same way Jesus himself did, courageously and faithfully bearing witness for God, even at the cost of their lives. Persevering fidelity to God in the face of implacable opposition from the world's mighty—this is how one conquers![32]

---

[32] See A. Yarbro Collins, "The Book of Revelation," in *The Origins of Apocalypticism in Judaism and Christianity*, vol. 1 of *The Encyclopedia of Apocalypticism* (ed. J. J. Collins; 3 vols.; New York: Continuum, 1998), 400–3. For Collins, it is especially significant that "one who conquers" is for John one who refuses to participate in any activity that pays divine honors to the emperor. G. K. Beale argues that one conquers by emulating Jesus' endurance of suffering (*The Book of Revelation: A Commentary on the Greek Text* [NIGTC; Grand Rapids: Eerdmans, 1999], 171–72).

This paradox of victory through apparent defeat by the overwhelming force of the empire is grounded, of course, in Jesus' own victory over evil. As one vision has it, the dragon (Satan) has been vanquished in heaven, and for this very reason turns in violent rage against God's faithful on earth—though only for a limited time (12:7–17). In celebrating this victory, the hymns that give substance to the heavenly liturgy interspersed throughout the visions of chapters 4–22 show that it is Jesus' faithfulness unto death that triumphs over evil and, as it were, buys freedom for the people of God (5:9–10; cf. 12:11). The mighty lion turns out to be none other than a slaughtered lamb (5:5–6).[33] Active, nonviolent resistance to oppressive earthly powers is the method of conquest; in a world that is terrorized by a beast masquerading as a gentle lamb, one prevails, if necessary, by surrendering life, but never surrendering one's allegiance to the one who sits, unseen, on heaven's throne.

As the seer's visions rush toward their denouement, Jesus appears to conquer in a more conventional manner. Attacked by ten kings aligned with the beast, the Lamb wins victory over them in battle (17:13–14). This decisive eschatological battle is narrated more expansively in 19:11–21. In both passages, the Lamb prevails because he exercises dominion over all earthly powers and rulers (17:14; 19:16). It is worth noting, however, that he wields power in justice (19:11), and his sword is the word he pronounces (19:15; cf. 1:16; 2:16; 19:21). Despite all the imagery of destruction in John's visions, the conquest he envisions is finally not a new system of domination (God's) overpowering another (Caesar's or Satan's), but the victory of divine justice and truth. Victory comes to the Lamb, and therefore to all who remain true to him, because God is the one who is seated on the throne. God reigns, and shares dominion with the Lamb. God's faithful, powerless though they may be, also share in this rule over the nations.

---

[33] See Carroll and Green, *Death of Jesus*, 144–45; cf. R. H. Mounce, *The Book of Revelation* (NICNT; rev. ed.; Grand Rapids: Eerdmans, 1998), 132.

And They Will Reign Forever

Contrary to all appearances, God is sovereign. That is the fundamental affirmation of Revelation.[34] The remarkable visions of this book enact the confident declaration of the heavenly liturgy: "The kingdom of the world has become [the kingdom] of our Lord and of his Christ, and he will rule forever" (11:15; cf. 17:14; 19:6, 16). God's reign, exercised through the co-regency of the Lamb (Jesus), means, of course, the demotion of the emperor, and it presupposes the defeat of the dragon (Satan) and the beast through whom Satan attacks God's faithful.

Of particular interest in this connection is the way John's Apocalypse draws God's people into that sovereign rule of God.[35] This is a dramatic case of power sharing. Two of the seven messages to the churches of Asia play this tune. As we have already seen, the letter to Thyatira promises power over the nations to the one who conquers, who persists in performing (keeping) the works of Jesus (2:26). Such a one will rule the nations "with an iron rod," an image drawn from Ps 2:9 and applied to Jesus himself in Rev 12:5; 19:15. This is an appropriate reward for Christians who shun the "deep things of Satan" (2:24), since the preceding message to Pergamum, site of "Satan's throne,"[36] makes clear that the only true rival to God's throne is that of Satan. John's visions are deeply ironic in their depiction of power; readers witness a reversal in which the oppressed, marginalized people who remain loyal to God displace Rome's power brokers.

---

[34] See M. E. Boring, "The Theology of Revelation: 'The Lord Our God the Almighty Reigns,' " *Int* 40 (1986): 257–69; cf. Roloff, *Revelation,* 29; R. Bauckham, *The Theology of the Book of Revelation* (NTT; Cambridge: Cambridge University Press, 1993), 8–9, 30–33; Beale, *Revelation,* 172–73.

[35] Cf. M. E. Boring, *Revelation* (IBC; Louisville: John Knox, 1989), 106–7; Bauckham, *Theology of Revelation,* 142–43.

[36] That is, the city from which the governor administers Roman imperial rule.

The seven messages conclude with this throne symbol. The church at Laodicea hears that the one who conquers will sit with Jesus on his throne, which is none other than the very throne of God (3:21). The sovereign rule of God is not "power over" the people, but "power with" the faithful, though of course this shared reign is "over" the nations who have opposed God's ways and instead served evil. In view of this interest in appropriate power, it is no surprise that John's visions concerning what must happen "after these things" (4:1) begin at the throne of God. In this pivotal throne scene, the Lamb steps forward to open the scroll that unveils the mysteries of the future and sets in motion the divine judgment against oppressive, coercive evil in the world. At the opening of the scroll, a "new song" is sung in heaven to celebrate the Lamb's redemption of people from every nation (5:9–10).[37] The closing lines of the hymn describe that redeemed people as a "kingdom and priests" (v. 10). John images the fashioning of a people with a phrase that echoes God's original forming of the nation (see Exod 19:6). But not only are they a "kingdom and priests" (a royal realm ruled by another), but they will themselves share in the rule: "[T]hey will reign on the earth."

Readers of John's Apocalypse will recall this prophetic declaration when they hear in chapter 20 of a coming millennial reign. Babylon's demise has been announced and mourned (ch. 18), and the "Word of God" has defeated the beast and his royal allies in a decisive battle. The outcome: a gruesome "marriage supper of the Lamb" (19:9) in which the vanquished become carrion, the main course for the birds who are the invited guests; and torment in a fiery lake for the beast and deceiver/pseudoprophet (19:11–21). With the forces of evil routed, all that remains is for Satan himself to be removed from the scene. This occurs at the start of chapter 20, as an angel captures the dragon, binds him, and confines him in the bottomless pit (vv. 1–3). Ominously, the period of Satan's confinement is set at

---

[37] On the meaning of this metaphor in John, see Carroll and Green, *Death of Jesus*, 145–47.

a thousand years, after which he "must be set loose for a short time [μικρὸν χρόνον]" (v. 3). Evil is so tenacious that it is not until a final battle subsequent to the thousand years that Satan is finally vanquished and joins the beast in the fiery lake (vv. 7–10).

The millennium of Satan's confinement coincides with a thousand-year reign of Christ on earth (20:4–7). He does not, however, rule alone. Consistent with the pattern we have discerned elsewhere in Revelation, Christ shares rule with the faithful—not all God's loyal people, but the martyrs, who have paid with their lives for their courageous witness for God and their refusal to worship or give allegiance to the beast. They are raised from the dead in anticipation of the final resurrection, and serve as priests to God (cf. 5:10). Like the figure of antichrist, the millennial reign has captured the imagination of generations of readers across the centuries, and has been the subject of various interpretations.[38] The concern here is not to fit the millennium into a larger historical system, but to register its role in Revelation. It expresses concretely John's prophetic message of power reversal—the defeated reign. Those faithful to God share honor and dominion with the one they have steadfastly served, while the powers are unmasked for what they are, stripped of any authority, and deposed. The End will show to be true what eyes of faith already perceive to be true: God reigns. If John is looking for "a few good martyrs"—Christians who will assert their faith with determined zeal even if it elicits a brutal, oppressive response from Rome—the promise of the millennial reign provides an attractive incentive. At the same time, the reign of the martyrs supplies the final answer to the question posed by the martyrs in 6:10: How long until they receive vindication? Their blood has been avenged (e.g., 19:1–3), and now they are truly vindicated.[39] Divine justice has delayed, but now is apparent to all.

---

[38] See Boring, *Revelation*, 202–8; Mounce, *Revelation*, 363–71; Roloff, *Revelation*, 223–26; Collins, "Book of Revelation," 409–11.

[39] Cf. Mounce, *Revelation*, 369; Bauckham, *Theology of Revelation*, 106–8. Bauckham argues that "the theological point of the millennium is solely to demonstrate the triumph of the martyrs" (107); it depicts the meaning, not the manner, of their vindication (108).

The culminating vision of the new Jerusalem likewise ends on the note of divine reign in which the faithful participate. John imagines a world so illuminated by divine light that no other light source will be needed, a world so filled with the divine presence that temples will be outmoded, a world so touched by divine healing that the tree of life will offer healing nourishment to the nations—yes, to the nations!—all year long. In such a world, God's loyal servants will reign not for a thousand years, but forever. There are surprising pictures in this eschatological city: the "healing of the nations" (22:2), the nations walking by the light of the Lamb (21:23–24a), and the kings of the earth coming into the city, bearing their glory (21:24b). This imagery may surprise, because in the previous visions the nations and their rulers were opposed to God and God's people, and stubbornly refused to repent when divine justice began to be executed (e.g., 9:20–21; 16:9, 11). They served the beast rather than the Lamb, and although the ten kings allied with the beast ultimately turn (with the beast) against the harlot (Rome), they continue to battle against the Lamb (17:12–18). They do so, to their own destruction (19:17–21). The presence of kings and nations in the new city of God is important. While elsewhere John is given little reason to hope that the world can be redeemed or will embrace change (repent), this use of symbols of power is transformative. Since the violent purging of evil that is so compellingly enacted in the visions of chapters 4–20 occurs only in a world imagined by the seer, the brighter vision of the closing scene of the book offers hope that God will prevail against evil by reclaiming and restoring, rather than destroying, the human and physical creation.[40] And yet, the recurring—and intensifying—cycles of judgment against evil underscore the tenacity and strength of evil. So the reader is given reason to hope, and therefore to persevere, but there is no room here for naïve optimism. If God's faithful are to rule forever, it will not be easy.

---

[40] See W. J. Harrington, *Revelation* (SP 16; Collegeville, Minn.: Liturgical Press, 1993), 217–20.

Divine Justice

The holy God, who alone is worthy of worship,[41] and who alone is sovereign, confronts the world's oppressive systems of coercion and domination with judgment. The working out of this divine justice—such a potent apocalyptic theme—is the motor that drives the visions in the central section of John's Apocalypse. Once again, the motif of divine judgment figures prominently in the messages of chapters 2–3, and then receives rich embellishment in the visionary narrative of the following chapters.

Thyatira learns, from the example of "Jezebel," that God [or the exalted Christ] will repay everyone for their actions (or "works," ἔργα, 2:23). Philadelphia likewise hears that Jesus disciplines those whom he loves (3:19). And Sardis finds encouragement in the promise that faithfulness will be honored, as symbolized by white clothing (3:4). The fate of God's martyrs appears to call God's justice into question (6:10: When will their oppressors finally be brought to justice?). But recurring cycles of visions picture God's judgment against evil, and the accompanying heavenly chorus ensures that the reader understands. The faithful will eventually receive their reward, and evil will be condemned (e.g., 11:18; 16:5–7; 18:4–6; 19:1–2). Following the last great eschatological battle, John narrates a conventional, though brief and restrained, judgment scene (20:11–15). None can escape accountability before God "according to their deeds [κατὰ τὰ ἔργα]" (20:12–13). The reader is reminded of this principle of accountability one last time in Jesus' closing speech (22:12). Jesus comes as judge, and he is coming soon.

The Coming One

The book of Revelation is replete with conventional apocalyptic themes, including those considered so far: the triumph of

---

[41] This is a prominent feature of Revelation. The dragon and the beast seek universal worship (13:4, 8, 15), which is due only to God. Even John must be reminded not to bow down in reverence before angelic mediators of revelation (19:10; 22:8–9).

divine forces over evil (or over the nations); eschatological judgment; the sovereign rule of God—although each theme is distinctly developed. Within this tapestry of apocalyptic motifs, the threads we have been tracing in this book—the parousia of Jesus, and the imminence of his appearance—are prominent. Revelation virtually begins by picturing the coming of the one (Jesus) "who is and who was and who is coming" (1:4):

> Look! He is coming with the clouds, and every eye will see him, even those who pierced him, and all the tribes of the earth will mourn over him. (1:7, drawing from Dan 7:13; Zech 12:10)

This first description of the coming of Jesus ties it closely to his death, and suggests both the cosmic conflict that will dominate the book and its outcome. The book ends on the same note, but from the vantage of the faithful community at worship:

> "And look! I am coming quickly" (22:7);
> "Look! I am coming quickly" (22:12);
> "Yes, I am coming quickly." Amen, come, Lord Jesus! (22:20).

Otherwise, the parousia of Jesus is mentioned once in the seven-bowl cycle (16:15) and plays an especially important role in chapters 2–3.

In the messages to Thyatira and Philadelphia, the exalted Christ clearly points to his parousia, in consolation but also admonition (2:25; 3:11).[42] The Christian community in Thyatira wins praise for its faithfulness and love (2:19), yet these words of congratulation pale in comparison to the sharp attack (2:20–24) on "Jezebel's" false teaching of cultural compromise (in John's view). Fresh from a stern warning of divine retribution against adherents of this teaching, the reader encounters an exhortation to constancy ("hold on to what you have") "until I come" (2:25). That the end-time *parousia* of Jesus is in view is evident from the following verse's reference to keeping Christ's works "until the end [ἄχρι τέλους]."

---

[42] For the verb "come," John uses ἥκω (2:25; cf. 3:3), and also the phrase ἔρχομαι ταχύ (3:11; cf. 2:16; 22:7, 12, 20).

The church at Philadelphia has undergone adversity but has proved faithful and is therefore assured of protection from "the hour of testing that is coming upon the whole world" (3:8–10). Jesus then announces his own imminent arrival, to reinforce his appeal that the community remain faithful (3:11). As in the case of Thyatira, the parousia promises respite from adversity and blessing for the community, but only if they keep the faith. Consolation is wedded to admonition.

Four further mentions of Jesus' coming do not expressly refer to the parousia (2:5, 16; 3:3, 20) but do employ manifestly eschatological imagery. Although the Ephesian church is commended for its persevering fidelity, it is reproved for diminished love (2:2–4). This forms the basis for an appeal to repent; failure to repent will mean Jesus' coming in judgment against the church (2:5). Pergamum is praised for keeping the faith despite the threat of persecution, but at the same time rebuked for tolerating the teaching of cultural accommodation by "Balak" and the Nicolaitans (2:13–15). The heavenly Christ then calls the community to repent and cautions that he will come against them as a battlefield foe if they do not (2:16). The church at Sardis is branded lifeless and urged to repent; if it does not, Jesus will come "like a thief," at an unknown hour (3:1b–3). (The image has a similar parenetic valence when it surfaces again in 16:15.) Finally, Laodicea is chastized for its complacency (3:15–18), again the basis for a summons to repentance (3:19). Jesus then appears at the door knocking, offering to "come in" and eat with any who will open the door (3:20).

While these passages hint at a coming of Jesus to the church apart from his end-time parousia, there are also clear eschatological signals. The analogy drawn to a thief's unforeseen intrusion is reminiscent of Luke 12:39–40 and 1 Thess 5:2. Jesus' "knocking at the door" is a stock end-time motif in the gospel tradition (e.g., Matt 25:10–12; Mark 13:34–36; Luke 12:36). These details suggest the possibility that John does not anticipate a separate parousia of Jesus to the church (targeting it particularly for its refusal to repent); rather, when Jesus comes at the End, it will mean either judgment or blessing for the church, depending on its conduct.

Even if this reading of the texts is not accepted, the combination of consolation and warning here reinforces the message John elsewhere delivers in relation to the parousia. Jesus comes in triumph; therefore, his parousia is good news to cheer the afflicted faithful. But Jesus comes in judgment; therefore, his parousia is bad news not only for world powers that oppose God's ways but also for those within the church who do not remain true to God. The image of Jesus' coming reassures but also warns.[43]

The End Is Near: Imminence and Delay in Revelation

Jesus is coming, and soon. John could not be more emphatic about that conviction.[44] Yet at the same time Revelation has various indicators of delay in the completion of history. Perhaps the most obvious, and surely the most poignant, mention of delay is voiced by the martyrs who long to see their vindication and the punishment of their slayers. How long must they wait? Their ranks must be swelled by still more witnesses-unto-death. Even when the faithful are overtaken by intense persecution, deliverance will not come immediately (6:9–11). John's message of hope is not for the fainthearted or for the gullible. Perseverance, or patient endurance, is a prime virtue in Revelation.

Between the blowing of the sixth and the seventh trumpets, a lengthy narrative interlude builds suspense, matching the angel's implicit admission that there had been a delay in the fulfillment of the divine mystery. But the heavenly messenger vows: "No more delay!" (10:5–7). Nevertheless, the ensuing judgment cycle (the bowls of divine wrath) and multiple enactments of

---

[43] In much the same way, the "coming" of the hour of God's judgment (14:7) and of the eschatological "harvest" reinforces appeals for fidelity but also, secondarily, reassures the righteous. The coming of Jesus is also the coming of God, "the one who is, and was, and is coming" (1:4, 8; cf. 4:8). The parousia of Jesus brings the eschatological triumph and judgment of God. See further Bauckham, *Theology of Revelation*, 63–64.

[44] See the survey and appraisal of these texts in Boring, *Revelation*, 68–74; cf. Schüssler Fiorenza, *Book of Revelation*, 49–50.

eschatological warfare move the reader toward that glorious fulfillment only through prolonged struggle. The implication is
clear: even when challenged by the Almighty, evil will not be
easily or swiftly vanquished. A thousand years free of Satan's de-
ception or the beast's coercion will not suffice to purge the cosmos of evil.

Still, the days of God's enemies are finite, as the numerical
symbolism of the central section of the book indicates. The temple's
outer courtyard will be profaned by the nations for forty-two months
(11:2); the beast will hold power for the same length of time (13:5).
This period of three and a half years (echoing the "time, two times,
and half a time" of Dan 12:6–7; cf. 12:11–12; 8:13–14) represents half
of a "complete" cycle of seven years. In other words, the powers of
evil will prevail for only a limited time.[45]

John and his late first-century audience know from experience that God's justice has been patient. The visions John narrates reflect that awareness. Within that setting, however, John
boldly affirms the imminent parousia of Jesus. Caesar may sit
comfortably on his throne, but his time is short. The book's first
verse and its penultimate verse direct the reader's attention to
what will occur in the near future. Indeed, John's entire revelation is characterized as a message concerning "what must soon
[ἐν τάχει] happen" (1:1). It "must [δεῖ]" happen because God is
the author both of the disclosure to John and of the events now to
unfold. John reminds us with identical wording (ἃ δεῖ γενέσθαι
ἐν τάχει, "what must soon happen") at the end of the book that
this is the substance of his prophetic teaching (22:6). Similarly,
the declaration "the time is near [ὁ γὰρ καιρὸς ἐγγύς]," introduced as an explanation for the beatitude John pronounces on
the reader and the hearers of this prophecy (1:3), reappears in
22:10 as an explanation for the command that John not seal the
prophetic words given to him. Revelation then closes on a note
of expectancy, oriented toward the imminent return of Jesus
(22:7, 12, 20).

---

[45] On the symbolic meaning of the forty-two months, see Roloff,
Revelation, 130; Bauckham, *Theology of Revelation,* 158.

Between these eschatological bookends, the theme of imminence—whether of the parousia and the deliverance associated with that event, or of divine judgment against evil—plays like a broken record. Several of these texts have already been considered in the discussion of Jesus' coming (2:16; 3:3; 3:11; 16:15; 22:7). Readers may count on his return in the near future, and this is good news, if they will preserve the integrity of their faith even at the cost of personal sacrifice. If they capitulate, however, their apostasy will mean that it is destruction that draws near.

A brief survey of the remaining imminence texts adds little to this picture. The devil (dragon) is rageful because he realizes he has just a little time left (ὀλίγον καιρόν, 12:12). The awaited seventh king among the beast's seven heads will necessarily (δεῖ) have a short tenure (ὀλίγον, 17:10), and the ten kings who will receive authority in alliance with the beast will have power for only "one hour" (17:12). Finally, the picture of sudden demise in "one hour" or "one day" becomes a refrain throughout the mourning songs of chapter 18. Babylon's divine judgment in the form of plagues and pestilence, mourning and famine, will descend in "one day" (v. 8). From the vantage of kings who have collaborated with the evil city, God's judgment will seem to have come in just "one hour" (v. 10). Other human beneficiaries of Roman might and wealth (merchants and ship owners) will share the same view: the city's vast wealth has been laid waste in "one hour" (vv. 17, 19). If justice has seemed slow in coming, one should not be deceived. God will intervene swiftly and decisively. Those who have been living faithfully and justly need not have concern; but for those who have been constant in their loyal service to oppressive evil, it will be too late. There will be no opportunity to change course.

A Rhetoric of Hope and Warning

The prophet John fits readers of the Apocalypse with a new set of lenses through which to view the world. They are bifocal lenses. Glimpsing signs of the future through the visions John reports, the audience discerns that the outcome of human history is in the trustworthy hands of the one in whom it began, in whom, indeed, all creation rests—the one who is first and last, alpha and omega, beginning and end. True to its apocalyptic heritage, Revelation imagines the future as an end (termination) of the evil powers that play with and ravage human welfare in the present. The parousia of Jesus in judgment upon evil plays a crucial role in that scenario of the future.

Yet John does not focus our gaze upon the future as one preoccupied with what will or may yet be. The point of the visions is to enable readers to view their present in a radically different way. Contrary to all the evidence, God reigns. John takes us behind the curtain of history, where we discover that God is sovereign. And God shares rule with Christ, who surrendered life out of his commitment to the divine ways, and with all the faithful, who will likewise bear witness to what they know to be true, no matter the cost. The promise of Jesus' coming—with all the other images of future deliverance and destruction in Revelation—works rhetorically to support the persevering commitment and faithfulness of the community in the moment of challenge that now confronts it. It is a rhetoric of warning for those who are complacent, or who are tempted to compromise to get along or get ahead. But it is also a rhetoric of consolation for all who will stay the course, trusting in the one who sits upon the throne.

# FOUR

THE PAROUSIA OF JESUS IN OTHER NEW TESTAMENT WRITINGS: *1 Peter, James, Hebrews, 2 Peter*

Eschatological hope, with the parousia of Jesus as a central and defining symbol, remained the common coin of broad segments of Christianity for several decades. The persistence and the wide distribution of such expectations are reflected in the New Testament writings to be examined in this chapter—1 and 2 Peter, James, and Hebrews—as well as in extracanonical documents of the early church, discussed in chapter 5. In this chapter, we will pay particular attention to the ways in which anticipation of Jesus' promised second coming supports the faith and moral life of the communities addressed by these "general epistles" of the New Testament.

FIRST PETER

First Peter addresses Christians who are truly "exiles of the diaspora" (1:1), that is, persons for whom the label "Christian" is increasingly problematic in Roman society and in pagan culture, and who therefore live in a

liminal zone within the Roman world. Their true home is
heaven, which is a good thing, because their participation in
their own social world is becoming precarious. The letter encourages and admonishes readers whose Christian identity has
brought suffering, with the aim of sustaining their commitment
to Christian faith and life despite adversity.[1] The author seeks to
engender hope, and the parousia of Jesus figures prominently as
a basis for hope. Though without the elaborate apocalyptic visions and the strongly negative appraisal of the Roman Empire
that mark John's Apocalypse, 1 Peter shares with that text a concern—in an environment hostile to Christian commitment—to
reinforce persevering faithfulness and to foster Christian hope.

Living in the Time of the End:
The "Apocalypse" of Jesus Christ

Employing a variety of images, 1 Peter situates its readers
in the time of the End. This is the era of fulfillment, the time of
salvation revealed to the ancient prophets and announced by
them in Scripture. The salvation, or deliverance, of the faithful
has been guarded until this time of the End, which is characterized, at the same time, as a period of intense testing (πειρασμός),
the end-time tribulation that is the necessary prelude to heav-

---

[1] The situation underlying 1 Peter is not general, state-sponsored
repression of Christians, but hardship stemming from more sporadic
and unofficial forms of opposition. For discussion of the social context of
the letter, see P. J. Achtemeier, *1 Peter* (Hermeneia; Minneapolis: Fortress, 1996), 28–58; L. Goppelt, *A Commentary on 1 Peter* (ed. F. Hahn,
trans. J. E. Alsup; Grand Rapids: Eerdmans, 1993), 7–15, 48–53; J. H.
Elliott, *A Home for the Homeless: A Sociological Exegesis of 1 Peter, Its Situation and Strategy* (Philadelphia: Fortress, 1981), 59–100. On the correlation of Jesus' suffering and that of the community in 1 Peter, see J. T.
Carroll and J. B. Green, *The Death of Jesus in Early Christianity* (Peabody, Mass.: Hendrickson, 1995), 139–42. I place 1 Peter in the last third
of the first century; although Peter, an elder and witness of the sufferings
of Jesus, is the stated author (1:1; cf. 5:1), this is likely a pseudonymous
writing. For a detailed presentation and evaluation of the evidence, see
Achtemeier, *1 Peter*, 1–43.

enly glory. As the "day of visitation" by God approaches, the faithful who endure suffering because of their Christian allegiance will follow Jesus' own path from suffering to glory. Images and motifs of apocalyptic pedigree thus permeate 1 Peter.[2]

Already the letter prescript identifies its recipients as God's elect, their destiny set by a gracious God and their present life marked by the Spirit for holiness and obedience (1:2). What is that destiny? Employing the images of rebirth through Jesus' resurrection, a permanent inheritance, salvation, and glory and honor (1:3–9), the author celebrates the eternal blessing that already exists in heaven for the faithful, and will soon be publicly disclosed. That inheritance—an apt reward for those who are now "dispersed exiles"—is being kept in heaven, and persons of faith are likewise being guarded for salvation (vv. 4–5). Although the present reality may seem to call such assurance into question, the adversity of this age will serve only to prove the genuineness of faith and will soon give way to honor (vv. 6–9). Therefore, to discerning eyes, the present is after all the era of fulfillment, promised long ago by the Hebrew prophets (1:10–12). The imminent future will reveal what faith already knows to be true.

Language of disclosure is prominent in 1 Peter, especially the noun ἀποκάλυψις ("revelation," "unveiling," "disclosure") and the verb ἀποκαλύπτω ("reveal," "unveil," "disclose"). Salvation is "ready to be revealed in the last time [ἑτοίμην ἀποκαλυφθῆναι ἐν καιρῷ ἐσχάτῳ]" (1:5). To prophets announcing the suffering and glory of Christ, it was "revealed" (ἀπεκαλύφθη) that their message was good news not for their own generation but for "you"—the Christian readers of the letter (1:12). The minds of the audience are thus aimed, in hope, toward the grace that approaches at the "revealing [ἀποκαλύψει] of Jesus Christ" (1:13). Peter, himself a witness of the suffering of Jesus, will also have a share in the "glory about to be revealed [μελλούσης ἀποκαλύπτεσθαι]" (5:1). The "apocalypse of Jesus Christ" (cf. 1 Cor 1:7; Gal 1:16) means a new way of perceiving the present,

---

[2] See Achtemeier, *1 Peter*, 105–7.

despite its afflictions, and renewed, expectant hope that deliverance from God is close at hand.

Not only Jesus' future coming but also his (past) earthly life is pictured as eschatological disclosure. Jesus was "manifested [φανερωθέντος] at the end of times [ἐπ' ἐσχάτου τῶν χρόνων]" and "raised up from the dead" (1:20–21). This gracious activity of God forms the basis for confidence or trust in God (1:21). The same verb, "appear" or "become manifest" (φανερόω), is used later also of Jesus' eschatological appearing (as a shepherd),[3] when the faithful will receive a glorious crown (5:4). Through such verbal and phraseological parallels, 1 Peter intimates a close association between the past suffering and glory of Jesus and the future glory of the faithful community for whom the present means suffering. To glimpse the decisive eschatological event, readers need look no farther than Jesus' own life of suffering and resurrection to divine glory. The pattern of the future, glorious revealing of Christ, and its offer of a share in God's glory to all the faithful who now suffer, may be discerned already in the life, faithfulness through suffering, and resurrection of Jesus.

---

[3] The author exhorts elders of the church to care for the flock in humility, not to seek power or personal gain (5:2–3). The shepherd metaphor (which of course has deep resonance in the Jewish scripture and tradition) links church leaders and Jesus. At his parousia, he will appear as the "chief among shepherds." The implications for church leaders are clear. They are to follow his example of humble service, and will then follow his path to divine honor. Elsewhere, 1 Peter forges a connection between household slaves and the pattern of Jesus' own life (2:18–25). He suffered undeservedly but to the end sustained his commitment to justice, and refused to retaliate against those who had wronged him. In the same way, household slaves should entrust their vindication to God, and meanwhile persist in doing what is right, even if they are punished for doing so. The author later extends this exhortation to the whole community (πάντες, "all," 3:8): all are called to find divine blessing through suffering for what is right (3:8–17; 4:12–19). This is no invitation to masochism but a summons to persevering commitment to God's ways, which in a world such as the author's—or ours—invariably brings opposition and hardship.

To summarize: the reader receives assurance of future deliverance and a share in divine glory, assurance that is grounded in the accomplished deliverance and present glory of Jesus. In fact, God has the promised inheritance ready and waiting. Those who trust God "know" their future, because they are able to "read" it in the prophetic promises of Scripture and especially in the life of Jesus. This reassuring message would be welcome consolation for 1 Peter's audience. The author intensifies their current experience of hostility by depicting it as a "fiery trial [πειρασμός]," a time of testing and adversity (4:12; cf. 1:6), and as a season (καιρός) of God's judgment (κρίμα), which may begin with the church but will eventually extend to the whole society (4:17). This is nothing less than the eschatological distress that precedes the End.[4]

Living in the midst of a disobedient and antagonistic people (2:7–9), readers are urged not to withdraw but to bear faithful witness for God in word, and especially in holy conduct (e.g., 2:11–12; 3:15–16). They are to declare the good news of divine mercy that has fashioned of them a new people of God (2:9–10). And the quality of their moral life will put the lie to any slanders directed at them by their neighbors but also elicit from the Gentiles praise of God on the "day of visitation [ἡμέρᾳ ἐπισκοπῆς]" (2:12).[5] Such a dramatic reversal of the

---

[4] For a recent collation and appraisal of the evidence, see M. Dubis, "The Messianic Woes in 1 Peter" (Ph.D. diss., Union-PSCE, 1997).

[5] It is striking that in a letter evidently addressed to Gentile believers (see 1:14, 18; 2:10; 4:3–4; cf. Achtemeier, *1 Peter*, 50–51), when the author speaks of "the Gentiles" as the ones who praise God, he is referring to outsiders to the community who must be convinced by Christians' good conduct that they are not blameworthy (2:12). The immediately preceding verses characterize the readers as God's elect people, using several scriptural images pointing to Israel (note, e.g., the echoes of Exod 19:6; Isa 43:20–21; Hos 2:23). They are no longer "Gentiles," but God's holy and elect nation. On this theme, see P. Perkins, *First and Second Peter, James, and Jude* (IBC; Louisville: John Knox, 1995), 43–44; Achtemeier, *1 Peter*, 163–68. Achtemeier proposes that the "controlling metaphor" in the theology of 1 Peter is the Christian community as God's people Israel (69–72); "In 1 Peter, the language and hence the reality of

present circumstance can only mean the arrival of the eschatological time of fulfillment. Or, as the author later puts it, "The
end of all things has drawn near [πάντων δὲ τὸ τέλος ἤγγικεν]"
(4:7).

From Suffering to Glory

First Peter situates its audience in the time of the End. This
contextualizing of the gospel supports a message of encouragement and admonition.[6] Before examining more closely this rhetorical function of the letter's eschatological claims, it is important
to develop the nexus between suffering and glory. Jesus' suffering is presented as the paradigm for the community's own experience, and as exemplary for its response to adversity.[7] Moreover, the recognition that Jesus' suffering was the prelude to his
exaltation engenders hope that those whose lives conform to the
pattern of his suffering will likewise follow him on the path to
glory.

The church, to be sure, is beset by adversity, harassed and
stigmatized in pagan culture. The label "Christian" is no badge
of honor but invites disdain (4:16). Yet this time of suffering that
tests faith (1:6–7; 4:12) is fleeting. It will last just "a little while
[ὀλίγον]," a point scored at both the beginning and the close of
the letter (1:6; 5:10). Present adversity, however, does not
simply run its course or cease; rather, the apocalyptic visitation
of God—featuring the revealing or appearing of Christ, and the
working out of divine judgment, starting with God's own
household—brings deliverance ("salvation") for the faithful.
Suffering gives way to vindication and honor at the glorious appearing (parousia, though the word is not used) of Jesus. Eschatological conviction enables the community's endurance in
the meantime.

Israel pass without remainder into the language and hence the reality of
the new people of God" (69).

[6] Note παρακαλέω ("encourage" or "exhort") in 5:1, 12.

[7] See further Carroll and Green, *Death of Jesus,* 140–41.

A Message of Hope and a Call to Persevering Fidelity

The readers of 1 Peter are already living in the time of severe hardship and testing that precedes the End—or, better, is itself part of the End (see especially 4:17). God's judgment has begun, but in an intriguing reversal, the target of that judging activity of God is, first of all, the church. Confronted with the rhetorical question "If [the judgment begins] with us, what will be the end [τέλος] of those who disobey the gospel?" (4:17), the reader can only shudder. What of the earlier charge to honor the emperor and all other people as well (2:17)? What of Jesus' postmortem proclamation to captive evil spirits that had been disobedient to God (3:18–20)?[8] And what of the expressed hope that "the Gentiles" would be led by their encounter with the Christian community's virtue to honor God (2:12)? First Peter directs its audience toward constructive and responsible engagement with the Roman world, but at the same time knows evil in its various guises. The letter closing—ominously, given the valence of the name in apocalyptic tradition—dispatches greetings from [the church] "in Babylon."[9] Christian readers will do well to

---

[8] On the interpretation of this difficult text, see Achtemeier, *1 Peter,* 239–74. He terms 3:19 "the most problematic, in this letter, if not in the NT canon as a whole" (252), seconding a remark by Luther (*Collected Works,* 12.367). Achtemeier concludes that "the spirits" to whom the risen Jesus preaches are not dead human beings from an earlier age, but (probably malevolent) supernatural beings (255). Jesus does not address them on his descent but as he ascends to heaven (258), and announcement of his triumph entails defeat and condemnation for the captive angelic beings (260–61). Such a reading of this elusive text squares well with the rhetorical situation and aims of the letter. First Peter, "with this emphasis on the triumph of Jesus over the powers of evil . . . encourages readers to remain faithful despite the pressure exerted on them by hostile forces in their contemporary world." The victory of Jesus over these spiritual beings ensures the victory of the faithful and therefore makes their own "resistance worthwhile" (261).

[9] The Roman conquest of Jerusalem in 70 C.E. evoked memories of the Babylonian destruction of the first temple in the early sixth century B.C.E. One finds frequent use of the name Babylon as a cipher for Rome, the contemporary destroyer of the Holy City and temple (e.g., 4 Ezra

honor the ruler of the empire, but not because of any inherent virtues! Still, the primary concern of the letter is the community's own faithfulness in a world defined by non-Christian values and beliefs.

The suffering of the community is temporary and soon will give way to participation in the glory that comes from God. This message of hope reassures Christian converts from pagan culture that the steep price they have paid for their new religious affiliation is a price well worth paying. There is no turning back to the old ways (4:1–6). Consolation therefore is closely tied to exhortation in 1 Peter. Church leaders are to emulate the "lead shepherd" as they care for their flock, if they would receive the honors of the victor when Jesus returns (5:2–4). The assertion that "the end of all things has drawn near" undergirds parenetic appeals for sensible and sober prayers and for mutual love within the community (4:7–8). The author appeals for persistence in holy conduct, and persevering commitment to the new faith, after the example of Jesus. The audience is urged: Keep the faith! Live in a way that is above reproach, so that your accusers will be able, in the end, to expose only their own deceit.

Although the church is hard pressed for the time being, readers may look to the future with hope. The ground of confidence and hope for persons of faith is the faithfulness of God, who has promised an inheritance and guards it even now. They may entrust their lives to a "faithful Creator" (4:19) and so lead faithful lives even when to do so means harassment and suffering. The coming of Jesus in the near future is potent symbol of the divine visitation that will soon deliver the oppressed faithful and judge the world.

Yet the parousia does not give new content to the destiny of the faithful or to the vocation of the Messiah. That content is already defined by Jesus' first "appearing," and attested by the prophetic scriptures. The end-time coming of Jesus, however, will provide full and open disclosure. The parousia in 1 Peter, in large measure, has to do with right discernment—an understanding of God and world that

---

3:1–2, 28; *2 Bar.* 11:1–2; 67:6–7; Rev 14:8; 16:19; 17:5; 18:2, 10, 21). See further Achtemeier, *1 Peter,* 353–54; Goppelt, *1 Peter,* 374–76.

sustains hope and supports the moral life of the community of faith during the turbulent period between Jesus' resurrection to glory and the eschatological glory of all God's people.

JAMES

From first to last, the Letter of James centers on community admonition and instruction. It is no wonder that it has regularly been described, since the publication of M. Dibelius's influential commentary, as a "parenetic letter."[10] In the opening and closing sections of the letter body James closely ties the moral formation of the community to the eschatological imagery of judgment, vindication, and the Lord's parousia (1:2–12; 4:11–5:11). Eschatological motifs, while submerged in the central part of the letter, reinforce and strengthen the moral appeals that form the heart and soul of James.[11]

Before exploring these admonitions and their relation to the eschatological themes of testing and judgment, we would be

---

[10] M. Dibelius, *James* (rev. H. Greeven; trans. M. A. Williams; ed. H. Koester; Hermeneia; Philadelphia: Fortress, 1975; orig. 1929). For critical engagement with this classification of the letter, see L. T. Johnson, *The Letter of James: A New Translation with Introduction and Commentary* (AB 37A; New York: Doubleday, 1995), 16–26. Johnson argues that while James has features of the parenetic letter (as well as of the diatribe), a case can also be made that it is a "protreptic discourse" (20–21); that is, it urges readers to embrace a profession—in this instance a "counter-cultural" vocation marked by friendship with God rather than friendship with the world—and the life of virtue that it entails.

[11] For the argument that the inclusio of James 1:2–12 and 4:6–5:12 provides an eschatological framework that shapes the reading of the entire letter, see T. C. Penner, *The Epistle of James and Eschatology: Rereading an Ancient Christian Letter* (JSNTSup 121; Sheffield: Sheffield Academic Press, 1996) esp. 210–12. Similarly, R. W. Wall describes "James as apocalyptic parenesis," in an essay bearing that title (*RestQ* 32 [1990]: 11–22). On the theme of eschatological judgment in James, see M. Klein, *"Ein vollkommenes Werk": Vollkommenheit, Gesetz und Gericht als theologische Themen des Jakobusbriefes* (BWANT 139; Stuttgart: Kohlhammer, 1995), 163–84.

well advised to pause at the very first verse, the letter prescript.
The sender of this missive identifies himself as a "slave
[δοῦλος][12] of God and of the Lord Jesus Christ," and his audience
as "the twelve tribes that are in the Diaspora" (1:1). The word
order of the opening phrase in Greek is striking: "James, of God
and the Lord Jesus Christ, a slave." James belongs first and fore-
most to God. In this letter's correlation of eschatology and ethics,
God is the key player. James presents a theocentric, eschatological moral vision. As the letter unfolds, there is considerable am-
biguity in the use of the word κύριος, here applied to Jesus but
elsewhere sometimes pointing to God (see, e.g., 5:10–11). So
when James speaks twice of the "coming of the Lord [τῆς
παρουσίας τοῦ κυρίου]" (5:7, 8), whose arrival is awaited, Jesus'
or God's?[13] We delay addressing that aspect of the parousia in
James until the end of our treatment of the epistle.

James addresses the twelve tribes (of Israel), dispersed
from the promised land. This designation contains an inherent
tension. On the one hand, the location of the audience in the Diaspora (cf. "exiles of the Diaspora" in 1 Pet 1:1) reminds readers
that they live on this side of the final fulfillment of the divine purposes for Israel—God's agenda for the people has unfinished
business. Yet the phrase "twelve tribes" implies the restoration
of the divided nation. This is, in fact, an eschatological hope: the

---

[12] T. B. Cargal holds that the author's self-designation as "slave" or
"servant" evokes the rich "servant of Yahweh" tradition and thus the
role of the "righteous sufferer" (*Restoring the Diaspora: Discursive Structure and Purpose in the Epistle of James* [SBLDS 144; Atlanta: Scholars
Press, 1993], 212).

[13] Johnson thinks "parousia of the Lord" reflects a "virtually tech-
nical Christian usage" in reference to Jesus (*Letter of James*, 313–14); the
parousia of God appears only in 2 Pet 3:12 (actually, it is the "day of
God"). The Lord who comes, and who is the judge (5:9), is therefore
Jesus—although Johnson (37) urges caution on the identification of
Jesus as the eschatological judge (cf. 4:12). Perkins disagrees, arguing
for the coming of God (*First and Second Peter, James, and Jude*, 88–89).
Penner suggests that the honorific title κύριος in 5:7 may be "deliberately
ambiguous," referring not only to God's judgment but also to the coming
of the Messiah (*James and Eschatology*, 170–71 n. 2).

Christian communities addressed by the letter not only participate in Israel's story, but also have a share in the renewal and
completion of the people of God.[14] But they have not yet "arrived"; for the time being, God's ways for Israel will govern the
moral life of this Diaspora community of faith.[15]

Moral Appeals

The moral vision James holds up for its audience is both
sapiential and prophetic; it taps both wisdom and apocalyptic
traditions of Judaism, as well as the popular moral philosophy of
Hellenistic culture.[16] What behaviors does the author commend?[17] And what conduct is blameworthy? I highlight five especially prominent moral concerns, each developed in the epis-

---

[14] Emphasized by Penner, *James and Eschatology*, 181–83; cf.
Perkins, *First and Second Peter, James, and Jude*, 95. Cargal (*Restoring
the Diaspora*, 45–49) takes seriously the metaphorical potential of "Diaspora" and proposes reading 1:1 retrospectively from 5:19–20. In the end,
James "challenges [readers] to accept the view that they are (also) the
'Diaspora' because they have 'wandered from the truth' " (49). The letter's instruction, however, has called the community back to the truth
and therefore moved them toward restoration.

[15] As Johnson puts it, "The designation [twelve tribes] clearly locates the composition within the symbolic world of Torah" (*Letter of
James*, 169).

[16] See Johnson, *Letter of James*, 26–48. Klein (*Vollkommenes Werk*,
64) observes that the chief difference between the moral teaching of
James and the popular moral philosophy of the Hellenistic world is the
eschatological perspective of this letter.

[17] The precise identity of "James" is unknown. For a sophisticated
recent rehabilitation of the traditional view that James, the brother of
Jesus, is the author, see Johnson, *Letter of James*, 89–123. Johnson offers
the brother of Jesus as a "reasonable candidate" (121), a position that
carries with it an early dating of the writing: James was executed in 62
C.E. by the high priest Ananus (see Josephus, *Ant.* 20.200; cf. Eusebius,
Hist. eccl. 2.23.4–8). Perkins regards composition by James highly unlikely and characterizes the author as a Hellenistic Jewish Christian
who made use of an appeal to the apostolic authority of James (*First and
Second Peter, James, and Jude*, 83–85).

tle by means of a contrasting pair of opposite traits: humility versus prideful arrogance that judges others; dependence upon God versus envious acquisitiveness; compassionate response to the needy versus contemptuous neglect and exploitative oppression of the poor; the implanted word that saves versus the uncontrolled speech of the foolish; and singleness of heart versus a divided self.

Humility versus Prideful Arrogance That Judges Others

In the course of a discussion of the destructive effects of envious desire, James cites Prov 3:34 LXX: "God [κύριος] opposes the arrogant but shows favor [δίδωσιν χάριν] to the lowly" (4:6). Arrogance destroys human community when it assumes the form of judgmentalism. This connection is clear in 4:11–12, where James asserts that those who presume to judge "the brother or sister" (v. 11) or "the neighbor" (v. 12) place themselves above God's law and therefore usurp the role that belongs only to God. As persons accountable to God, readers are directed to show mercy rather than judge the other (2:12–13). Not the self-assured, but the humble will be exalted by God (4:10).

Dependence upon God versus Envy

James draws a sharp contrast between the "wisdom from above" that is praiseworthy, and wisdom that derives from earth (3:15–17)—or between friendship toward God and friendship with the world (4:4).[18] Wisdom of this world is driven by prideful boasting and envy, which inevitably undermine solidarity and community harmony (3:13–4:10). The author unmasks the hubris that underlies all ambitious scheming for gain and advantage, and exposes its futility (4:13–17). The very one who plans tomorrow's business agenda has no more security than "mist that appears for a little while [ὀλίγον], and then

---

[18] A point emphasized by Johnson throughout his commentary (*Letter of James*).

vanishes" (v. 14). The only human security belongs to those who acknowledge their complete dependence upon a gracious God, who gives every good and perfect gift (1:5, 16–18; 4:6–8, 15). As for the complaint that human sin and misery result from God's testing—that is, tempting—of people, the author counters that sin has its root deep within, in a person's unhealthy desires (cf. 4:1–3).

Reversal of Rich and Poor

Arrogance and envy, according to James, keep company with wealth. Indictment of the rich, and of those who show partiality to them, is a major theme of the letter (1:9–11; 2:1–7; 5:1–6). With the help of Isa 40:6–7, James observes that the wealthy have no more permanence than grass (1:10–11; cf. "mist" in 4:14). It is no accident that the concrete illustrations of "doing the law" or of "good works" involve compassionate response to persons afflicted by poverty and need (e.g., 1:27; 2:8–17). The rich, by contrast, not only show contempt for and neglect the poor but also exploit and oppress them (2:6; 5:4–6).[19] If the social world inhabited by readers of James shows partiality to the wealthy, God favors the poor, who will be heirs of the divine realm (2:5).[20]

The Saving Word versus the Dangers of Speech

The divine word planted within the person of faith is "able to save" (1:21)—provided, of course, the believer enacts the word in works (ἔργα) of compassion and mercy. Prayers spoken in faith are the vehicle of divine healing and forgiveness (5:13–18). But the spoken word can be a source of great harm;

---

[19] Note that James distinguishes its readers ("you") from the rich who oppress them (2:6). Although the woe-oracle of 5:1–6 is also cast in the second person plural, the rich who are upbraided in the epistle are apparently not members of the community but outsiders.

[20] James is not alone in asserting this countercultural view of the place of the poor in the world God is fashioning; see, e.g., Luke 1:46–55; 6:20b, 24; 16:19–31; 1 Cor 1:26–29; *1 Enoch* 94–105.

the tongue is difficult to control (3:1–12; cf. 4:11; 5:12).[21] The inclination to boast (3:5) and judge (4:11) has already been mentioned. One should be quick to hear, but slow to speak. James associates quick speech with anger, and anger runs counter to the divine purpose for human relationships (1:19–20). Human speech is also problematic when it comes from a divided self (1:6–8; 3:9–12).

Singleness of Heart versus the Divided Self

James commends singleness of purpose, constancy, and unwavering faith (1:2–6; 5:11–12). Faith that struggles with doubt—the condition of a person with a "divided mind [or self, δίψυχος]" (1:8)—hinders reception of God's generous gifts. Another dimension of the wholeness or integrity James advocates is congruence between faith professed and enacted, or between faith and works. Yet some people speak out of both sides of the mouth, offering praise to God while cursing human beings fashioned in God's likeness (3:9–10). For James, this is not authentic faith; devotion to God and compassionate care for the other person are inextricably tied.

Eschatological Test and Reward (1:2–12)

We have sketched important dimensions of the moral life James directs his audience to embrace, as well as the attitudes and actions they must avoid. With imagery of reversal, judgment, and temporality, the parenesis of the letter hints at its eschatological grounding. How do eschatological themes of judgment and parousia reinforce the letter's shaping of the moral life of the community? We begin by noting the motifs of eschatological test, endurance, and reward with which the argument of James opens.

---

[21] On the topic of "speech" in James and in its cultural environment, see W. R. Baker, *Personal Speech-Ethics in the Epistle of James* (WUNT 2.68; Tübingen: J. C. B. Mohr [Paul Siebeck], 1995).

The experiences of trial or testing (πειρασμός) are something to be celebrated rather than feared (v. 2). Why? The testing of faith leads to endurance (ὑπομονή, the same word favored in Revelation), which is necessary if one is to be whole (vv. 3–4). Verses 9–11 then paint a vivid picture of the reversal of status that will befall the rich and the poor. James reminds readers of the ephemeral quality of the activities, the wealth, and the very life of the rich person. Trials "proving" one's faith—faith that is confirmed through patient endurance—and an eschatology of one's personal existence combine to suggest that an eschatological perspective orients readers to the parenetic instruction that follows.[22] This hunch is supported by the image of reward that clinches the argument (v. 12). A beatitude in form, this verse promises the "crown of life" to those who persevere through trial (ὑπομένει πειρασμόν).[23] This clearly is an eschatological incentive to faithful living out of one's convictions in a less than supportive environment. Many of these motifs surface again toward the close of the epistle, and the eschatological horizon becomes much more distinct.

"The Judge Is at the Door!": *Judgment and the Parousia of the Lord (4:11–5:11)*

The end of personal existence (personal eschatology) figures again in the exhortation of 4:13–17. The image of mist that swiftly vanishes suggests the precariousness of an individual's presumption to be able to plan tomorrow's agenda of trading and accumulating profits (v. 14). This is vintage wisdom teaching in line with Ecclesiastes, for example, and the message of Jesus.[24] One lives for only a "little while," and only by the mercy of God

---

[22] This is the view of Penner, *James and Eschatology*, 197–201.

[23] The crown (στέφανος) was awarded to the victors in athletic competitions, or in recognition of distinguished service. See Johnson, *Letter of James*, 188.

[24] See Eccl 5:13–17; 6:1–2; Luke 12:16–21; cf. also Prov 27:1; Sir 11:18–19; and for a similar Stoic view, Epictetus, *Disc.* 1.1.17; 3.21.12.

(vv. 14b–15). The unit concludes with the observation that any-one who knows "the good" (καλόν) and fails to perform it sins. And the reader of James knows the good and right thing to do! This is an appropriate bridge to the woe-oracle against the rich in 5:1–6, for they do not perform the works God requires.

The woe-oracle opens (v. 1) with a call to the rich to weep and wail at the miseries that are coming upon them, yet the im-ages that follow intimate that divine justice is already at play. Judgment against the wealthy has begun to be felt, in the form of moth-eaten clothing and rusting precious metals (vv. 2–3). But this is only the beginning. Accompanying the depletion and dete-rioration of earthly treasure is the accumulation of treasure "in the last days [ἐν ἐσχάταις ἡμέραις]" (v. 3b). James then under-scores the gravity of the sin of the rich. They have not just accu-mulated wealth for themselves; they have done so by cheating, oppressing, and even killing the righteous (vv. 4–6). So the trea-sure of the end time means not comfort but misery. This "day of slaughter" will not be one to "fatten their hearts" (v. 5). These two notes of end-time reversal and judgment (treasure "in the last days," "day of slaughter") are sounded only briefly, but hear-ers of James's discourse cannot miss the ominous warning to those who exploit others for the sake of their own profit.[25]

The rhetoric shifts abruptly at 5:7. The author turns from the rich who have (ostensibly) been the audience of 5:1–6 and now addresses the believing community ("brothers and sis-ters"). The inferential particle οὖν ("therefore") signals that the appeal for patient waiting for the Lord's coming is undergirded by the negative example of the rich and their demise: "Be pa-tient, therefore." This call to patience recalls the virtue of patient endurance (ὑπομονή) in chapter 1 (vv. 2–3, with the related verb in v. 12), though the verb μακροθυμέω ("bear in patience") ap-

---

[25] If the rich are outsiders to the community, as seems likely (see 2:6), the harsh words of 5:1–6 do not issue a summons to repent, but an-nounce certain judgment. Cf. Perkins, *First and Second Peter, James, and Jude*, 131. On the eschatological dimension of this indictment of the op-pressive rich, see Johnson, *Letter of James*, 321.

pears in 5:7–8, with the related noun in 5:10. One should not overplay the distinction in terms.[26] Both ὑπομονή (ch. 1) and μακροθυμία (ch. 5) are associated with the experience of adversity ("testing" in ch. 1, "suffering" in ch. 5). Moreover, with the introduction of Job's patient endurance in 5:11 (both ὑπομονή and the cognate verb appear), the author closely links the two terms. Job models patient endurance in the face of severe trials, the same quality commended by the author at the start of the letter and now reinforced at the end.

But there is a new wrinkle. Patience must "suffer long" (μακροθυμία) before the Lord's return. An agricultural metaphor develops the point: just as farmers wait patiently during both early and late rains before expecting the harvest, the hearers of James should patiently await the Lord's parousia (5:7–8a). The imagery presupposes the experience of parousia delay; nevertheless, as with virtually every other New Testament writing, acknowledgment of delay goes hand in hand with reaffirmation of imminent hope: "The coming [parousia] of the Lord has drawn near [ἤγγικεν]" (5:8b). The temporal nearness of the parousia is good news for the reader, who may welcome the Lord in confidence. Confidence, but not complacency: 5:9 immediately returns to the motif of judgment. The one who is coming—indeed, who "stands at the door"—is "the judge." The specific moral appeal supported by this picture of imminent eschatological judgment aims to prevent a potential threat to community solidarity: "Do not grumble against one another, brothers and sisters, so that you may not be judged" (cf. Matt 7:1).

Although the audience is urged to be patient, the author sustains hope oriented toward a parousia waiting just on the horizon. And though the one who draws near comes as judge, this is bad news only for those (notably the rich) who fail to do what is right (who refuse to be shaped by the moral teaching of the letter). The genuine faith and righteousness of the community will

---

[26] As Johnson does, for example (*Letter of James,* 312–13). He thinks μακροθυμία connotes a more active stance than ὑπομονή and involves a superior party's bearing with one lower in status.

receive public recognition and honor (recall the "crown" of 1:12). But is the coming one Jesus or God?

The prescript identifies the author as "slave of God and the Lord Jesus Christ" (1:1). And the conventional, and therefore expected, early Christian usage is the parousia of Jesus. Chapter 5, however, contains several references to the κύριος that clearly seem to point to God (v. 4, "Lord Sabaoth"; v. 10, prophets speaking in the Lord's [God's] name; v. 11, in the light of Job's endurance, the purpose of the Lord, and the mercy of the Lord [God]). The imminent parousia of the κύριος in vv. 7–8, therefore, is probably the coming of God to judge the unjust and vindicate the just. Of course, early Christian readers schooled in traditions that feature the parousia of *Jesus* would (appropriately) associate Jesus with eschatological justice. On either reading, divine justice honors the patient waiting and patient endurance of the faithful. Eschatology and ethics join hands to shape a community fit for the "day of the Lord."

HEBREWS

The Letter to the Hebrews presents a striking blend of spatial (vertical) and temporal (horizontal) categories. For example, the true sanctuary is located not on earth (in the Jerusalem temple) but in heaven (e.g., 9:11, 24), and it is there that Jesus' perfect priestly sacrifice opens up access to God, to the "throne of grace" (4:16). Yet Hebrews begins by situating readers in the time of God's decisive, final revelation at "the end of these days" (1:2) and anticipates Jesus' "second coming" in the near future (9:28; cf. 10:25). This juxtaposition of spatial and temporal imagery has prompted sustained debate on the cultural location of the book and its author, and has also resulted in quite divergent accounts of the eschatological perspective in this "message of exhortation" (13:22).[27]

---

[27] On the genre of Hebrews, see W. L. Lane, *Hebrews* (WBC 47A–B; 2 vols.; Dallas: Word, 1991), 1:lxix–lxxv; H. W. Attridge, *The Epistle to the Hebrews* (Hermeneia; Philadelphia: Fortress, 1989), 13–14. This is a

C. Spicq holds that the spatial dualism of Hebrews (e.g., its contrast between the true, heavenly tabernacle and the earthly "copy") reflects its indebtedness to Philo and Alexandrian Judaism.[28] C. K. Barrett, on the other hand, argues that "eschatology is the determining element" in the thought of Hebrews and describes its pedigree as "apocalyptic Judaism," not "Platonic idealism."[29] Other scholars have sought to mediate between the two poles of spatial (Hellenistic, Neoplatonist, or gnostic) and temporal (apocalyptic). G. W. MacRae assigns the apocalyptic eschatology of the homily to its audience and the Alexandrian (spatial) perspective to the author. The author does not correct but reinforces the eschatological hope of readers through imagery drawn from Philo's Alexandria: "It is only by faith in the invisible divine reality that apocalyptic hope can be sustained."[30] This proposal, while intriguing, is impossible to test; and one should

----

homily driven by parenetic interests. The "preacher" appeals for persevering fidelity to Christian commitment in the face of fading hope (e.g., 10:23), a hostile environment (10:32–33), and the lure of the patterned life and liturgy of the synagogue. Hebrews is fitted with a conventional epistolary conclusion (13:22–25). Parenetic appeals are supported by extensive christological argument grounded in complex scriptural exegesis.

[28] See, e.g., C. Spicq, "Le philonisme de l'Épître aux Hébreux," *RB* 56 (1949): 542–72; *RB* 57 (1950): 212–42. E. Käsemann contends that the author of Hebrews addressed the challenge of adapting Jewish apocalyptic conceptions to a Gentile world influenced by gnostic syncretism (*The Wandering People of God: An Investigation of the Letter to the Hebrews* [trans. R. A. Harrisville and I. L. Sandberg; Minneapolis: Augsburg, 1984]). Highlighting the motif of pilgrimage in Hebrews, Käsemann hears echoes in the book of the gnostic journey of the liberated self from the enslaving material world to the spiritual world.

[29] C. K. Barrett, "The Eschatology of the Epistle to the Hebrews," in *The Background of the New Testament and Its Eschatology* (ed. W. D. Davies and D. Daube; Cambridge: Cambridge University Press, 1956), 366, 375–76, 389. See also B. Klappert, *Die Eschatologie des Hebräerbriefs* (Theologische Existenz heute 156; ed. K. G. Steck and G. Eicholz; Munich: Chr. Kaiser, 1969).

[30] G. W. MacRae, "Heavenly Temple and Eschatology in the Letter to the Hebrews," *Semeia* 12 (1978): 179–99; the quotation is from p. 195.

press the question whether the spatial and temporal categories are not part of one (culturally complex) religious perspective. Klappert suggests that Hebrews actually "radicalizes" the eschatological character of the Christ event by means of Alexandrian (spatial) dualism, so that the confession of the heavenly high priest is interpreted as a confession of hope.[31] And L. D. Hurst points out that the imagery of a heavenly temple and a heavenly Jerusalem—existing in heaven now, but to appear on earth at the End—is very much at home in Jewish apocalyptic literature.[32] It would be a mistake, however, to assign the eschatology of Hebrews to an apocalyptic milieu that had no room for the influence of Neoplatonist thought, as witnessed in Philo's Alexandria. Hebrews and its eschatology reflect the rich cultural mix of Hellenistic Judaism in the early imperial period.

Living in the Time of the End

The author looks back on the decisive moment in history. God formerly spoke through the prophets, but at "the end of these days" (or "in these last days") divine disclosure has come through the Son, who has already accomplished purification for sins—once for all time, we will later learn (7:27; 9:12, 26; 10:14)—and been installed in power at God's right hand (1:1–3). He will inherit "all," but only as the one who was the agent in the creation of the universe. Creation and consummation, eschatology and protology are wedded in the one who bears the very character of God.

The images of "purification for sins" and a seat "at the right hand" of God signal themes of fundamental importance in Hebrews. Precisely as the one through whom God deals decisively with human sin, Jesus changes forever the shape and destiny of human life. As the "great high priest" who leads the way into the heavenly sanctuary, he is the "pioneer and perfecter" of faith

---

[31] Klappert, *Eschatologie*, 59.

[32] L. D. Hurst, "Eschatology and 'Platonism' in the Epistle to the Hebrews," *SBLSP 1984* (ed. K. H. Richards; Chico, Calif.: Scholars Press,

(12:2), the one who opens up access to God, the ground for confident hope. That he has a seat of power in heaven (1:3, 13; 8:1; 10:12) underscores his honor and exaltation—divine honor vindicating the one who "despised the shame" of the human court (12:2).[33] At the same time, this exaltation motif, drawn from Ps 110:1, also depicts the present as the era of eschatological conflict, when the enemies of God's Son are being subjected to his rule. Interest in demonstrating the supremacy of Jesus to the angels leads the author from Psalm 110 to Psalm 8, and both psalms link honor from God to the subjection of enemies (or all) under his "feet" (Ps 8:6, quoted in Heb 2:8). As the writer observes, however, "we do not yet see everything subject to him" (2:8b; cf. 10:13). It is the "world that is coming," not the world as it now is, that God has subjected to Christ (2:5). These are the last days, and human destiny has been rerouted from condemnation to salvation, yet not all God's enemies have been vanquished. The world in which people of faith live still poses difficult challenges to faithfulness. A "Sabbath rest" awaits, but only those who persevere in faith and obedience will enter it (3:7–4:13). Their share in Christ is secure, *if* they hold their confidence "to the end [μέχρι τέλους]" (3:14). The promise is sure, but its fulfillment belongs to the eschatological future.[34]

Challenges to Fidelity and Appeals for Perseverance

Memory of Israel's wilderness wandering undermines complacency. Disobedience to God prevented that generation's

---

1984), 41–74; cf. idem, *The Epistle to the Hebrews: Its Background of Thought* (SNTSMS 65; Cambridge: Cambridge University Press, 1990).

[33] For an analysis of Hebrews using the "honor-shame" model, see D. A. deSilva, *Despising the Shame: Honor Discourse and Community Maintenance in the Epistle to the Hebrews* (SBLDS 152; Atlanta: Scholars Press, 1995).

[34] This is the conclusion reached by J. Laansma, *"I Will Give You Rest": The Rest Motif in the New Testament with Special Reference to Mt 11 and Heb 3–4* (WUNT 2.98; Tübingen: J.C.B. Mohr, 1997), 272, 293, 307, 314.

entry into the promised rest. Now, for the audience of Hebrews, there is no rest for the weary, or for the unwary. The people must remain faithful to God if they are to enjoy the promised salvation. What obstacles to community fidelity must be overcome? It appears that external pressures, including "hostility, abuse, imprisonment, and dispossession of goods," have tested the group's faith and endurance (see 10:32–34).[35] The epistle's recurring appeals for unwavering confidence (e.g., 4:14–16; 6:11–12; 10:23, 35) and its frequent warnings against lapsing from true faith (e.g., 6:4–6; 10:37–39), suggest that the author views the threat to community fidelity to be grave. In such a setting, it is imperative that the people continue to gather for corporate worship (10:25).

The author responds to this perceived danger with vigor. Hebrews is laced with sharp warnings of the impending destruction that will befall the apostate and the rebellious. We focus here only on moral appeals and warnings that are painted in distinctly eschatological hues. Belief in resurrection from the dead and "eternal judgment" belongs to the basics of Christian instruction (6:1–2). For those who have "tasted" the "powers of the coming age" (associated with the Holy Spirit) and then fall away from faith, there is no further opportunity to repent (6:4–6). Divine judgment is no trivial matter. The situation of the readers is more hopeful, however, because the author is confident that they will in patient, persistent faith inherit the promised salvation (6:9–12). Their hope will remain firm to the end (ἄχρι τέλους, 6:11). Abraham is a paradigm of patient faith finally receiving the promise (6:13–15). It is to such persevering faith that Hebrews summons its hearers.

---

[35] See N. C. Croy, *Endurance in Suffering: Hebrews 12:1–13 in Its Rhetorical, Religious, and Philosophical Context* (SNTSMS 98; Cambridge: Cambridge University Press, 1998), 162–64, 217. Croy maintains that Hebrews counters these external forces in three ways: (1) the athletic metaphor of the race or contest (ἀγών), which promises an eschatological reward to those who endure; (2) exemplars of faith; and (3) the interpretation of suffering as (nonpunitive) divine παιδεία or instruction (summarized on pp. 217–18).

The realization that Jesus, by virtue of his perfect sacrifice, has led the way into the heavenly sanctuary, inspires confident hope in the faithful (10:19–24). So that hope may not waver, mutual encouragement and regular public assembly of the congregation are necessary—"and much more so, as you see the day drawing near [ἐγγίζουσαν]" (v. 25). What day? The ensuing passage leaves no doubt: it is the "day of God's judgment" (10:26–31). The approach of divine judgment reinforces the appeal for constancy of faith. This pairing of stern warnings and positive encouragement is characteristic of the parenesis of the epistle. Memory of the recent experience of adversity shows the need for perseverance (ὑπομονή) if one is to receive the promise (10:36). A citation from the prophet Habakkuk (2:3–4) supports the claim that divine judgment is imminent: "For yet a little while, and the one who is coming will come and will not delay [χρονίσει]" (10:37). The ensuing warning against "shrinking back" indicates that the coming one draws near to judge those whose faith falters (10:38–39).

Hebrews also employs a metaphor drawn from the arena of athletic competition to summon readers to enduring commitment. The life of faith is an ἀγών, a race (12:1). Readers must stay the course and finish the race, following in the footsteps of Jesus, who endured (ὑπέμεινεν) his ἀγών, the cross, and was awarded a place of honor by the throne of God (12:2). This athletic metaphor "commends an eschatological perspective as a way of viewing and coping with suffering."[36] As the great heroes of faith in Israel's history refused to surrender their trust in God's promises despite great suffering, the hearers of the epistle are urged to persevere as well (ch. 11). The future city of God to which Israel's faithful looked expectantly still beckons to the people of God (11:10, 16; cf. vv. 39–40).

Living in Hope: The Imminence of the Parousia

Although the term *parousia* does not appear in Hebrews, there is mention of a "second appearing" of the Christ (9:28)—

---

[36] Croy, *Endurance in Suffering*, 221.

the closest the Bible comes to the traditional expression "the second coming of Jesus." We have seen that the prospect of eschatological judgment (that is, God's judgment) figures prominently in Hebrews. The certainty and the near approach of judgment reinforce appeals for a life of enduring commitment to God. Christ appeared once for all time (ἄπαξ) at the close of the ages (συντελείᾳ τῶν αἰώνων) to remove sin through his sacrificial offering (9:27, recalling 1:3). Because this "first coming" of Jesus dealt definitively with the problem of sin, his second appearing does not need to answer sin with judgment. Instead, he will come to bring to salvation all who are waiting expectantly for him (9:28). The parousia is an image of hope for the faithful.

The community addressed by Hebrews lives in the time of the End, the time of fulfillment. Yet, like their ancestors in faith, they have not yet entered the promised rest, not yet taken up residence in the glorious city of God. There is no room for comfortable self-assurance and complacency. And the prospect of a day of accounting before God counters any temptation to withdraw from the rigors of Christian life in a hostile environment. But if the readers will hold fast their commitment through adversity, and if they will persevere in faith and obedience, they may live in confident hope, awaiting Jesus' return as their salvation.

2 PETER

The gospels preserve the tradition that Jesus promised his return before the generation of his contemporaries came to an end (e.g., Mark 13:24–30; cf. 9:1). As we have seen, New Testament writings generally affirm the belief that Jesus' parousia and associated eschatological events would occur within that first Christian generation. Even documents from the last decades of the first century, when delayed fulfillment of God's eschatological promise had to be admitted and explained, almost invariably reaffirmed expectation of an imminent eschaton, with

John's Gospel a notable exception.[37] Recognition of delayed fulfillment and continued vitality of eschatological hope could and often did coexist.[38] Yet as a new century began, the problem of delay, at least in some circles, led to skepticism: if God had not delivered on the promised eschatological completion, then why hold on to such beliefs as eschatological judgment or the glorious parousia of Jesus? This is ultimately a question of theodicy, for the march of history calls into question divine justice.[39] And it is a matter of God's faithfulness and the reliability of the prophetic word. Second Peter must respond to these troubling theological questions.

A Response to "False Prophets"

In 2 Peter, eschatological instruction is no theoretical concern. Teachers or prophets within the Christian communities known to the author have ridiculed conventional eschatological convictions and evidently invited readers into a world free of the constraints imposed by such notions as divine judgment. To counter these dangerous teachings, the writer dispatches a letter cast in the form of a testament or farewell message from Simeon Peter (see 1:12–15). The testament genre enjoyed broad

---

[37] John retains eschatological imagery, though the element of imminence is missing (see ch. 3 above).

[38] See C. L. Holman, *Till Jesus Comes: Origins of Christian Apocalyptic Expectation* (Peabody, Mass.: Henrickson, 1996); J. D. G. Dunn, "He Will Come Again," *Int* 51 (1997): 42–56; R. Bauckham, *Jude, 2 Peter* (WBC 50; Waco: Word, 1983), 310; idem, "The Delay of the Parousia," *TynBull* 31 (1980): 3–36; J. T. Carroll, *Response to the End of History: Eschatology and Situation in Luke–Acts* (SBLDS 92; Atlanta: Scholars Press, 1988).

[39] A critical dimension of 2 Peter, according to J. H. Neyrey, *2 Peter, Jude* (AB 37C; New York: Doubleday, 1993), e.g., 122–27; cf. also Bauckham ("Delay of the Parousia," 7–8), who suggests that the problem of parousia delay is not simply a matter of unfulfilled prophecy but the "apocalyptic version of the problem of evil" (7). A "universal challenge" to the divine righteousness necessitated "a universal righting of wrongs, an elimination of evil on a universal, even cosmic, scale" (8).

appeal.[40] It blended (1) reminiscence of the author's life; (2) moral appeals and exhortations; and (3) predictions of the fortunes and challenges awaiting the hearers. The attribution of authorship was fictional; this was a stock feature of the testamentary literature. In the case of 2 Peter, Bauckham terms the ascription to the apostle Peter a "transparent fiction."[41] Not only the letter's self-presentation as a testament from Peter, but also the concluding warning against "destabilizing" instruction that is based on misreadings of the letters of Paul (3:15b–17) align the author's message with the church's foundational and authoritative tradition. It is this tradition—a vigorously eschatological tradition with clear moral implications—that readers are directed to "remember" (1:12, 13, 15; 3:1, 2).

2 Peter and Jude

Comparison of 2 Peter with the Letter of Jude turns up significant correspondences. Of particular interest for this study is the relationship between 2 Pet 3:1–3 and Jude 17–18:[42]

Beloved, I am now writing to you this second letter; in these [letters] I am arousing in your memory a sincere understanding,	Beloved,

---

[40] Examples drawn from Jewish literature: Tob 14:3–11; 4 Ezra 14:28–36; *T. Moses; T. 12 Pat.; T. Job; Jub.* 21–22, 35, 36; *1 Enoch* 91–104; *2 Bar.* 77–86; cf. Gen 49; Deut 33; Josh 23–24; John 13–16; Acts 20:18–35; 2 Tim 3–4. On 2 Peter as testament or farewell speech, see C. H. Talbert, "II Peter and the Delay of the Parousia," *VC* 20 (1966): 139–40; Bauckham, *Jude, 2 Peter,* 131.

[41] Bauckham, *Jude, 2 Peter,* 134–35. He points out that the fiction of genuine prophecy—predicting the emergence of false prophets (2:1–3; 3:3–7)—is not consistently maintained. The author sometimes shifts to present-tense descriptions of the teachers (e.g., 2:10b–22). Bauckham provides a helpful discussion of the pseudonymous authorship of the letter (133–34, 158–62).

[42] See Bauckham, *Jude, 2 Peter,* 283; Neyrey, *2 Peter, Jude,* 227. For evaluation of the literary connections between the two documents, see

so that you will remember [μνησθῆναι] the words spoken beforehand by the holy prophets, and also the command from the Lord and Savior through your apostles.	remember [μνήσθητε] the words spoken beforehand by the apostles of our Lord Jesus Christ, that they said to you,
Knowing this, first of all, that in the last days [ἐσχάτων τῶν ἡμερῶν] scoffers [ἐμπαῖκται] will come scoffing, who will go out in accordance with their own passions. (2 Pet 3:1–3)	In the last time [ἐσχάτου χρόνου] there will be scoffers [ἐμπαῖκται], who will go out in accordance with their impious passions. (Jude 17–18)

If, as seems quite probable, 2 Peter is the later text and its author has used Jude as a source document, the eschatological warning present in Jude has been expanded and applied to a new situation.

Jude warns of the intrusion of false teachers within the community of faith (vv. 3–4), and points to several scriptural instances of divine judgment against evil (vv. 5–11). The implication is clear: the contentious members of the congregation will likewise be condemned. Reinforcing his appeal to readers to remain faithful and seek to rescue others from the trap set by the false teachers, the author places predictions on the lips of both Enoch (vv. 14–16) and the apostles (vv. 17–18). In an apparent quotation from the extracanonical *1 Enoch* (1:9), Jude presents Enoch's prophecy of the parousia: "The Lord will come[43] with his holy myriads."[44] And the purpose of this eschatological coming

---

Bauckham, *Jude, 2 Peter*, 141–43; Neyrey, *2 Peter, Jude*, 120–22. Both commentators follow the majority opinion that 2 Peter borrows from Jude as a literary source.

[43] Literally "came" (aorist tense). This verb expresses prophetic certainty, and is therefore future in sense. See Bauckham, *Jude, 2 Peter*, 93; Neyrey, *2 Peter, Jude*, 80.

[44] The "Lord" God in *1 Enoch* becomes the "Lord" Jesus in Jude (cf. v. 17). Notice that 2 Peter does not preserve the quotation from *1 Enoch*, for reasons we can only guess. The same is true of the possible allusion to *T. Moses* in Jude 9–10. See Bauckham, *Jude, 2 Peter*, 139–40.

is to judge (v. 15). The apostles predicted that "in the last time" scoffers would come, driven by impious passions and fomenting division in the congregation (vv. 18–19). The readers, by contrast, are to wait for divine mercy that will issue in eternal life (v. 21). The parousia will mean mercy for those who persist in faith and love, but judgment for others, even for community members who turn from piety to unholy passions. We find, then, a familiar pattern: eschatological imagery in service of parenetic appeals.

Jude leaves to the reader's imagination the content of the scoffers' mocking. Second Peter embellishes the prophecy of end-time false teachers by specifying the substance of the opponents' critique: "Where is the promise of his parousia? For from the [day] the fathers fell asleep [i.e., died], everything continues just as it has been from the beginning of creation" (3:4). What is the nature and likely derivation of this objection to the community's eschatological faith? And what counterarguments does the author advance?

The Position of the Opponents

The Christian teachers opposed by 2 Peter evidently ridicule the notion that there will be an eschatological judgment or a triumphant parousia of the Lord. Judging from the author's strenuous defense of prophetic speech (1:19–21) and disavowal of elaborate myths (1:16) in the section immediately preceding the introduction of the false teachers, they may be denying the validity of prophetic revelation, and they may be inventive mythmakers themselves. All this in a letter purporting to be from Peter, authoritative voice for the gradually emerging "catholic" church. This combination of elements, together with the letter's correlation of "heresy" and exaggerated moral freedom or licentiousness, has convinced Talbert that the opponents are gnostic Christians with an overly realized, spiritualized eschatology.[45] Readers are urged to take seriously divine judgment and accountability to God for moral conduct.

-----

[45] Talbert, "II Peter." Talbert concludes that the letter "was written to serve as a defense against Gnosticism" (142), and that the develop-

This is an attractive explanation, but other possibilities should be considered. Neyrey stresses that the profile of the opponents glimpsed through the author's attack would have been very much at home in the Hellenistic world of late antiquity. The idea of divine judgment by fire and water—a judgment cosmic in scope—was common among Jews and Greeks alike (cf. 2 Pet 3:6–7, 12).[46] From Stoics came the image of the world consumed by fire at the end of its historical cycle. Moreover, Epicurean philosophical teaching rejected divine providence, and that view carried with it a denial of divine judgment and of the credibility of prophetic oracles. Certainly a delay in the fulfillment of divine promises (or of a prophetic oracle) would be taken as support of the Epicurean posture. Yet challenges to conventional views of providence and divine activity were by no means confined to Epicurean circles; such skepticism enjoyed broader currency during this period.[47] It is plausible that 2 Peter is responding to a Christian view that has been shaped by Epicurean-style skepticism regarding divine providence.

Bauckham appropriately adds a third cultural tradition to the mix, that of apocalyptic Judaism.

---

ment of eschatological themes must be read in relation to the gnostic challenge. The motifs of parousia and judgment in 2 Peter "motivate moral behavior" (143).

[46] Neyrey, *2 Peter, Jude*, 203. He points to Luke 17:26–30; *T. Naph.* 3.5; Josephus, *War* 5.566; Philo, *Mos.* 2.53–65; Plato, *Tim.* 22B-C; Lucretius, *R. nat.*, 5.341–44, 383–415; 6.660–737; Seneca, *Nat.* 3.27–30; Origen, *Cels.* 1.19–20. See also Justin, *1 Apol.* 20; *2 Apol.* 7.1–3; Irenaeus, *Haer.* 1.7.1; 5.35.2; 6.36.1; Cicero, *Nat. d.* 2.118; cf. C. P. Thiede, "A Pagan Reader of 2 Peter: Cosmic Conflagration in 2 Peter 3 and the *Octavius* of Minucius Felix," *JSNT* 26 (1986): 79–96. Neither Irenaeus nor Origen favors the notion of a world conflagration. Thiede thinks Irenaeus, in agreement with 2 Peter, anticipates a new world, but does not accept cosmic destruction by fire (86). Origen ties both deluge and conflagration to sin and pictures the conflagration as a matter not of annihilation but purification (87).

[47] See Neyrey, *2 Peter, Jude*, 122–28. Against Talbert, Neyrey locates the opponents of 2 Peter in popular skepticism influenced by Epicurean ideas, not in gnostic thought.

Second Peter represents, in fact, an intriguing blend of ideas drawn from Greek popular philosophy and apocalyptic Jewish traditions.[48] Bauckham thinks the teachers opposed by 2 Peter combined eschatological skepticism and moral libertinism. In the context of Hellenistic culture, they aimed to "disencumber Christianity of its [culturally embarrassing] eschatology and its ethical rigorism."[49] The author responds by vigorously reaffirming apocalyptic hope centered on the parousia of the Lord and the certainty of eschatological judgment.

The wide currency of the religious and philosophical debates that appear to underlie the position of the opponents makes any precise identification difficult. For that reason, the specific proposal of a gnostic threat in the community is less convincing, although it cannot be excluded. Whatever the particular derivation of the "heresy" that has prompted the author to send this sharp rejoinder, how does 2 Peter frame a response?

An Apology for Eschatological Faith

The credibility of the prophetic promise rests on its source: a trustworthy God. God's voice revealed the majestic glory of the beloved Son at the transfiguration Peter had witnessed (1:16b–18). Not speculative myths but this concrete experience of divine majesty in the world informs the author's affirmation of the Lord's glorious future coming (1:16a). If the opponents dismissed (eschatological) prophetic revelation, there is irony in the way the author introduces the teachers in chapter 2, as Bauckham has noted. Those within the congregation who reject the validity of prophecy unwittingly confirm its truth, since they are the very false prophets prophesied to arise before the End.[50]

---

[48] Bauckham, *Jude, 2 Peter*, 154: a blending of Greek and apocalyptic ideas "is precisely the way in which the author tries to interpret and defend the apostolic message in a postapostolic generation."

[49] Ibid., 156.

[50] Ibid., 295.

The First Argument: Creation and Judgment

Second Peter 3:4–10 employs a chiastic structure to present the opponents' critique and its rebuttal:

A – Scoffers ask, "Where is his promised coming?" (v. 4a).

    B – Then add, "[E]verything continues just as it has been from the beginning of creation" (v. 4b).

    B′ – The reply to B: The creator used the medium of creation (water) to execute judgment (the deluge), and that same creative, judging word will destroy the wicked (vv. 5–7).

A′ – And then the reply to A, in two steps:

(1) The promised coming is delayed because of the patient mercy of God (vv. 8–9).

(2) Nevertheless, the day of the Lord will come "like a thief," and the elements (στοιχεῖα) will be dissolved by fire (v. 10).

Verses 3:11–15 then exploit the parenetic potential of this eschatological teaching. If this is what the future looks like (cosmic destruction by fire, and the approaching "day of the Lord"), then what manner of living fits the circumstance? The author appeals for holy, godly, and peaceable living by persons of faith who wait expectantly for God's eschatological judgment and creation of a new cosmic order.[51]

Does the constancy of the created world really support the view that there will be no eschatological judgment? Read again! The sovereign and just God has exercised judgment in creation from the beginning, in fact using the waters of creation to good effect as instrument of divine judgment. The problem with the teachers' belief is not that they believe the world is unchanging, but, instead, that they draw the wrong inference from the world's constancy.[52] In fact, the continuity of God's creating,

---

[51] The verb προσδοκάω, rendered here "wait expectantly," appears in 3:12, 13, 14.

[52] See S. Meier, "2 Peter 3:3–7—An Early Jewish and Christian Response to Eschatological Skepticism," *BZ* 32 (1988): 255–57.

judging word ("that same word," 3:7) links creation and eschaton. Just as the wicked were overtaken by destructive judgment in the flood (cf. Noah, and also Lot—water and fire—in 2:4–8), morally bankrupt teachers in the time of the End—the time of the congregation 2 Peter addresses—will face the bar of divine justice.[53]

The Second Argument: God's Patient Mercy

The argument now takes a positive turn, as the author offers a more hopeful explanation for parousia delay. The End has not come as expected, but that is not due to any failure of divine providence. Far from calling God's sovereignty into question, the slow fulfillment of the old promise has God's purposive activity as its very cause. God is patient and merciful, "slow to anger, and abounding in steadfast love," one might almost insert, drawing from the classic Psalter text (103:8; cf. Exod 34:6).[54] Yet divine patience has another face, captured in another line from the same psalm: God vindicates and grants justice to the oppressed (103:6). God's patient mercy has as its intended outcome the repentance of all (3:8–9, 15). Judgment approaches, yet there is still time to avert it through a reoriented mind and life. A faithful people who reflect God's holiness may even "hasten" the appearance of the "day of the Lord" (3:12). The problem of parousia delay is not entirely out of the readers' hands. Their part is to order their lives around the holy ways of God.

------

[53] For discussion of this typological argument, in which each scriptural instance of judgment prefigures the eschatological judgment, see Bauckham, *Jude, 2 Peter*, 249. He rightly perceives that the interest in 2 Peter is not cosmology but faith's affirmation of judgment against evil. Like their precursors, the false teachers will face judgment. At bottom, this is a matter of theodicy, of divine justice.

[54] This connection between delay and divine patience appears also in *2 Bar.* 12:4; 21:20–21; 24:2; 48:29; 59:6; 85:8; cf. Bauckham, *Jude, 2 Peter*, 16–19.

The Third Argument: Reaffirmation of Parousia Expectation

Reasserting eschatological judgment, the author also reaffirms the parousia hope that has been questioned, indeed ridiculed. Borrowing an image from the gospel tradition of Jesus' own teaching, 2 Peter cautions that the parousia (the "day of the Lord," 3:10a) will come "like a thief" (cf. Matt 24:42–44; 1 Thess 5:2; Rev 3:3; 16:15). The metaphor obviously suggests sudden and unexpected intrusion of an unwelcome and menacing event. Yet the other side of the coin is more hopeful. If the letter's hearers remain alert, ready, and waiting, the End will not catch them unawares. The patience of God will then bring not their demise but their salvation (3:15).

Nevertheless, true to the predominantly parenetic thrust of the letter, the depiction of the parousia in 2 Peter centers on eschatological judgment. And there are fireworks (3:10b, 12)! Unlike Stoic schemes of world conflagration, 2 Peter envisages a new heaven and a new earth that will be eternal (1:11; 3:13, 18). This move, subsuming the fire that will engulf the world under the providential care of a sovereign—and just—God, illustrates the weaving together of divergent cultural traditions (Greek popular philosophy and Jewish apocalyptic tradition) in this letter. In the scenario of the future proposed by 2 Peter, God's purposes in the eschaton ultimately target not destruction but salvation and new creation.

Eschatological Parenesis

Major sections of 2 Peter are dominated by vivid descriptions of the moral deficiencies of the opponents. An unflinching catalog of the vices of these advocates of freedom (2:17–22) shows them as ripe for the judgment that is surely coming, no matter how confidently they deny it. Eschatological faith supports moral seriousness and accountability. The letter's closing leaves no uncertainty: as readers wait expectantly for the day of the Lord, they are to lead holy and godly lives (3:11). After all, the "new heavens and new earth" that are coming will be the home of "righteousness" (3:13). If 2 Peter's message has hit the mark, the congregation will shun harmful "heresy," and will embrace both the authoritative theological tradition and the moral life it sanctions. They will be found blameless and at peace when Jesus returns and the world finally glimpses the face of God's holy justice.

 FIVE

THE PAROUSIA OF JESUS IN SECOND- AND THIRD-CENTURY CHRISTIANITY

by Jeffrey S. Siker

In this chapter we consider Christian approaches to the parousia of Jesus during the period between the end of the New Testament era and the rise of Constantine at the beginning of the fourth century. For the purposes of this study we will focus on Christian writings ranging from the apostolic fathers in the early second century through the theologian Origen and his successors in the middle of the third century.

A good place to get a foothold in the large amount of primary and secondary literature is the pivotal and controversial study by Martin Werner, *The Formation of Christian Dogma,* originally published in 1941.[1] Werner

---

[1] The English translation (*The Formation of Christian Dogma: An Historical Study of Its Problems* [New York: Harper & Brothers, 1957]) is an abbreviated translation of the German original, *Die Entstehung des christlichen Dogmas.*

appropriately dedicated his book to Albert Schweitzer, who early in the twentieth century had pioneered a renewed appreciation for earliest Christianity as a movement infused with radically apocalyptic eschatological notions of the impending End.[2] Werner argued that the so-called delay of the parousia was experienced by the early Christians as a serious crisis, and that many early Christian writings reflect this struggle with parousia delay. He could point to such early second-century texts as 2 Pet 3:3–4, which warns "that scoffers will come in the last days with scoffing, following their own passions and saying, 'Where is the promise of his coming?' " The author of 2 Peter appears to be addressing the disturbance of the early church at the delay of the parousia.[3]

---

[2] Schweitzer was in turn influenced by J. Weiss's emphasis on Jesus as an eschatological figure, especially in Weiss's seminal book *Jesus' Proclamation of the Kingdom of God*, first published in German in 1892 and finally translated into English in 1971 (Philadelphia: Fortress, 1971). The most groundbreaking book was Schweitzer's *The Quest of the Historical Jesus*, published originally in 1906 and translated into English in 1910 (New York: Macmillan, 1968). But also important were Schweitzer's *The Mystery of the Kingdom of God* (trans. W. Lowrie; New York: Dodd, Mead, 1914 [orig. 1901]) and his most significant book on Paul, *The Mysticism of Paul the Apostle* (trans. W. Montgomery; New York: Macmillan, 1955 [ET orig. 1931]), in which he argued that apocalyptic eschatology was also the key to Paul's thought. Again, as for Schweitzer's influence on Werner, there is a telling comment by Morton Enslin on the dust jacket of the English translation of Werner's *The Formation of Christian Dogma:* "It can be soberly said that this volume by Werner is the one which Schweitzer would have written had he set his hand to it."

[3] In a significant article C. H. Talbert argues against this view of 2 Peter. Talbert writes, "II Peter can be regarded as evidence for a serious disturbance within the Church over the delay of the *Parousia* only if the problem of eschatology is not treated in relation to the problem of heresy about which the entire document is concerned. Such a method of exegesis is surely incorrect. . . . nowhere does the author say that the whole Church was disturbed by a delayed *Parousia*. Rather . . . the only ones who appear to consider the delay of the *Parousia* a problem are the heretics [gnostics], the outsiders" ("II Peter and the Delay of the *Parousia*," *VC* 20 [1966]: 142). See the discussion of 2 Peter in chapter 4 above.

Although at the end of the twentieth century scholars generally recognize that Werner overstated his case and pushed the evidence too far, it is still common in studies of early Christianity to claim that the delay of the parousia forced early Christians to revise their theology in significant ways as they geared up for a longer haul through history than they had imagined would happen.[4] Thus, the argument goes, we move from an apocalypticist like Paul in the middle of the first century, with his fervent expectation of the End coming very soon, to a writing like the Gospel of John, with its heavily realized eschatology, by the end of the first century of the common era. By the time Constantine comes on the scene at the beginning of the fourth century, Christianity has wrestled sufficiently with the failure of the parousia to materialize that, apart from the occasional Montanist, Christianity has essentially become deeschatologized, with expectations

---

[4] This view appears in various standard introductions to the New Testament. See, e.g., R. A. Spivey and D. M. Smith, *Anatomy of the New Testament* (4th ed.; New York: Macmillan, 1988), 58, where the authors relate how the church "had to face the problem posed by the delay of the expected *parousia* . . . and the end of the world." Also see S. Harris, *The New Testament: A Student's Introduction* (2d ed.; Mountain View, Calif.: Mayfield, 1995), 187, where in reference to John's Gospel Harris states: "The failure of the *Parousia* to occur during the lifetimes of Jesus' original followers may have created a crisis of belief that John's transformation of Jesus' story effectively addresses." In response to such assumptions, see the corrective comments of N. T. Wright, *The New Testament and the People of God* (Minneapolis: Fortress, 1992), 342–43. Wright puts the situation well: "A good deal has been made, this century, of the idea that the earliest and most Jewish Christians confidently expected the imminent end of the space-time universe, and that the development of Christianity was marked by the fading of this expectation. . . . [but] it is quite clear that the expectation of a coming great reversal, with Jesus returning as judge, continued unabated in the second century and beyond, with no apparent embarrassment or signs of hasty rewriting of predictions. All sorts of charges were being rebutted by apologists, but there is no sense that Christianity had changed its character, or been put in jeopardy, by the failure of Jesus to return within a generation of Easter. A full reappraisal of the nature and place of eschatology within early Christianity seems called for."

regarding the parousia of Jesus a distant hope at best. Or so the argument goes.

While there is some merit to this way of perceiving early Christian responses to the so-called delay of the parousia, I argue that instead of a relatively smooth transition away from fervent end-time expectations over the first few centuries, there was in fact an unresolved tension in Christian eschatology from the very outset, a tension that can be seen throughout Christian tradition. This tension is between Christians who had fervent expectations of the parousia as an event soon to take place and those who did not have any real expectations of an impending second coming, or for whom such eschatological language was at best muted. There is, of course, a continuum of thought from radically imminent expectations of the parousia represented in Paul's Thessalonian correspondence, on the one hand, to the radically deeschatologized gnostic understandings of spiritual salvation here and now.[5] There is much between these two poles. But both poles are present in the first century, in the second and third centuries, and also in our own day and age.

In our own day one can certainly see the tensions between fundamentalist Christians who argue for the parousia being very close at hand[6] and what we have come to call mainstream Protestants and Catholics who make retirement plans without a thought about the parousia of Jesus. Although it is not exactly the same, we can also see a parallel tension in the scholarly debate over the historical Jesus. Some scholars argue vigorously that Jesus was indeed an apocalyptic preacher who expected the End soon,[7] while others contend

---

[5] See the discussion below.

[6] Imminent eschatological approaches are perhaps best exemplified by the television ministry of Jack van Impe and his wife Rexella, or by Hal Lindsey's well-known book, *The Late Great Planet Earth* (Grand Rapids: Zondervan, 1971).

[7] See, e.g., E. P. Sanders, *The Historical Figure of Jesus* (London: Penguin, 1993), and J. Meier, *A Marginal Jew: Rethinking the Historical Jesus,* vol. 2: *Mentor, Message, and Miracles* (ABRL; New York: Doubleday, 1994).

just as vehemently that Jesus was a noneschatological wisdom teacher without fervent expectations of the End.[8] In my judgment, it is a mistake to insist that early Christian expectations were consistently one way or another, or that Christianity started out eschatologically charged only to diminish in hope and expectation over time. Instead, both strands have always been present, and both can be seen in second- and third-century Christian writings as well.

We can make a running start into the second and third centuries by touching briefly on the appearance of both strands of thought about the parousia in the New Testament writings. We find a good example in 1 Corinthians. On the one hand, Paul, the clearly apocalyptic preacher, is convinced that the End is so imminent that people should not get married if they can stand not to (1 Corinthians 7). In the same community, however, we find Christians—apparently prominent Christians from the community—arguing that they are already living the resurrected life of the Spirit. Recall Paul's biting sarcasm: "Already you have all you want, already you have become rich. Quite apart from us you have [already] become kings!" (4:8).

When we turn to second- and third-century Christian writers we discover the same tension, if with more stops along the continuum between these two poles of imminent and realized eschatology. In general we see at one end of the spectrum Christians who advanced a thoroughgoing eschatology with the parousia close at hand; on the other end we find Christians who lack any real sense of the parousia. In the middle emerges a centrist position, with various Christians advocating a moderate eschatology that looks to an eventual but not imminent parousia—a position that remains a prominent option at the end of the twentieth century.

---

[8] See, e.g., M. Borg, *Jesus: A New Vision* (San Francisco: Harper & Row, 1987), and J. D. Crossan, *The Historical Jesus: The Life of a Mediterranean Jewish Peasant* (San Francisco: Harper, 1991), along with the publications of the Jesus Seminar.

DIDACHE AND EPISTLE OF BARNABAS

We can begin our study of second- and third-century Christian sources by surveying the apostolic fathers, a disparate and somewhat artificial collection of writings from the early to middle second century. The *Didache* and the *Epistle of Barnabas* are noteworthy for their emphasis on what appears to be an imminent parousia. In a section of the *Didache* dealing with prayer after the celebration of the Eucharist (10:5–6), we find this prayer: "Remember, Lord, thy church, to deliver it from all evil and to make it perfect in thy love, and gather it together in its holiness from the four winds to thy kingdom which thou hast prepared for it. . . . Let grace come and let this world pass away. Hosannah to the God of David. . . . *Maran atha,* Amen." The cry of "maranatha" (our Lord come!) has a significant parallel in 1 Cor 16:22. In both cases it expresses a desire for the parousia to happen soon. The *Didache* (with apparent reliance on Matthew 24) concludes with warnings of the coming apocalyptic judgment of God: "Watch over your life. . . . be ready, for you know not the hour in which our Lord comes" (16:1).[9]

The *Epistle of Barnabas* also warns its readers of the coming End: "The final stumbling block is at hand of which it was written, as Enoch says, 'For to this end the Lord has cut short the times and the days, that his beloved should make haste and come to his inheritance.' . . . Wherefore let us pay heed in the last days, for the whole time of our life and faith will profit us nothing, unless we resist, as becomes the [children] of God in this present evil time" (4:3, 9).

The *Epistle of Barnabas* also provides an eschatological reading of the creation story from Genesis. Noting that God created the world in six days and that on the seventh day God made an end of it, Barnabas says: "Notice, children, what is the meaning of 'He made an end in six days'? He means this: That the Lord will make an end of everything in six thousand years, for a

---

[9] See V. Balabanski, *Eschatology in the Making: Mark, Matthew and the Didache* (SNTSMS 97; Cambridge: Cambridge University Press, 1997), 206–9.

day with him means a thousand years. . . . So then, children, in six days, that is, in six thousand years, everything will be completed" (15:4). What will happen after these six thousand years? Barnabas explains: since God rested on the seventh day, it means that "when his Son comes he will destroy the time of the wicked one, and will judge the godless, and will change the sun and the moon and the stars, and then he will truly rest on the seventh day" (15:5). But still that is not the end of the story. For since elsewhere in scripture God says, "Your new moons and the sabbaths I cannot endure" (Isa 1:13), Barnabas writes, "Do you not see what he means? The present sabbaths are not acceptable to me, but that which I have made, in which I will give rest to all things and make the beginning of an eighth day, that is the beginning of another world" (15:8). Thus, for Barnabas, Christ's second coming will eventually inaugurate a totally new age, an eighth day of creation at the end of the appointed time. Barnabas is the first Christian on record to make this argument about history being a week of ages, but he will not be the last, as this notion will get picked up later in the second century by Irenaeus, and in the third century by Hippolytus. Unfortunately, Barnabas does not say where he thinks he is in the six-thousand-year countdown, but he clearly thinks he is living in the final times.

APOCALYPSE OF PETER AND
EPISTULA APOSTOLORUM

In both the *Didache* and the *Epistle of Barnabas,* the parousia of Jesus seems close at hand. The warnings are to be prepared for the imminent coming of Christ with judgment. A similar concern for the impending coming of Christ can be found in some of the early Christian writings categorized as New Testament Apocrypha. In particular the *Apocalypse of Peter* (typically dated between 135 and 150 C.E.) and the *Epistula Apostolorum* (middle to late second century) anticipate the imminent return of Christ. The *Apocalypse of Peter* begins with these words: "The Second Coming of Christ and Resurrection of the Dead which Christ revealed through Peter to those who died for their sins, because they did not keep the commandment of God, their creator."[10] With apparent dependence on apocalyptic materials from Matthew 24, the *Apocalypse of Peter* proceeds to warn of the suddenness of the parousia: "The coming of the Son of God shall not be plain; but as the lightning that shines from the east to the west" (ch. 1).

Similarly, *Ep. Apos.* 16–17 has the risen Christ speak about his second coming. The disciples ask him, "In what kind of power and form are you about to come?" Jesus responds, "Truly I say to you, I will come as the sun which bursts forth; thus will I, shining seven times brighter than it in glory, while I am carried on the wings of the clouds in splendor with my cross going on before me, come to the earth to judge the living and the dead."[11] The disciples then ask when this will happen: " 'O Lord, how many years yet?' And he said to us, 'When the hundred and fiftieth year is completed, between pentecost and passover will the coming of my Father take place.' "[12]

1 CLEMENT AND SHEPHERD OF HERMAS

While several Christian writings from the second century attest to an imminent sense of the parousia, two other writings from the apostolic fathers, *1 Clement* and the *Shepherd of Hermas,* present similar warnings about being prepared, but have a somewhat less immediate sense of an impending parousia. The author of *1 Clement* writes, "Let us not be double-minded, nor let our souls be fanciful concerning his excellent and glorious gifts. Let this Scripture be far from us in which he says, 'Wretched are the double-minded, who doubt in their soul and say, "We have heard these things even in the days of our fathers, and behold we have grown old, and none of these things has happened to us." Oh, foolish men, compare yourself to a tree. . . .'

---

[10] "The Apocalypse of Peter," in *The Apocryphal New Testament* (ed. J. K. Elliott; Oxford: Oxford University Press, 1993), 600.

[11] *Apocryphal New Testament,* 565–66.

[12] Ibid., 566.

See how in a little time the fruit of the tree comes to ripeness. Truly his will shall be quickly and suddenly accomplished, as the Scripture also bears witness that 'he shall come quickly and shall not tarry' " (*1 Clem.* 23.2–5; last phrase quoting Isa 13:22 LXX). As B. Daley observes, the eschatological themes sounded in *1 Clement* "are presented as being in continuity with creation, the expected culmination of the orderly process of history rather than a crisis that has suddenly come upon us."[13]

In the initial section of Visions the *Shepherd of Hermas* addresses the question of the parousia directly to the "ancient lady" who mediates the visions to him: "And I began to ask her about the times, if the end were yet. But she cried out with a loud voice saying, 'Foolish man, do you not see the tower still being built? Whenever therefore the building of the tower has been finished, the end comes. But it will quickly be built up; ask me nothing more' " (3.8). The tower appears to be the Shepherd's way of talking about the church. The building is not yet complete. The time is not yet at hand for the End to come. This motif finds clearer articulation later in a section from the Similitudes (Parables):

> And on that day the building was finished, but the tower was not completed, for it was going to be built on to, and there was a pause in the building. And the six men commanded all the builders to retire a little and rest, but they commanded the maidens not to go away from the tower. And it seemed to me that the maidens had given up looking after the tower. But after they had all gone away and were resting I said to the shepherd: "Why, sir," said I, "was the building of the tower not completed?" "The tower," said he, "cannot yet be completed unless its lord come and test this building, in order that if some stones prove to be rotten, he may change them, for the tower is being built according to his will." . . . And the shepherd asked the maidens if the lord of the tower had come. And they said that he was about to come, to examine the building. (9.5.1–2, 7)

Here, then, we have a vision of building steadily towards the coming of the Lord, but no sense that the End is right at hand. Rather, the Lord first has to come and inspect how the building

---

[13] B. Daley, *The Hope of the Early Church: A Handbook of Patristic Eschatology* (Cambridge: Cambridge University Press, 1991), 10.

is going, to check and see if any part of the building needs to be replaced. This is a builder who wants to get it right and is patiently waiting until the tower is finished as designed. But still we can see that the Shepherd does not want his audience to become complacent, lest they think the Lord will never come. He is coming, but not quite yet.

JUSTIN MARTYR

When we turn to the Christian apologists of the mid-second century, Justin Martyr stands out for his teachings regarding the parousia.[14] For Justin the notion of "two advents of Christ" has become a clear doctrine grounded in Scripture. In his *First Apology* (ch. 52) Justin writes, "The Prophets have foretold two comings of Christ: the one, which already took place, was that of a dishonored and suffering man; the other coming will take place, as it is predicted, when He shall gloriously come from Heaven with His angelic army."[15] Similarly, in his *Dialogue with Trypho the Jew* Justin says, "It also was foretold by the Patriarch Jacob . . . that there would be two Advents of Christ, and that in the first He would be subject to suffering, and that after this Advent your people would have neither prophet nor king, and that the Gentiles who believe in the suffering Christ would look forward to His second coming" (ch. 52).[16] Here Justin has added a twist of anti-Jewish rhetoric to his understanding of the parousia. The parousia will be for the Gentiles who have accepted the first coming of Christ. Later in the *Dialogue* Justin uses the parousia as an occasion to criticize Jewish ritual sacrifice: "And do not suppose that Isaiah or the other Prophets speak of sacrifices of blood or libations being offered on the altar at His second com-

---

[14] On Justin's eschatology in general, see especially L.W. Barnard, "Justin Martyr's Eschatology," *VC* 19 (1965): 86–98.

[15] *The Fathers of the Church*, vol. 6: *Writings of Saint Justin Martyr* (trans. T. B. Falls; Washington, D.C.: Catholic University Press of America, 1948), 89.

[16] Ibid., *Saint Justin Martyr*, 226.

ing, but only of true and spiritual praises and thanksgivings" (ch. 118).[17] Somewhat like the *Shepherd of Hermas,* Justin thinks that God has intentionally held bringing history to a close with the parousia so that the full number of those chosen by God might be included before the second coming (see *1 Apol.* 45).

GNOSTIC CHRISTIANITY

Whereas Justin Martyr joins the *Shepherd of Hermas* in the notion of a planned divine pause before the parousia, and hence a slackening of imminent expectations regarding the End, in the middle of the second century we meet a completely different approach to the parousia in various gnostic writings. Perhaps the clearest place to see this gnostic Christian view of the parousia— or rather this view of a nonparousia—is in the Valentinian *Treatise on the Resurrection* (also known as "To Rheginus"). The author writes,

> The savior swallowed death. . . . for I mean that laying aside the corruptible world, he exchanged it for an incorruptible eternal realm. And he raised himself up, having swallowed the visible by means of the invisible, and gave us the way to our immortality. So then, as the apostle said of him, we have suffered with him, and arisen with him, and ascended with him. Now, since we are manifestly present in this world, the world is what we wear (like a garment). From him (the savior) we radiate like rays; and being held fast by him until our sunset—that is, until our death in the present life—we are drawn upward by him as rays are drawn by the sun, restrained by nothing. This is resurrection of the spirit, which swallows resurrection of the soul along with resurrection of the flesh (45–46).[18]

Eschatology here is fully realized. Resurrection is a spiritual resurrection. The believer has already suffered, risen, and ascended with Christ back to the fullness of God. There is no need for parousia, for a second coming, since all was accomplished in the

---

[17] Ibid., 330.

[18] In *The Gnostic Scriptures: A New Translation with Annotations and Introductions* (ed. and trans. B. Layton; Garden City, N.Y.: Doubleday, 1987), 321.

first. This restoration to the spirit of the heavenly world enlightens the believer and brings rest (see also *Gos. Philip* 71.15).

Another gnostic writing, the *Gospel of Mary*, has a similar view of realized eschatology. In this apocryphal Gospel the resurrected Christ speaks to his disciples, "Peace be with you. Receive my peace to yourselves. Beware that no one lead you astray, saying 'Lo here!' or 'Lo there!' For the Son of man is within you" (8:13–19).[19] The passage is reminiscent of Luke 17:20–21: "The kingdom of God is not coming with things that can be observed; nor will they say, 'Look, here it is!' or 'There it is!' For, in fact, the kingdom of God is among [or within, ἐντὸς] you." Rather than looking for the coming of the Son of Man in the future, the *Gospel of Mary* directs the faithful gnostic to look within oneself here and now.

WESTERN FATHERS FROM IRENAEUS TO CYPRIAN

Irenaeus

At the end of the second century, Irenaeus takes an approach to the parousia that differs greatly from that of the gnostic Christians he opposed. For Irenaeus the second coming of Christ is simply the logical and graceful end of the whole of salvation history that God began in creation. Like Justin, Irenaeus states that "all the prophets announced His two advents: the one, indeed, in which he became a man subject to stripes, and knowing what it is to bear infirmity . . . but the second in which He will come on the clouds, bringing on the day which burns as a furnace, and smiting the earth with the word of His mouth" (*Haer.* 4.32.1).[20] Irenaeus confidently pronounces that when Christ re-

---

[19] The *Gospel of Mary* [Magdalene] comes from the Berlin Gnostic Codex (8502, I), and its original composition is typically dated in the middle or late second century. See *The Nag Hammadi Library* (ed. J. M. Robinson; San Francisco: Harper & Row, 1977), 470–74.

[20] *The Ante-Nicene Fathers* (ed. A. Roberts and J. Donaldson; 1885–1887; 10 vols., repr. Peabody, Mass: Hendrickson, 1994), 1:506. Hereafter, *ANF.*

turns he will bring judgment against the Marcionites, the Valentinians, and the Ebionites, along with other schismatic Christian groups. One aspect of Irenaeus's eschatology that stands out is his emphasis on a thousand-year millennial reign. This millennial kingdom is basically a place in which Christians will get acclimated to life in God's kingdom. As he puts it, Christians will enter God's kingdom, "which is the commencement of incorruption, by means of which kingdom those who shall be worthy are accustomed gradually to partake of the divine nature" (*Haer.* 5.32.1). Practice in a quasi-heavenly state prepares the believer ultimately for the real thing after the millennium.

Irenaeus "is [also] convinced that the world will come to an end six thousand years after creation (*Haer.* 5.28.3). He does not offer any precise reckoning of when this will be, but situates the Incarnation of the Word 'in the last times.' "[21]

Tertullian

In the Latin West, and late second and early third century North African Christianity, the most prominent figure is Tertullian. He is a particularly interesting player in the history of Christian eschatological views because of his conversion later in life to an exuberant and spirited Montanist perspective.[22] The parousia of Christ was of central concern to Tertullian, for with it came all he devoted himself to: the glory of Christ, the resurrection of the body, judgment of the world, and the new world. For Tertullian the parousia showed how essentially disjunctive life as a Christian and life in the world were.[23] Not only does Athens have nothing to do with Jerusalem, this world of sin and rebellion has nothing to do with the coming kingdom of God and the reign of Christ. For Tertullian the End is near at hand, and violently so.

---

[21] Daley, *Hope of the Early Church*, 231 n. 8.

[22] See T. D. Barnes, *Tertullian* (rev. ed.; Oxford: Oxford University Press, 1985), 131–42.

[23] See E. Osborne, *Tertullian, First Theologian of the West* (Cambridge: Cambridge University Press, 1997), 214–24.

The violence of the End has connections both to the life of martyrdom lifted up by Tertullian, and to his vision of God's vengeful and radical judgment against the world. More than Irenaeus, Tertullian has a developed notion of the "interim state," the time when souls await judgment in the aftermath of the parousia. In his view, all souls—righteous and wicked alike—await judgment in Hades, but they wait in two separate regions of Hades. In his treatise *De Anima* ("On the Soul") he argues that "the soul undergoes punishment and consolation in Hades in the interval, while it awaits its alternative of judgment, in a certain anticipation of gloom and glory" (58).[24]

Like Irenaeus, Tertullian also holds that the second coming of Christ will inaugurate a millennial age. In his treatise *Adversus Marcionem* Tertullian states that the heavenly Jerusalem is on the verge of being revealed in all of its glory. He writes,

> [T]he word of the new prophecy which is a part of our belief [i.e., Montanism], attests how it foretold that there would be for a sign a picture of this very city exhibited to view previous to its manifestation. This prophecy, indeed, has been very lately fulfilled in an expedition to the East. For it is evident from the testimony of even heathen witnesses, that in Judea there was suspended in the sky a city early every morning for forty days. As the day advanced, the entire figure of its walls would wane gradually, and sometimes it would vanish instantly. We say that this city has been provided by God for receiving the saints on their resurrection, and refreshing them with the abundance of all really spiritual blessings (*Marc.* 25).[25]

Tertullian was so convinced of the impending end of the age that he believed there had already been a sighting of the new heavenly Jerusalem in Judea over a forty-day period. With the virtual advent of the new Jerusalem the End was at hand, and the heavens were poised to welcome the newly resurrected saints.

---

[24] *ANF* 3:235. See also Daley, *Hope of the Early Church*, 36.

[25] *ANF* 3:342–43. The "expedition to the East" refers to the military expedition of Severus against the Parthians. See also Osborne, *Tertullian*, 214–19.

Hippolytus

Hippolytus, who died as a martyr around 235 C.E., continues the eschatological emphasis seen in Irenaeus and in Tertullian. He was extremely interested in eschatological matters, as evidenced by his commentary on Daniel and by his treatise on Christ and the antichrist. Hippolytus's commentary on Daniel repeats the notion found earlier in Irenaeus and Barnabas that the world is in its sixth and final millennium. According to Hippolytus, Christ was born midway through the last millennium of history, and so the end of history is not due until five hundred years after Christ's birth.[26] "For the first appearance of our Lord in the flesh took place in Bethlehem, under Augustus, in the year 5500; and He suffered in the thirty-third year. And 6,000 years must needs be accomplished, in order that the Sabbath may come, the rest, the holy day 'on which God rested from all His works.' . . . From the birth of Christ, then, we must reckon the 500 years that remain to make up the 6,000, and thus the end shall be."[27]

As Dunbar points out, the persecution of Christians under the emperor Severus in 201–202 C.E. brought with it a renewed interest in apocalyptic themes.[28] Hippolytus emphasized the nearness of the end of the age primarily as a pastoral matter, to encourage his congregations in the face of persecution. His interest, then, was not merely speculative.

Cyprian

In the middle of the third century in the Latin West, Cyprian, the bishop of Carthage in North Africa (248–258 C.E.), likewise employed eschatological themes with a pastoral crisis in view.

---

[26] *Comm. Dan.* 4.23–24. On Hippolytus, see Daley, *Hope of the Early Church*, 38–41; and also D. G. Dunbar, "The Delay of the *Parousia* in Hippolytus," *VC* 37 (1983): 313–27.

[27] Hippolytus, "Fragments from Commentaries": "On Daniel" 2.4 (*ANF* 5:179).

[28] Dunbar, "Delay of the *Parousia* in Hippolytus," 315.

Shortly after he became bishop a persecution broke out under Decius in 250 C.E., and then again under Valerian in 257–258. In addition to these problems was the added difficulty of an extensive plague in North Africa in 252–254 C.E. These very difficult times led Cyprian to conclude that the End must be near. In his "Exhortation to Martyrdom" (addressed to Fortunatus), Cyprian writes, "You have desired, beloved Fortunatus, that since the burden of persecutions and afflictions is lying heavy upon us, and in the ending and completion of the world the hateful time of Anti-christ is already beginning to draw near, I would collect from the sacred Scriptures some exhortations for preparing and strengthening the minds of the brethren, whereby I might animate the soldiers of Christ for the heavenly and spiritual contest."[29] Like others before him, Cyprian saw himself and the Christians under his care as living at the end of the age: "[S]ix thousand years are now nearly completed since the devil first attacked man."[30]

EASTERN FATHERS: CLEMENT OF ALEXANDRIA AND ORIGEN

Clement of Alexandria

The primary concerns of the Latin West in the third century were practical and pastoral issues arising from sporadic persecution, and patristic writers generally upheld a real belief in the impending end of the age. In the Greek-speaking churches of Alexandria and the East we find different approaches to the parousia of Jesus and to eschatological convictions in general. At the beginning of the third century Clement of Alexandria was the head of the catechetical school educating Christians in Alexandria, though he would soon be forced to leave because of the persecution under Severus in 202 C.E. Clement drew extensively on Platonic and Stoic thought, and had an interest in more spec-

---

[29] "The Treatises of Cyprian" (*ANF* 5:496, preface, 1).
[30] "The Treatises of Cyprian" (*ANF* 5:496, preface, 2).

ulative theology. Clement argued that human beings were destined to grow into perfection, indeed that perfection was attainable through stages of learning. The Christian who attained such knowledge was the true gnostic. Clement was not overly concerned with the second coming of Christ, because he believed that Christians could already in this life contemplate the mystery of God in their souls, and that such divine education would merely be extended into the resurrection life. Any punishment in the afterlife was purely cleansing and educational, leading the individual to a deeper understanding of the mystery of God.[31]

Origen

Origen (d. 254/255 C.E.) was the most significant and daring Christian thinker of the third century. Origen followed in the path of Clement at Alexandria in his philosophical interests, but he went beyond Clement's concern to harmonize Christian beliefs with Greek cosmology and ethics.

Origen's approach to the parousia was to take the apocalyptic passages of the New Testament in both literal and metaphorical senses.[32] This can be seen in his *Commentary on Matthew,* especially in his treatment of Matt 16:27, "For the Son of Man shall come in the glory of His own Father with His angels" (so Origen's version of the passage).[33] Origen begins his comments on this verse by noting that the Son of Man has indeed not come in his glory; rather, he came in suffering and affliction. Origen goes on to comment about the various kinds of glory the Son of Man will manifest—the glory of the Father as well as his own glory with the angels. For Origen this does not imply that there will be no literal second coming, though the literal second coming is not the

---

[31] As Daley notes, "Clement can be considered the first Christian exponent of the doctrine of purgatorial eschatological suffering" (*Hope of the Early Church,* 47).

[32] So B. Daley, "Eschatology," *Encyclopedia of Early Christianity* (New York: Garland, 1990), 311.

[33] Origen, *Comm. Matt.* 12.29–34 (*ANF* 9:465–68).

deepest meaning to be gleaned from the text. "But we say these things not rejecting even the second coming of the Son of God understood in its simpler form" (*Comm. Matt.* 12.30).[34] Thus for Origen the second coming of Christ in history is not to be rejected, but if one stops with this level of meaning one misses out on the deeper significance of Matthew's language about the coming of the Son of Man. Although Origen goes on to ask, "But when shall these things happen?" he does not really answer the question.

In Matt 16:28, Jesus declares that there are some standing there who will not taste death before they see the Son of Man coming with his kingdom. Origen first offers a "simpler interpretation" of the passage. He states that the transfiguration of Jesus in Matthew 17, which follows immediately afterward, could be seen as a fulfillment of Jesus' statement in 16:28, for they see the face of Jesus shining with glory. But this reading is for those who are spiritual babes: "Now this interpretation about the three Apostles not tasting of death until they have seen Jesus transfigured, is adapted to those who are designated by Peter as newborn babes longing for the reasonable milk which is without guile" (*Comm. Matt.* 12.31, referring to 1 Pet 2:2).[35]

The more spiritual reading of the passage comes in Origen's explanation of what Christ means in the light of Matt 28:20: "I am with you all the days, even until the consummation of the age." Origen comments:

> Plainly we shall not be compelled to admit that those who see the Son of man coming in His own kingdom shall taste of death, after being deemed worthy of beholding Him in such guise. But . . . the urgent necessity was to teach us that "until the consummation of the age" He would not leave us but be with us all the days; so also in this case I think that it is clear to those who know how to look at the logical coherence of things that He who has seen once for all "the Son of man coming in His own kingdom," and seen Him "in His own glory," and seen "the kingdom of God come with power," could not possibly taste of death after the contemplation of things so good and great.[36]

---

[34] *ANF* 9:466.

[35] Ibid.

[36] *Comm. Matt.* 12.34; *ANF* 9:468.

The coming of the Son of Man, then, refers in a deeper sense to the awareness of the spiritually mature that Christ is present to the believer forever. The contemplation of this great truth means that the believer in Christ will not die in any ultimate sense.

Origen also discusses the parousia in his comments on the apocalyptic material in Matthew 24. He explains the literal sense of the text in a straightforward manner, referring to false prophets and persecutions in his own time. For the more advanced Christian, however, he offers an allegorical interpretation of the second coming. As Daley observes, for Origen one "can speak of another 'second coming of Christ,' in which he becomes present to the souls of those *veri perfecti* [perfect individuals] who can understand his divine beauty; 'to this second coming is joined the end of this world in the one who reaches maturity.' "[37] Matthew's description of "famines" in 24:7 is read by Origen in a spiritual sense as a reference to the Christian's hunger for a deeper understanding of Scripture. Origen also refers to plagues (apparently importing Luke's reference to plagues in 21:11), which he interprets as the false teachings of the gnostics and heretics. The infamous "desolating sacrilege" of Matt 24:15 is rendered by Origen as any false interpretation of Scripture, and the clouds on which the triumphant Christ returns are, in Origen's view, the writings of the apostles and prophets.[38]

If Origen allegorizes the apocalyptic sections of the gospels, how does he treat the book of Revelation? In general Origen opposes millenarian interpretations of the Apocalypse as being too Jewish and too literal. Those Christians who have a literal interpretation of the new heavenly Jerusalem, for example, are guilty of

> adopting a superficial view of the letter of the law, and yielding rather in some measure to the indulgence of their own desires and lusts, being disciples of the letter alone. . . . They especially desire to have again, after the

---

[37] Daley, *Hope of the Early Church,* 48. Daley is quoting from Origen's *Commentary on Matthew* (32).

[38] *Commentariorum Series in Matthaeum,* 37–52. See Daley, *Hope of the Early Church,* 48–49.

> resurrection, such bodily structures as may never be without the power of
> eating, and drinking. . . . Those, however, who receive the representations
> of Scripture according to the understanding of the apostles, entertain the
> hope that the saints will eat indeed, but that it will be the bread of life,
> which may nourish the soul with the food of truth and wisdom.[39]

We see, then, that Origen takes most of the scriptural references to future events associated with the second coming of Christ in a symbolic way as pointing to the individual Christian's growth towards a deepened understanding of salvation.

As for when and how the parousia will come, Origen writes, "[T]his should not be understood to happen suddenly, but gradually and by steps, as the endless and enormous ages slip by, and the process of improvement and correction advances by degrees in different individuals."[40] Here we see Origen's notion of divine education and purification of the soul, indeed, repeated education, until all are saved. Eventually the state of *apokatastasis,* complete restoration of the universe, will occur. Origen's understanding of *apokatastasis* involves the notion of recapitulation, so that the end of the age restores the universe to the way it was in the beginning at creation. Origen addresses a chapter in *De Principiis* to the end or consummation of things (1.6). Here he states that "the end is always like the beginning: and, therefore, as there is one end to all things, so ought we to understand that there was one beginning" (1.6.2).[41]

Origen's contribution to Christian understandings of eschatology and the second coming of Christ left a considerable wake. Theologians after him responded either with admiration or with criticism for his views. The most significant critic of Origen was Methodius of Olympus, though Methodius himself was greatly indebted to Origen. Methodius was a Christian of the Greek East in the mid-third century who maintained expectations of the parousia of Christ within a more imminent millen-

---

[39] Origen, *De Principiis* 2.11.2–3 (*ANF* 4:297).

[40] Ibid., 3.6.6 (from Daley, *Hope of the Early Church*, 49).

[41] See also the discussion in Daley, *Hope of the Early Church,* 58–59.

nial framework than that found in Origen. Methodius also disagreed significantly with Origen's emphasis on spiritual resurrection, arguing instead for a more physical understanding of the resurrection of the body.[42]

CONCLUSION

We have now explored various approaches to the second coming of Christ in second- and third-century Christianity. We have seen significant variety in the thought of the writings surveyed. Some appear to have expected an imminent parousia of Christ: *Didache, Epistle of Barnabas, Apocalypse of Peter, Epistula Apostolorum,* and Tertullian. Some saw a slight calm before the storm of the parousia: *1 Clement, Shepherd of Hermas,* Justin Martyr, Irenaeus, Hippolytus, and Cyprian. Others argued for a more spiritual and less literal or imminent interpretation of the second coming of Christ: Clement of Alexandria, Origen, and gnostic writings such as the *Treatise on the Resurrection* and the *Gospel of Mary.* All three approaches, as well as others along the continuum, can be found in varying forms throughout second- and third-century Christian reflections on the parousia of Christ.

Advocates of these different positions could each claim support from various proof-texts in the first-century Christian writings that became canonical. And so does Christianity at the threshold of the twenty-first century find itself with divided views on the second coming of Christ. Perhaps that is to be expected, since the significance of Christ's first advent generated so much discussion among the early Christians and continues to do so to this day at the dawn of a new millennium.

---

[42] Ibid., 60–64.

SIX

THE PAROUSIA OF JESUS AND JEWISH MESSIANIC HOPES

by Claudia J. Setzer

I always wince a bit when my non-Jewish students ask, "Is it true that Jews are still waiting for the Messiah?" The word "still" seems to carry some pathos. But I also wince because it is so difficult a question to answer. Truthfully, in some ways we are waiting and in some ways we are not. Messianism in the broad sense of the longing for a redeemed, repaired world has always been a feature of Jewish history. Sometimes the longing has coalesced into a sharp desire for a specific messianic figure to appear. Yet the Pharisees and later the rabbis turned away from active messianism, domesticating the longing under their program of Torah observance and creating a religion still ambivalent about messianic figures.

The longing for redemption, sometimes coupled with the expected appearance of a particular messianic figure, percolates throughout Jewish history. The earliest notion of a messiah emerges with Israel's anointed kings in 1 and 2 Samuel and 1 and 2 Kings. King David is called God's son, and while he will not return after death, his dynasty is eternal. God is centered in Jerusalem and rules forever through his servant David. His offspring are to rule Israel in safety and prosperity. The power of this image never completely disappears. Even today, Jewish high school students have in their repertoire of camp songs, "David, King of Israel, Lives."

In the first century, peasant leaders of liberation movements arose, drawing on the memory of a popular, anointed king and promising deliverance from political oppression.[1] In the second century C.E., the rebel leader Bar Kokhba claimed for himself the title "Prince of Israel," combining religious conservatism and revolution. Even today, flashes of messianism appear in Jewish communities. West Bank settlers are frankly messianic,[2] and some elements within the Lubavitcher Hasidim understand the last Rebbe, Menachem Mendel Schneerson, to be the Messiah.[3] The liberal Jewish periodical *Tikkun* and its Christian counterpart *Sojourners* preach a message of social justice that uses traditional language of redemption.

---

[1] See R. Horsley, "Popular Messianic Movements around the Time of Jesus," *CBQ* 46 (1984): 471–95; idem, "Palestinian Jewish Groups and Their Messiahs in Late Second Temple Times," in *Judaisms and their Messiahs at the Turn of the Christian Era* (ed. J. Neusner, W. S. Green, and E. Frerichs; Cambridge: Cambridge University Press, 1987), 14–29; R. Horsley and J. S. Hanson, *Bandits, Prophets, and Messiahs* (Minneapolis: Winston, 1985), ch. 3.

[2] These communities are hybrids of classic Zionism (originally a secular movement) and fervent religious observance. See S. Sharot, "Religious Zionism in Israel—A Return to Messianism," in *Messianism, Mysticism, and Magic* (Chapel Hill: University of North Carolina Press, 1982), 225–37; A. Ravitzky, *Messianism, Zionism and Jewish Religious Radicalism* (trans. M. Swirsky and J. Chipman; Chicago: University of Chicago Press, 1996); and for a popular treatment, J. Winokur, "The Settlement," *Natural History* 105 (December 1996–January 1997): 38–49.

[3] The Rebbe's death did not destroy the hope that, in some way, he would be an agent of redemption. See *The New York Times,* 25 February 1996, 33, 38. The organization Lubavitch World Headquarters issued a statement disclaiming the interpretation of the Rebbe as Messiah (*The New York Times,* 8 February 1996).

Yet active messianism has never been universal or continuous among Jews. Some ancient thinkers and communities functioned quite well without such expectations. Philo neutralized the idea of a messiah by spiritualizing and dehistoricizing both the messianic figure and the messianic age.[4] The Maccabees, for all their pious nationalism and belief in resurrection, did not expect a Davidic messiah.[5] The Mishnah, though formulated during a period of political resistance and defeated nationalism, fairly ignores the implications of the whole idea of a messiah, but nominally includes messiah as a category within its system of classification.[6] The rabbis, Akiba notwithstanding, seemed to discourage active messianism and transmute it into an abstract spiritual longing that served their agenda of Torah observance.[7]

Because of this diverse evidence, we cannot know how much or how many ancient Jews fervently waited for a messiah to appear in their time. Recent discussions of messianism have minimized its prevalence in early Judaism. Scattered and disparate references are insufficient to produce a theory of widespread and uniform messianic expectation.[8] Criticizing the earlier model of a Judaism drenched in eschatological expectancy, W. S.

---

[4] R. Hecht, "Philo and Messiah," in Neusner, Green, and Frerichs, *Judaisms and Their Messiahs,* 139–68.

[5] J. Goldstein, "How the Authors of 1 and 2 Maccabees Treated the 'Messianic' Promises," in Neusner, Green, and Frerichs, *Judaisms and Their Messiahs,* 69–96.

[6] J. Neusner argues that the Mishnah is essentially ahistorical, presenting a taxonomy of a timeless, idealized world rather than interpreting history ("Mishnah and Messiah," in Neusner, Green, and Frerichs, *Judaisms and Their Messiahs,* 265–82).

[7] Neusner suggests that the rabbis use the messiah myth, but subordinate salvation to the sanctification of daily life achieved through Torah observance. Thus the messiah becomes not so much the apocalyptic judge on the clouds of heaven, but the rabbi-messiah who will come when Israel fulfills the commandments ("Mishnah and Messiah," 278–82).

[8] This skepticism characterizes the volume by Neusner, Green, and Frerichs, *Judaisms and Their Messiahs,* as well as the *Anchor Bible Dictionary* entries, "Messiah" (M. de Jonge, 4:777–88) and "Messianic Movements in Judaism" (R. Horsley, 4:791–97).

Green judges it "finally unpersuasive because it uses so little to account for so much."[9] Any sweeping or universal theory of messianism in early Judaism is naturally suspect. Nor would anyone reasonably argue a continuous and unbroken line of messianic thought.

J. J. Collins suggests, however, that "the pendulum of scholarly opinion has swung too far."[10] A variety of eschatological figures do emerge regularly in different communities. These figures play several roles, but primarily they are expected to return to judge the guilty and vindicate the righteous. Their expected appearance makes sense of the present suffering by putting it in the context of a larger drama and promising relief.

Looking at the broad spectrum of Jewish messianic hopes, Jesus' parousia is not out of place. It fits with the expectation that at the end of days, a figure will appear to make things right, judging and punishing the wicked and defending the righteous. Multiple eschatological figures populate Jewish apocalyptic literature as the champions of final justice, either as present at final judgment or in the role of judge. The "one like a son of man" at the end of days in Daniel 7 becomes the "Son of Man" in the Similitudes in *1 Enoch* who "will open all the hidden storerooms . . . remove the kings and mighty ones from their comfortable seats . . . and crush the teeth of the sinners" (46:3–4). At the same time, the "Elect One" will be sent and "shall sit on the seat of glory" (45:3). *Second Baruch* notes the "Anointed One" who will return in glory (30:1; 39:7). The *Apocalypse of Abraham* refers to a future day when the trumpet will sound and "my Chosen One, having in him one measure of all my power . . . will summon my people, humiliated by the heathen" (31:1). In the *Testaments of the Twelve Patriarchs,* Judah and Levi are agents of redemption. The *Testament of Judah* (24.1, 4) uses the eschatological meta-

---

[9] W. S. Green, "Introduction: Messiah in Judaism: Rethinking the Question," in Neusner, Green, and Frerichs, *Judaisms and Their Messiahs,* 1–13.

[10] J. J. Collins, *The Scepter and the Star* (New York: Doubleday, 1995), 4.

phors of "a Star from Jacob" (Num 24:17), "a man from my pos-
terity like the Sun of righteousness," and "the Shoot of God." The
"prophet like Moses" will return (Deut 18:18; cf. Acts 3:22; 7:37).
In John he is called simply "the Prophet" (6:14; 7:40, where he is
distinct from the Messiah). Scenes of the end of days and the just
meting out of punishment and blessings are frequent in this literature (e.g., *Apoc. Zeph.* 8:5; *1 Enoch* 71:16–17).

In addition to these idealized messianic figures in literary
works, peasant society produced concrete examples of popular
"kings" who led liberation movements, driven or enhanced by
the memory of eschatological prophets. R. Horsley argues that
the insurrectionist movements in Palestinian society in the first
and second centuries were revivals of ancient Israelite patterns
of popular, anointed "kings," men of humble origins who rise up
to liberate the people from oppressive rule and restore economic
and social parity.[11]

If we consider the concept of Jesus' parousia more nar-
rowly and specifically, as a human being, a preacher or teacher
who returns from the dead to spark the end of days, obviously
there are far fewer parallels in Jewish life and literature. The
New Testament shows that such a notion is not absent from first-
century Judaism. Herod mistakenly thinks that Jesus is John the
Baptist returned from the dead. The transfiguration shows that
Moses and Elijah are expected to return. The author of Revelation thinks that Domitian is Nero *redivivus* (17:11). Three figures
in particular evoked speculation: Enoch, Elijah, and the Righteous Teacher of the Qumran scrolls.

ENOCH

A terse biblical notice of Enoch (Gen 5:18–24) gives rise to a
rich set of traditions.[12] "After the birth of Methuselah, Enoch

---

[11] Horsley and Hanson, *Bandits, Prophets, and Messiahs*, ch. 3.

[12] See E. Schürer, G. Vermes, and F. Millar, *The History of the Jewish People in the Age of Jesus Christ* (rev. ed.; 3 vols.; Edinburgh: T&T
Clark, 1973–87) 3:250–77.

walked with God for three hundred years, and had other sons and daughters. He lived three hundred and sixty-five years. Enoch walked with God, and then was seen no more, because God had taken him away" (vv. 22–24). Enoch's mysterious disappearance was understood by many as a bypassing of death (e.g., Heb 11:5).[13] More significantly, Enoch's strange passage suggested he had been shown the secrets of the universe, that he had special knowledge of the mysteries of heaven and earth, including a vision of the end of days.

Enoch's vision is elaborated in the noncanonical work *1 Enoch,* particularly in the latest stratum, the Similitudes (Parables) of Enoch (chs. 37–71). Dates proposed for the Similitudes range from the first century B.C.E. to the end of the first (possibly early second) century C.E.[14] In his vision Enoch foresees the congregation of the righteous avenged and sinners delivered into their hands. At this final judgment "my Elect One shall sit on the seat of glory" (45:3). Another figure is the "Son of Man" who "will open all the hidden storerooms" and "crush the teeth of the sinners" (46:3–4). Enoch also sees "the One to whom belongs the time before time. And his head was white like wool, and there was with him another individual, whose face was like that of a human being" (46:1). Like many other apocalyptic works, the Similitudes derive from the "one like a son of man" in Daniel 7 and the "suffering servant" in Isaiah 40–55. Enoch is not identified with these people but is a witness to their appearance.

Enoch's vision of the end of days translates into his presence in the final drama. In *Jubilees* Enoch himself is a judge or the scribe of the judge: "[Enoch] was taken from among the children of men, and we led him to the garden of Eden for greatness and honor. And behold, he is there writing condemnation and

---

[13] For a discussion of New Testament use of the heroes of the Hebrew Bible, see P. Eisenbaum, *The Jewish Heroes of Christian History: Hebrews 11 in Literary Context* (SBLDS 156; Atlanta: Scholars Press, 1997).

[14] See J. C. VanderKam, *Enoch: A Man for All Generations* (SPOT; Columbia: University of South Carolina Press, 1995), 132.

judgment of the world . . . that he might relate all the deeds of the generations until the day of judgment" (4:23–24). According to Hippolytus (*Antichr.* 43) and Tertullian (*An.* 50.5), in Rev 11:1–13 he and Elijah are witnesses to the final judgment.[15]

In a later work, the *Apocalypse of Elijah* (latter half of the third century C.E.), Enoch and Elijah actually carry out the punishment of those who persecute the righteous: "After these things, Elijah and Enoch will come down. They will lay down the flesh of the world, and they will receive their spiritual flesh. They will pursue the son of lawlessness and kill him, since he is not able to speak" (5:32). Enoch is elsewhere paired with Elijah, no doubt because of the similar mystery around their deaths (*Apoc. Zeph.* 9:4; Josephus, *Ant.* 9.27–28; Philo, *QG* 1.85–86). He is also linked to Moses, who experienced a mysterious death. According to Philo, both Enoch and Moses were "translated" to immortality.[16]

Enoch's popularity does not extend into rabbinic literature. Only one possible Tannaitic reference to Enoch appears embedded in a later work.[17] The occasional references in the later midrashic materials waver between Enoch as a wicked and as a righteous character.[18] Far more frequent in later literature is the other biblical character who seems to avoid death.

ELIJAH

Like Enoch, Elijah is "taken up" and disappears from earth (2 Kgs 2:1–14). His mysterious departure spawns a set of tradi-

---

[15] Others suggest the two figures point to Moses and Elijah. See M. E. Boring, *Revelation* (IBC; Louisville: John Knox, 1989), 146; cf. R. H. Mounce, *The Book of Revelation* (rev. ed.; NICNT; Grand Rapids: Eerdmans, 1998), 216–17.

[16] See Philo, *Post.* 40–44; *Mut.* 34–38; *QG* 1.86; *Abr.* 17–26, 47; *Praem.* 15–21; *Sacr.* 8–10.

[17] See M. Himmelfarb, "A Report on Enoch in Rabbinic Literature," in *SBLSP 1978* (ed. P. Achtemeier; 2 vols.; Missoula, Mont.: Scholars Press, 1978), 1:259–69.

[18] See VanderKam, *Enoch,* 161–68, for a discussion of Enoch in the rabbinic literature and Targumim.

tions that depict him as an intermediary between heaven and earth. As early as Malachi, these traditions included the expectation of his return as the harbinger of the messianic age: "Look, I shall send you the prophet Elijah before the great and terrible day of the Lord comes" (4:5). In Sirach, Elijah is to come at the appointed time (48:10). The gospels contain eight distinct passages that express or imply the expectation that Elijah will return at the dawn of the new age. (1) When King Herod hears of Jesus he thinks he is John the Baptizer raised from the dead; "But others said 'It is Elijah.' Others again, 'He is a prophet like one of the prophets of old' " (Mark 6:14–16; cf. Luke 9:7–9). (2) When Jesus asks, " 'Who do people say that I am?' They answered 'Some say John the Baptizer, others Elijah, others one of the prophets' " (Mark 8:27–30 par.). (3) At the transfiguration Jesus is joined by Moses and Elijah (Mark 9:2–10 par.). (4) The disciples then ask him,

> "Why do the scribes say that Elijah must come first?" He replied, "Elijah does come first to set everything right. How is it then, that the scriptures say of the Son of Man that he is to endure great suffering and be treated with contempt? However, I tell you that Elijah has already come and they have done to him what they wanted as the scriptures say of him."

Here Jesus implies that Elijah is John the Baptizer (Mark 9:11–13; cf. Matt 17:10–13). (5) In Matt 11:14 Jesus is explicit: "John is the destined Elijah, if you will but accept it." (6) Similarly, in Luke 1:17 the angel predicting John the Baptizer's birth says he will be possessed "by the spirit and power of Elijah." (7) In Jesus' cry from the cross, some bystanders assume he is calling Elijah (Mark 15:33–36; Matt 27:45–49). (8) Finally, John the Baptizer testifies before the priests and Levites from Jerusalem that he is not the Messiah, Elijah, or the prophet (John 1:19–23).

As K. Lindbeck observes, since Malachi explicitly refers to Elijah as the forerunner of the end of days, it is surprising how rarely he figures in early Jewish materials.[19] The flourishing of

---

[19] My thanks to Kristen Lindbeck for discussing with me her dissertation on Elijah in rabbinic literature, as well as providing me with bibliography. See "Story and Theology: Elijah's Appearances in the Bab-

Elijah motifs in later materials, however, suggests to some scholars the existence of an Elijah apocryphon in antiquity,[20] or at least a rich set of traditions about Elijah in an oral, biblical culture.[21] J. L. Martyn presents the thesis that Jesus was identified with Elijah in some Jewish-Christian circles known to John, but that this identification was later suppressed by the evangelist.[22] Clearly, the conception of Elijah as one who would return to inaugurate the new age was current.[23] All four gospel authors feel called to account for Elijah in their schemata of salvation. In the mid-second century, Justin refers to the expectation that Elijah will be forerunner to the Messiah as a Jewish belief and places it in Trypho's mouth (*Dial.* 8.49).

We have seen above that the *Apocalypse of Elijah* pictures Elijah returning along with Enoch to chase out the lawless one and avenge the righteous (5:32). The Tannaitic literature contains only a handful of references to Elijah, often in the form of a statement that doubtful matters are to be left "until Elijah comes." A *baraita*, or Tannaitic statement, assumes the Messiah would not come unless Elijah came first.[24] In another text Elijah appears: "And seven covered the whole (history of) the world. They are the following. Adam saw Methuselah; Methuselah saw

---

ylonian Talmud" (Ph.D. diss., Jewish Theological Seminary of America, 1999).

[20] See M. E. Stone and J. Strugnell, *The Books of Elijah: Parts 1 and 2* (SBLTT 18; Pseudepigrapha 8; Missoula, Mont.: Scholars Press, 1979).

[21] D. Frankfurter, *Elijah in Upper Egypt* (Minneapolis: Fortress, 1993), 55. Frankfurter suggests that Elijah may have become a type for any kind of prophetic discourse.

[22] J. L. Martyn, " 'We Have Found Elijah,' " in *Jews, Greeks, and Christians* (ed. R. Hamerton-Kelly and R. Scroggs; Leiden: Brill, 1976), 181–219.

[23] In disagreement with M. Faierstein ("Why Do the Scribes Say That Elijah Must Come First?" *JBL* 100 [1981]: 75–86) who rejects the view that Elijah as the forerunner of the Messiah was widespread in first-century Judaism.

[24] See *b. Erub.* 43a–b. Faierstein argues that the uniqueness of this reference in Tannaitic literature suggests it may be influenced by the gospel tradition ("Why Do the Scribes Say?" 83–85).

Shem; Shem saw Jacob; Jacob saw Serah; Serah saw Ahijah; Ahijah saw Elijah, and Elijah lives and exists until the Messiah shall come."[25] We have seen that Elijah rarely figures in the early rabbinic and other Jewish materials. Could his prominence in Christian texts be a factor? Was he taken over by Christians to such an extent that early rabbinic and other Jewish groups downplayed his importance?

Elijah's role expands in later rabbinic literature and he appears in many guises, as the friend to scholars and martyrs, the friend to the poor, and the teacher, but he also retains his role as the forerunner of the Messiah.[26] Every Passover seder table contains a cup for Elijah, stressing the continued hope of redemption.

THE RIGHTEOUS TEACHER

Apocalyptic expectation at Qumran produced an array of eschatological figures and titles, some of which probably overlap, including: "the messiahs of Aaron and Israel," one priestly and one Davidic;[27] also "the Prince of the Congregation"; "the Interpreter of the Law"; "the Examiner of the Many"; "the One who will teach righteousness in the end of days" (CD MS A 6:10–11); "the Prophet" (1QS 9:10); "the Righteous Teacher"; and "the unique Teacher." These figures function along standard apocalyptic lines, judging the wicked and raising up the righteous. But a unique slant at Qumran is the importance of a teacher. A new set of laws is expected at the end of days, as well as a figure who will teach and interpret them.

---

[25] ʾAbot R. Nat. B 38, translation from A. Saldarini, *The Fathers According to Rabbi Nathan* (SJLA 11; Leiden: Brill, 1975), 231. Saldarini dates the work before 200 C.E.; most assign it to the second or third century (12–16).

[26] See S. Segal, *Elijah: A Study in Jewish Folklore* (New York: Behrman's, 1935); L. Ginzberg, *Legends of the Jews* (7 vols.; Philadelphia: Jewish Publication Society, 1909–38) 4:193–236.

[27] See Collins (*Scepter and Star,* 74–95) for a discussion of these titles and possible interpretations.

The Righteous Teacher is a figure from the past, likely a priest and founder of the community, who suffered persecution from within the community as well as from the Wicked Priest without. He instructed the men of the community in "the first precepts" (CD MS B 20:31–32). Two references hint that his return is expected, assuming he is the same figure as "the Unique Teacher": "The Unique Teacher was gathered in until there arises the Messiah from Aaron and from Israel" (CD MS B 20:1), and "the Unique Teacher was gathered in until the end of all the men of war who turned away; with the Man of the Lie there will be about forty years" (CD MS B 20:14–15). There will be a teacher to come at the end of days (CD MS A 6:10–11), but whether or not this is the same Righteous Teacher who was prominent from the early days of the community is unclear. Most scholars do not identify the past and future teacher as the same person, but P. Davies and M. Wise have made a convincing case that they are identical.[28] Collins notes that messianic expectation is "a network of interlocking references" and multiple titles may serve for one or many figures.[29]

Collins points to the distinctive type of the eschatological teacher as a counterpart to the militant messiah.[30] The radical nature of the teacher is evident in two other examples of popular resistance. Judas the Galilean, the leader of a popular revolt after the death of Herod, is called a "sophist" (Josephus, *War* 2.117–118). He is compared to the revered teachers of the Fourth Philosophy who conspired with their students to pull down the Roman eagle at the temple gate (*War* 1.648–655; *Ant.* 17.149–154).

CONCLUSION

Summary

The concept of an eschatological figure is part of the larger vision of the end of days. Like resurrection (Dan 12:1–3;

---

[28] Discussed in Collins, *Scepter and Star*, 102–23.
[29] Ibid., 64.
[30] Ibid., 122.

2 Maccabees 7), the idea of final judgment is an answer to the problem of suffering and to the question of theodicy. One day all will be made right: the martyred just ones will confront their oppressors, the wicked will be punished and the suffering righteous exalted. Wisdom of Solomon is characteristic: "At the day of reckoning, the just man will confront his oppressors" (5:1). Equally important, the wicked will show remorse. This rectifying of wrongs and answering of the problem of suffering is accomplished by other thinkers with the idea of the immortality of the soul (e.g., Philo; 4 Maccabees) or the belief in individual reward. Members of the Fourth Philosophy, for example, visualize "greater rewards after their deaths at the hands of the Roman executioner" (Josephus, *War* 1.651–653).

The parousia of Jesus does not fit perfectly with any of the models we have seen. Collins notes that belief in a Davidic messiah was the primary messianic mode among Jews, but there were also minor messianic strands, like the priestly messiah or the Son of humanity (Man). From these strands Christianity wove its own distinctive messianic theory. Reflection on Jesus' life and death in light of the Hebrew Bible and Jewish apocalyptic tradition produced the idea of a suffering messiah who would return, triumph over the world, and vindicate his righteous followers.[31]

Many Jews did not go in this direction. The Pharisees turned inward, concentrating on their own brand of pious community. The Mishnah, Neusner contends, is concerned not with history, but with sanctification in the here and now.[32] In the Talmuds, the messiah idea is subordinated to Torah: the Messiah will not come until Israel perfectly observes the Torah. Perhaps because of Israel's attempts to force its own salvation in the war against Rome, the disastrous results of the Bar Kokhba revolt, and also as a reaction against Christianity, the rabbis neutralized messianism. While they retained the idea of longing for a messiah, they did not encourage chasing after one. A Tannaitic

---

[31] See D. Juel, *Messianic Exegesis* (Philadelphia: Fortress, 1988).
[32] Neusner, "Mishnah and Messiah," 281.

source reads, "He [Rabban Yochanan ben Zakkai] used to say: If there were a plant in your hand and they should say to you, 'Look, the Messiah is here!' Go and plant your plant, and after that go forth to receive him" (*'Abot R. Nat.* B 31).

The Parousia as a Response to Jewish Objections

Yet Jews and Judaism may have contributed to the formation of the idea of Jesus' parousia in a more direct way. Graham Stanton proposes that the "two advents" schema in Matthew takes shape in response to Jewish charges that Jesus' life and death did not fit Jewish messianic expectations or fulfill scriptural prophecies.[33] Justin and Origen claim that Jews objected that Jesus' life of suffering and humiliation proved he could not be the glorious Messiah. These Christian writers counter with the explanation that there were two advents, the first one humble and the second one, yet to come, glorious.

Though the evidence of Jesus' second coming as an answer to Jewish complaints is not explicit until the mid-second century, Stanton argues that it is operative already in Matthew's Gospel. He notes that Matthew stresses Jesus' earthly life as the Son of David by expanding Mark's three references to nine. Furthermore, in four of the six passages that come from Matthew's own hand, the claim that Jesus is the Son of David provokes negative Jewish reaction (2:3; 9:27–34; 12:22–24; 21:9, 15).[34] Not only does Matthew juxtapose the themes of Jesus as Davidic messiah with Jewish disbelief, but he heightens the contrast between Jesus' humble earthly life and his future coming in glory (cf. 16:21–23 and 16:27–28; 21:5 and 25:31–46). Stanton concludes that not only in Justin and Origen, but also in the *Ascents of James* and Matthew's Gospel, the two-advent schema arises as a response to Jewish objections that Jesus cannot be the Davidic messiah because his life fails to fulfill scriptural prophecies.

---

[33] G. Stanton, *A Gospel for a New People* (Louisville: Westminster John Knox, 1993), 185–91.

[34] Ibid., 180–85.

The parousia fits within broader disputes over humiliation and glory that point to Jewish objections. Both the crucifixion and the resurrection seemed to draw fire from Jews, and provoked Christian defenses from Scripture.[35] Paul notes that Christ crucified is a scandal to the Jews (1 Cor 1:23), showing that the cross was a problem for Jews as early as the 50s. Paul's complex argument about Jesus taking on the curse of the law in Galatians 3 and his turning inside out Deut 21:23, "Cursed be everyone who hangs on a tree," suggest that someone objected to the manner of Jesus' death on the basis of this verse. A hundred years later, Justin goes to great lengths to refute the idea that the Messiah could not be crucified. Furthermore, he attributes this objection to the Jew Trypho (*Dial.* 32.1; 89.1; 90.1; and by implication 10.3 and 38.1).

Similarly, the resurrection of Jesus produced friction between Jews and believers in Jesus. Matthew clearly alludes to this conflict in the scene that closes the Passion Narrative. The chief priests and Pharisees ask Pilate for a guard at the tomb lest the disciples steal the body and claim he has risen from the dead (27:62–66). This dispute also marks the scene in which the chief priests and elders bribe some soldiers to say the body was stolen (28:11–15). This claim that the body was stolen, Matthew tells us, is still current in his own time (v. 15). Apologetic touches in the gospels attest to the physical reality of the resurrection (Luke 24:36–42; John 20:26–29). The apocryphal *Gospel of Peter* presents an elaborate apologetic for the resurrection in the context of severe anti-Jewish polemic. Justin presents scriptural proof for the resurrection, as well as transmitting the Jewish accusation from Matthew that the body was stolen (*Dial.* 32.3–6; 106.8; 108.2). Finally, Celsus's Jew argues against the resurrection, noting it was reported only by a "hysterical female" (Origen, *Cels.* 2.55).

Embedded in these reports and Christian defenses from Scripture are Jewish critiques of Jesus' earthly life and its failure

---

[35] For a more detailed discussion, see C. J. Setzer, " 'You Invent a Christ!' " *USQR* 44 (1991): 315–28.

to match a dominant strain in messianic thought that pictured a glorious figure whose return would herald an age of peace and security. How much apologetic was self-generated after reflection on the Bible by Christians, especially Jewish Christians, and how much was reactive to outside complaints, is not always clear. But these examples suggest that a good deal of Christology was honed by Christians in response to their Jewish neighbors.

SEVEN

CENTURIES OF WAITING
The Persistence of Apocalyptic Hope

We have discovered that the expectation of Jesus'
parousia—whether pictured as victory over enemies,
judgment against evil, or deliverance of the faithful—left
its stamp on nearly every New Testament writing and remained a vital, credible hope into the fourth century, even
though history did not promptly end as expected. One of
the truly remarkable features of Christian history, in fact,
is the persistence of apocalyptic hope across two millennia of the church's existence. Understandably, occasions
of acute social crisis have called forth particularly intense
expressions of apocalyptic enthusiasm (or terror!). Yet eschatological hope, even when submerged, has never been
very far from the surface of Christian thinking about the
world and about history. This chapter traces a few of the
most interesting moments and figures in that story.

EARLY LATIN CHRISTIANITY AND
AUGUSTINE OF HIPPO

Latin Christianity of the fourth century could produce strident chiliasm such as that advocated by

Lactantius (ca. 240–320).[1] An eminent scholar of rhetoric who after his conversion to Christianity was forced to leave his post, Lactantius penned his *Divine Institutes* (314–323) during the imperial administration of Diocletian. Tapping both biblical and pagan sources, he pictured the world as aging and on the verge of ruin in its final age (7.14). The End would not arrive for another two centuries, that is, the year 500 (7.25), but the eschatological era was already underway and would witness the demise of Rome, the emergence of the antichrist in the form of a Syrian tyrant, and the triumphant return of Christ. The faithful who pass muster in a fiery judgment will join others raised from the dead and participate in a millennial reign of Christ on earth (7.17–21). After this thousand-year period, evil will be unleashed one last time and vanquished by God; the world will be ravaged but God's people will enter into angelic existence while sinners face perpetual misery (7.27).[2]

Other fourth-century Latin theologians, while not abandoning the traditional eschatological framework (the parousia, antichrist, resurrection, judgment), preferred a more spiritual, allegorical interpretation of the Bible's apocalyptic materials. Hilary of Poitiers (ca. 315–367) and Ambrose of Milan (ca. 334–397), for example, both modulated the cosmic eschatological scenario out of interest in the personal end and judgment of individuals.[3] Over the course of the fourth century, Christianity moved from the margins of the Roman social order into the center of power, and the threat of persecution receded. It is not surprising that apocalyptic fervor was less pronounced; nevertheless,

---

[1] The term *chiliasm* refers to expectation of a literal millennial reign in which eschatological events occur within human history, in an earthly setting.

[2] My summary of Lactantius's exposition is indebted to the sketch by B. E. Daley ("Apocalypticism in Early Christian Theology," in *Apocalypticism in Western History and Culture*, vol. 2 of *The Encyclopedia of Apocalypticism* [ed. B. McGinn; New York: Continuum, 1998], 18–19); see also B. McGinn, *Visions of the End: Apocalyptic Traditions in the Middle Ages* (New York: Columbia University Press, 1979), 24.

[3] See Daley, "Apocalypticism in Early Christian Theology," 20–21.

the close of the fourth and the beginning of the fifth century give evidence of growing pessimism about history and renewed interest in its approaching, catastrophic end—a posture made all the more compelling when the Visigoths, led by Alaric, sacked Rome (410).

The social turbulence of the era no doubt helps to account for the great scholar Jerome's ambivalence toward apocalyptic notions. Jerome (331–420) seems to have viewed the millennial reign of Revelation 20 as a picture of the church's growth in a postpersecution age and could think of the coming of Christ not only as a public, eschatological event but also as personal encounter with Christ at an individual's death.[4] Confronted with Rome's fall to Alaric, however, Jerome, like many others, perceived connections between the eschatological prophecies of Scripture and the contemporary political scene (e.g., *Comm. Isa.* 6.14.1; *Comm. Ezek.* 11.38).

The towering intellectual figure of this era was, of course, Augustine (354–430), bishop of Hippo, and his ideas about Christian eschatology exerted enormous influence. Augustine acknowledges that biblical prophecies point to actual future events, but that does not mean the chronology of the End can be known.[5] In early writings, Augustine referred to the schema of a "week" of ages, and correlated the seventh, "sabbath" age with the millennium of Rev 20:1–6 (e.g., *Sermon* 259.2), but he came to conceive of the millennium as an era of peace for the church within history, prior to the distress of the End (e.g., *City of God* 20.7–9). His preaching in the aftermath of the fall of Rome presented this traumatic event not as a sign of the approaching eschaton but as the occasion for conversion and the extension of divine mercy ("Sermon on the Fall of the City").

The *City of God* is a massive interpretation of history, which includes Augustine's reflections on Rome's decline. If

---

[4] Ibid., 27–28.

[5] See the discussion in B. E. Daley, *The Hope of the Early Church: A Handbook of Patristic Eschatology* (Cambridge: Cambridge University Press, 1991), 131–50.

Eusebius of Caesarea a century earlier had closely linked the fortunes of the church and the empire, Augustine decisively distinguished the two. God's realm does not depend on the success or survival of imperial Rome. Again the misfortunes of Rome do not signal the imminent completion of history, which may not be calculated. Even while affirming the traditional expectation of end-time events such as the appearance of the antichrist and the coming of Christ in judgment, Augustine reads in the apocalyptic texts of Scripture a perennial struggle between good and evil within the human self (*City of God* 20.7, 19). This "de-apocalypticizing" of millennial teaching—locating the millennial reign within the church's history, though not as a triumphalist vision of the church—shaped the conventional eschatological wisdom for centuries to come.

JOACHIM OF FIORE

One of the most fascinating figures in the rich history of Christian apocalypticism is the abbot Joachim of Fiore (ca. 1135–1202). Yet his apocalyptic vision of history, inspired by his visionary experience in the years 1183–84, was not the rediscovery of an ancient tradition that had long remained silent. The year 500 C.E., for example, evidently became the focus for heightened apocalyptic speculation in some circles (e.g., *Apocalypse of Thomas,* perhaps written about the same time as the *City of God*).[6] Then, near the close of the sixth century, Pope Gregory (the Great)—in the wake of the incursions of the Lombards into northern Italy, the spread of the bubonic plague, and continuing corruption in the church—regarded the End as imminent, although there was still time for repentance.[7] Weakened by attacks from Slavs and Arabs during the seventh century, the Byzantine Empire was ripe for millennialist thinking. Where Augustine had taken pains to distinguish the destiny of God's

---

[6] Cf. the discussion above of Lactantius. See further Daley, "Apocalypticism in Early Christian Theology," 37–38.
[7] Ibid., 42.

realm and that of Caesar, Byzantine apocalypses like the *Apocalypse of Pseudo-Methodius* (ca. 690 C.E., responding to the Arab conquest of Syria) once again forged a strong connection between the emperor and Christ. Rome is the last great empire, and the last emperor will soon surrender his world rule to God through the dramatic symbolic gesture of placing his crown upon the cross. After the emperor's death, antichrist will rise to power at Jerusalem, only to be vanquished by the returning Christ.[8] Although the extent of apocalyptic fervor associated with the approach of the year 1000 has been exaggerated, expectation of an imminent End was a recurring feature of medieval piety.[9]

Apocalyptic hopes were intertwined with efforts to reform the medieval church. B. McGinn has argued convincingly that popular movements of resistance and protest possessed no monopoly on millennialist ideas. Ecclesial and civil authorities, too, could appeal to such views.[10] Among a variety of models for relating millennialist ideas to church reform during this period, the approach of Joachim of Fiore stands out for its comprehensiveness and the extent of its influence.[11] Joachim, out of his deep investment in the monastic life and concern for the reform of the church, developed a complex and thoroughly apocalyptic theology of history. The system of symbols the abbot constructed is evocative, even if his exposition of them is obscure and wearisome. For Joachim, the history of the world has been predetermined by God, and Scripture reveals its course and its meaning.[12] History has a Trinitarian structure, unfolding in three distinct epochs attributed to Father, Son, and Spirit. The third era, or *status,* that of the Spirit, was about to begin; in fact, Joachim believed that the

---

[8] D. Olster, "Byzantine Apocalypses," in McGinn, *Apocalypticism in Western History,* 60–64.

[9] See B. McGinn, "Apocalypticism and Church Reform: 1100–1500," in idem, *Apocalypticism in Western History,* 74–75.

[10] See, e.g., McGinn, *Visions of the End,* 32.

[11] Ibid., 78–81.

[12] B. McGinn, *The Calabrian Abbot: Joachim of Fiore in the History of Western Thought* (New York: Macmillan, 1985), 190.

monastic order, which would be of central importance in this third age, already marked its beginning.[13]

Joachim tenaciously held to the belief that the End was near; although its precise time could not be predicted, the end-time events were imminent. The contemporary scene—including the growing Islamic challenge, bitter conflict between pope and emperor, and ecclesiastical corruption—signaled the imminent appearance of the "great Antichrist." Moreover, the persecution of the church by the imperial power (which for Joachim was thus far removed from the benign "last emperor" of Byzantine apocalypses) was a sure indicator that this historical era was nearing its end. The dawning age of the Spirit would bring an idyllic "sabbath" for the church on earth. As McGinn has shown, this vision of a future, thoroughly monastic church amounts to a "radical critique" of the existing church and papacy.[14] In the apocalyptic spirituality of Joachim of Fiore, fervent apocalyptic hope does not express disengagement from this world or its institutions but instead energizes the drive for ecclesial reform.

THE REFORMERS

The age of the Reformation again witnessed an upsurge of interest in apocalyptic ideas. Anabaptist leaders like Thomas Müntzer and John of Leyden were stridently millennialist in their views. But Luther, Calvin, and Zwingli were more cautious. P. Boyer suggests that Lutheran and Reformed (Calvinist) traditions, reacting against Anabaptist radical millennialism, "began with a strong amillennial bias and suspicion of end-time speculation," a bias they still retain.[15] Certainly in the case of Luther, however, it would be a mistake to distance the Reformer from urgent eschatological expectations. Luther, to be sure, insisted that God's reign would not be established by human activ-

---

[13] Ibid., 186, 189.

[14] Ibid., 192.

[15] P. Boyer, *When Time Shall Be No More: Prophecy Belief in Modern American Culture* (Cambridge: Harvard University Press, 1992), 60–61.

ity, and that evil and good would remain locked in fierce combat until the final judgment. Nevertheless, he often gave expression to an acute eschatological sensibility. He went so far as to publish a chronology of world history, the *Supputatio annorum mundi* (1541); his calculations led him to situate his own age in the final period of history.

The challenges posed by the Ottomans (representing, to Luther, "Gog") and by the papacy (for Luther, "Antichrist") were interpreted by the Reformer in imagery drawn from biblical apocalyptic texts. Luther hoped and anticipated that deliverance from these "powers of darkness" was close at hand. Calvin was more circumspect about eschatological concerns. It is revealing that the one New Testament book on which he did not write a commentary was the book of Revelation. Calvin's reading of history did not share the pessimism and apocalyptic concern of Luther. The Calvinist interest in shaping civil life within this world was generally not driven by apocalyptic urgency—although one should not repeat the familiar, and misleading, contrast between imminent eschatological beliefs and responsible moral engagement with the world. For Calvin, the timing of the parousia was unknowable; in the meantime, the church's task was to proclaim the gospel to all the world. The return of Christ and the resurrection of the faithful would culminate in the establishment of God's eternal rule, which, until then, exerts itself in the form of Christ's spiritual rule in the lives of individual believers.

ESCHATOLOGY IN THE "NEW WORLD"

From the very beginning of European exploration of the Americas, perceptions of this "new world" were caught up with apocalyptic notions. This land of promise, for the "Christ-bearer" Christopher Columbus as for countless others who followed in his wake, was the new Jerusalem in which divine prophecies for the end time were to be fulfilled.[16] Millennialist hopes played a

---

[16] On Columbus, see A. Milhou, "Apocalypticism in Central and South American Colonialism," in *Apocalypticism in the Modern Period*

significant role in the Christian piety that marked the "new" England. Premillennialist systems, represented by Cotton Mather (1663–1728), and postmillennialist views, represented by Jonathan Edwards (1703–1758), both found eloquent advocates in colonial New England.

Predicting the End: The Millerites

Without doubt, one of the most fascinating chapters in the history of Christian eschatological speculation is associated with the name of William Miller (1782–1849).[17] After his conversion in his mid-thirties, Miller became an ardent student of prophetic scriptures, arriving at the conclusion that the end of history would soon occur. Beginning in 1831, Miller traveled extensively in New York and New England, and he published his views in 1836.[18] Joshua Himes joined the cause, organizing conferences and spreading the word through newspapers and periodicals. The basic message was that Christ's return was imminent, and would be followed by a thousand-year reign (on earth) of Christ with the saints. Though at first reluctant, Miller predicted that the second coming of Christ would happen between March 21, 1843 and March 21, 1844. When March 1844 came and went, Miller conceded his mistake, but refused to give up his imminent eschatological hope. At the

---

and the Contemporary Age, vol. 3 of The Encyclopedia of Apocalypticism (ed. S. J. Stein; New York: Continuum, 1998), 3–5. For later developments in North American Protestantism, see Boyer, When Time Shall Be No More, 80–112; R. Smolinski, "Apocalypticism in Colonial North America," in Stein, Apocalypticism in the Modern Period, 36–71; J. H. Moorhead, "Apocalypticism in Mainstream Protestantism, 1800 to the Present," in Stein, Apocalypticism in the Modern Period, 72–107; J. H. Smylie, "A New Heaven and New Earth: Uses of the Millennium in American Religious History," Int 53 (1999): 143–57.

[17] See the analysis of the Millerite movement in S. D. O'Leary, Arguing the Apocalypse: A Theory of Millennial Rhetoric (New York: Oxford University Press, 1994), 93–133.

[18] W. Miller, Evidence from Scripture and History of the Second Coming of Christ about the Year 1843.

prodding of one of the Millerite movement's evangelists, Miller and Himes adjusted their clocks and forecast the End on October 22, 1844. The failure of this revised prophecy prompted intense public ridicule and effectively brought the Millerite movement to an end.

In the decades following this evident disconfirmation of millennialist faith, however, Ellen White and others picked up the pieces and forged a new millennialist organization that would have staying power into the next century (and even the next millennium), the Seventh-Day Adventists. Under some circumstances, disconfirmation of eschatological prophecies can lead beyond disillusionment and abandonment of the faith to revitalized and reinvigorated eschatological conviction.[19]

From Scofield to Lindsey

About the same time that the Millerite movement was flourishing in the United States, John Nelson Darby (1800–1882) popularized millennialist thinking in Britain. Darby believed human history unfolds in discrete phases; in each of these dispensations, God relates to humanity in a distinctive manner—hence, the label "dispensational premillennialism" for this eschatological system. In contrast to apocalyptic prophets like Miller, Darby denied that current events could be fitted into an eschatological timetable. In fact, he regarded the present dispensation, the age of the church, as a great historical "parenthesis" between the time of Jesus and the kingdom age of the end time. Events prophesied for the end time—including, notably, the advent of antichrist and the woes of the great tribulation—would occur only after the rapture—a concept and term thought to have been introduced by Darby—of the faithful. Removed from earth before the onset of eschatological distress, true believers would

---

[19] See the classic study of cognitive dissonance in apocalyptic sects authored by social psychologists L. Festinger, H. W. Riecken, and S. Schachter, *When Prophecy Fails* (New York: Harper Torchbooks, 1964).

be united with Christ and spared the ordeals of those left behind on earth.

On several lecture tours of the United States, Darby introduced his dispensational premillennialist system to American evangelical preachers. A host of "prophecy conferences" sustained interest in the topic, with the annual Niagara Bible Conference, spanning more than two decades at the close of the nineteenth century, the most influential. Turning away from attempts to reform society or otherwise build God's realm on earth, these prophecy enthusiasts focused on the urgent missionary task of "saving" individuals before the rapture. It remained, however, for Cyrus Scofield (1843–1921) to consolidate the movement with his *Scofield Reference Bible,* first published in 1909. Scofield's Bible embellished the text of Scripture with a commentary conveniently placed below the biblical text on the page. The commentary hammered home the dispensational premillennialist system, and the visual proximity of commentary to text has enhanced the authority of the eschatological approach for many readers, from Scofield's time to the present day.

This approach to Christian eschatology has been vigorously advocated for half a century at Dallas Theological Seminary, one of whose graduates, Hal Lindsey (b. 1930), became the great popularizer of dispensational premillennialism for the last third of the twentieth century. Lindsey's *Late Great Planet Earth* (1970) claimed that with the reconstitution of the state of Israel in 1948, the apocalyptic countdown had begun. One by one, current political events found a place in the eschatological scenario clearly prophesied in Scripture. Although Lindsey did not predict the End with the precision of a William Miller, he left his readers in no doubt: theirs was the "terminal generation." Naturally, Lindsey has had to calibrate his prophetic system to make room for subsequent historical developments that disconfirmed his bold prophetic message—first framed as it was in America of the late 1960s, embroiled in its own cultural apocalypse, particularly the Vietnam War.

Countless television evangelists—from Jack Van Impe to Pat Robertson—have fanned the flames of urgent apocalyptic hope throughout the last decades of the twentieth century.[20] Doomsday speculation has also been nourished in secular soil, fed by fears such as ecological catastrophe, societal collapse, and nuclear holocaust. An apt illustration of the secular co-opting of genuinely religious apocalyptic expectancy was the "Y2K" craze, the so-called millennium bug. Some analysts warned that the Y2K problem would cause computer-dependent economic and political systems to "crash," leading to social conditions not that far removed from the Apocalypse's eschatological tribulation. No doubt many of these ominous warnings were exaggerated and extreme, but they did fix the attention of a whole generation on the turn of the millennia in a way that was surely unprecedented in human history. The fact that the third millennium of the common era actually begins in 2001 (there was no year 0), and the further observation that the third millennium after Jesus' birth likely began a few years ago (Herod the Great died in 4 B.C.E.) are beside the point. A generation of Americans generally impatient with historical study and absorbed in the present moment are, for a time at least, oriented toward an uncertain future. Yet their view of the future seldom makes meaningful connection with the richly layered and textured apocalyptic hope of the first Christians. One of the aims of this book has been to enable readers to begin to make those connections. What would an appropriate "parousia hope" look like at the start of the twenty-first century?

HOPEFUL REALISM AT THE DAWN OF A NEW MILLENNIUM[21]

An authentic Christian eschatology for the third millennium of the church's existence must be equal measure hope and

---

[20] For a sample of Robertson's views, see P. Robertson, *The New World Order* (Dallas: Word, 1991).

[21] I borrow the phrase "hopeful realism" from the title of a volume of programmatic essays by D. F. Ottati, *Hopeful Realism: Reclaiming the Poetry of Theology* (Cleveland: Pilgrim, 1999).

realism. Why should Christians continue to think—and to hope—eschatologically? There is, first of all, a nonnegotiable concern with justice. The present world does not reflect the divine purpose for the whole human family, and in fact the observer of current events discerns no trends even toward the "kinder, gentler" society President George Bush anticipated. Dehumanizing oppression and cruelty, a new world order that features ethnic cleansing rather than cooperation, domestic abuse, teen violence on a terrifying scale, a widening chasm between the rich and the poor and between the powerful and the powerless—these may not be the precise facts and figures presented in apocalyptic texts like Revelation, but the contemporary drama of human suffering is all too familiar to the reader of Jewish and Christian apocalyptic literature. Christians place their trust in a faithful and just God, and therefore they must continue to look toward the fulfillment of God's purposes for humankind.

But not just for humankind. Christian eschatological reflection, at its best, expresses a continuing concern with the entire cosmos. The horizon of Christian hope is the whole created order; Christian faith does not mean a sectarian preoccupation with the fortunes and future of one's own marginalized group. The concern of the church is with all people, all nations, all the earth. The church is called to embody and to declare good news of liberation and restoration—and in a world such as ours to do so persistently, tenaciously, and gracefully.

The world as we know it is a canvas still being painted by the divine artist. For all these reasons, eschatological hope is a necessary feature of Christian faith. The alternatives—whether an egocentric reduction of vision and concern to one's own personal salvation, or despair in the face of the oppressive evil of the present—will not sustain vibrant Christian faith in the next millennium. God is not through with the creative and restorative project that extends to the whole human family, and to the entire world. There is unfinished business on the divine agenda with the cosmos.

As to the form and content of eschatological hope, there is no one prescribed pattern. Scripture provides a rich variety of

images and expectations for the consummation of God's purposes in creation. And subsequent Christian tradition attests the
sometimes helpful, often bewildering ways in which biblical imagery can be deployed. Yet the main contours of a Christian eschatology for the third millennium that is grounded in the
witness of Scripture, and also responsive to the world of contemporary experience, can be discerned. Evil in its many guises—
including every form of dehumanization and oppression—is not
the final word, and those who serve and perpetuate evil systems
of domination will answer for what they have done. Persons and
communities of faith are summoned to persevere in their commitment to a faithful God, despite powerful forces that move
them toward despair or passive resignation. Trusting in the sure,
liberating work of God, they sustain faith and hope in the
meantime.

The central New Testament image of the triumphant return
of Christ need not be interpreted literally, as if Jesus would actually ride the clouds back to earth in a show of glory and power
visible to all. But this potent symbol of Christian hope must be
taken seriously, for it points to the completion of God's work of
life and salvation for this planet and all who call it home. In the
meantime, people of faith will wait in patient hope. Yet they will
not wait passively, relinquishing any concern with the shaping
of human life. God's sovereign purpose will bring all creation to
its intended flourishing, but, as ever, God will co-opt persons
and communities of faith to participate in the difficult work of
making it so.

When? The answer Jesus gave in the eschatological discourses of the gospels and in Acts 1 still holds true: We do not
know and cannot know the time. Yet a critical implication of
early Christian thought about the times—which was driven by
the conviction that the End, though unpredictable, was at hand—
was a seriousness and urgency about the church's mission and
about the Christian's moral responsibility. Expectation of an imminent parousia also provided hope and assurance that would
enable the suffering faithful to persevere through trial. But if
Jesus is not returning tomorrow—or ten or fifty years from

now—from what source will twenty-first century persons of faith draw the moral seriousness, the fervent commitment to mission, the hope and assurance that can sustain one through adversity?

It is probably fair to say that for many Christians, personal eschatology has become the functional equivalent of the collective imminent eschatology of the earliest Christian generation. One does not know when one will die, and in any case we are given only a few years of life. (Perhaps social institutions like churches, not just individuals, might benefit from such a self-understanding.) The parousia of Jesus as cosmic judge and liberator is thus transformed into a personal coming of Jesus to the individual at the moment of death. This personalizing of parousia hope is not a bad thing. It can provide perspective and challenge to faithful living in many of the ways that the corporate eschatology of the earliest Christians did. At the same time, it is crucial to acknowledge the limits of this approach to eschatology. The communal, social, and cosmic concern of God—and therefore of God's people—can be lost.

In the twenty-first century as in the first, communities of faith must develop resources and strategies for sustaining moral and religious commitment over the long haul. We cannot wink at evil, assuming that it is soon to vanish. We must resist it strenuously, and work together with all persons of goodwill to construct more just and humane social systems. Yet if a reading of Jewish and Christian apocalyptic texts reveals anything, it is that oppressive evil is tenacious and powerful. We must do what we can now as people of God, yet we await a future that only God can fashion, living by trust in a faithful creator—Maranatha: Come, sovereign one!

BIBLIOGRAPHY

Achtemeier, Paul J. *1 Peter.* Hermeneia. Minneapolis: Fortress, 1996.

Allison, Dale C., Jr. *The End of the Ages Has Come: An Early Interpretation of the Passion and Resurrection of Jesus.* Philadelphia: Fortress, 1985.

———. "The Eschatology of Jesus." Pages 267–302 in *The Origins of Apocalypticism in Judaism and Christianity.* Vol. 1 of *The Encyclopedia of Apocalypticism.* Ed. John J. Collins. New York: Continuum, 1998.

———. *Jesus of Nazareth: Millenarian Prophet.* Minneapolis: Fortress, 1998.

Altizer, Thomas J. J. "Modern Thought and Apocalypticism." Pages 325–59 in *Apocalypticism in the Modern Period and the Contemporary Age.* Vol. 3 of *The Encyclopedia of Apocalypticism.* Ed. Stephen J. Stein. New York: Continuum, 1998.

Anderson, Charles P. "Who Are the Heirs of the New Age in the Epistle to the Hebrews?" Pages 255–77 in *Apocalyptic and the New Testament: Essays in Honor of J. Louis Martyn.* Ed. Joel Marcus and Marion L. Soards. JSNTSup 24. Sheffield: JSOT Press, 1989.

Anderson, Paul N. *The Christology of the Fourth Gospel.* WUNT 78. Tübingen: J. C. B. Mohr (Paul Siebeck), 1996.

Attridge, Harold. *Hebrews.* Hermeneia. Philadelphia: Fortress, 1989.

———. " 'Let Us Strive to Enter That Rest': The Logic of Hebrews 4:1–11." *HTR* 73 (1980): 279–88.

Baarlink, Heinrich. *Die Eschatologie des synoptischen Evangelien.* BWANT 120. Stuttgart: Kohlhammer, 1986.

Baker, William R. *Personal Speech-Ethics in the Epistle of James.* WUNT 2.68. Tübingen: J. C. B. Mohr (Paul Siebeck), 1995.

Balabanski, Vicky. *Eschatology in the Making: Mark, Matthew, and the Didache.* SNTSMS 97. Cambridge: Cambridge University Press, 1997.

Barkun, Michael. "Politics and Apocalypticism." Pages 442–60 in *Apocalypticism in the Modern Period and the Contemporary Age.* Vol. 3 of *The Encyclopedia of Apocalypticism.* Ed. Stephen J. Stein. New York: Continuum, 1998.

Barnard, Leslie W. "Justin Martyr's Eschatology." *VC* 19 (1965): 86–98.

Barnes, T. D. *Tertullian.* Rev. ed. Oxford: Oxford University Press, 1985.

Barrett, C. K. "The Eschatology of the Epistle to the Hebrews." Pages 363–93 in *The Background of the New Testament and Its Eschatology.* Ed. W. D. Davies and David Daube. Cambridge: Cambridge University Press, 1956.

———. *The Gospel according to St. John.* 2d ed. Philadelphia: Westminster, 1978.

Bassler, Jouette M., ed. *Thessalonians, Philippians, Galatians, Philemon.* Vol. 1 of *Pauline Theology.* Minneapolis: Fortress, 1991.

Bauckham, Richard J. *Jude, 2 Peter.* WBC 50. Waco: Word, 1983.

———. "The Delay of the Parousia." *TynBull* 31 (1981): 3–36.

———. *The Theology of the Book of Revelation.* NTT. Cambridge: Cambridge University Press, 1993.

Bauer, David R., and Mark Allan Powell, eds. *Treasures New and Old: Contributions to Matthean Studies.* Atlanta: Scholars Press, 1996.

Bayer, H. F. "The Preaching of Peter in Acts." Pages 257–74 in *Witness to the Gospel: The Theology of Acts.* Ed. I. Howard Marshall and David Peterson. Grand Rapids: Eerdmans, 1998.

Beale, Gregory K. *The Book of Revelation: A Commentary on the Greek Text.* NIGTC. Grand Rapids: Eerdmans, 1999.

Beasley-Murray, George R. *Jesus and the Kingdom of God.* Grand Rapids: Eerdmans, 1986.

———. *Jesus and the Last Days: The Interpretation of the Olivet Discourse.* Peabody, Mass.: Hendrickson, 1993.

Beker, J. Christiaan. *Paul the Apostle: The Triumph of God in Life and Thought.* Edinburgh: T&T Clark, 1980.

———. *The Triumph of God: The Essence of Paul's Thought.* Trans. Loren Stuckenbruck. Minneapolis: Fortress, 1990.

Berger, Peter L., and Thomas Luckmann. *The Social Construction of Reality: A Treatise in the Sociology of Knowledge.* New York: Doubleday, 1966.

Best, Ernest. *The First and Second Epistles to the Thessalonians.* London: Adam and Charles Black, 1972.

Betz, Hans Dieter. *Galatians: A Commentary on Paul's Letter to the Churches in Galatia.* Hermeneia. Philadelphia: Fortress, 1979.

Black, C. Clifton. "First, Second, and Third John." Pages 363–469 in vol. 12 of *NIB.* Ed. Leander E. Keck et al. Nashville: Abingdon, 1998.

Blank, Josef. *Krisis: Untersuchungen zur johanneischen Christologie und Eschatologie.* Freiburg: Lambertus, 1964.

Bock, Darrell L. "The Son of Man and the Debate over Jesus' 'Blasphemy.' " Pages 181–91 in *Jesus of Nazareth: Lord and Christ: Essays on the Historical Jesus and New Testament Christology.* Ed. Joel B. Green and Max Turner. Grand Rapids: Eerdmans, 1994.

Boer, Martinus C. de "Paul and Apocalyptic Eschatology." Pages 345–83 in *The Origins of Apocalypticism in Judaism and Christianity.* Vol. 1 of *The Encyclopedia of Apocalypticism.* Ed. John J. Collins. New York: Continuum, 1998.

——. "Paul and Jewish Apocalyptic Eschatology." Pages 169–90 in *Apocalyptic and the New Testament: Essays in Honor of J. Louis Martyn.* Ed. Joel Marcus and Marion L. Soards. JSNTSup 24. Sheffield: JSOT Press, 1989.

Borg, Marcus J. *Jesus: A New Vision.* San Francisco: Harper & Row, 1987.

——. "A Temperate Case for a Non-Eschatological Jesus." *Forum* 2 (1986): 81–102.

Boring, M. Eugene. *Revelation.* IBC. Louisville: John Knox, 1989.

——. "The Theology of Revelation: 'The Lord Our God the Almighty Reigns.' " *Int* 40 (1986): 257–69.

Boyer, Paul. "The Growth of Fundamentalist Apocalyptic in the United States." Pages 140–78 in *Apocalypticism in the Modern Period and the Contemporary Age.* Vol. 3 of *The Encyclopedia of Apocalypticism.* Ed. Stephen J. Stein. New York: Continuum, 1998.

——. *When Time Shall Be No More: Prophecy Belief in Modern American Culture.* Cambridge: Harvard University Press, 1992.

Brown, Alexandra R. *The Cross and Human Transformation: Paul's Apocalyptic Word in 1 Corinthians.* Minneapolis: Fortress, 1995.

——. "Latter Days." In *Eerdmans Bible Dictionary.* Grand Rapids: Eerdmans, forthcoming.

Brown, Raymond E. *The Death of the Messiah: From Gethsemane to the Grave. A Commentary on the Passion Narratives in the Four Gospels.* 2 vols. New York: Doubleday, 1994.

———. *The Epistles of John.* AB 30. Garden City, N.Y.: Doubleday, 1982.

———. *The Gospel according to John.* 2 vols. AB 29–29A. Garden City, N.Y.: Doubleday, 1966–70.

Bultmann, Rudolf. *The Gospel of John: A Commentary.* Philadelphia: Westminster, 1971.

Burnett, Fred. *The Testament of Jesus Sophia: A Redaction-Critical Study of the Eschatological Discourse in Matthew.* Washington, D.C.: University Press of America, 1981.

Caird, George B. *The Revelation of St. John the Divine.* HNTC. New York: Harper & Row, 1966.

Cargal, Timothy B. *Restoring the Diaspora: Discursive Structure and Purpose in the Epistle of James.* SBLDS 144. Atlanta: Scholars Press, 1993.

Carlston, Charles E. "Eschatology and Repentance in the Epistle to the Hebrews." *JBL* 78 (1959): 296–302.

Carroll, John T. "Present and Future in Fourth Gospel 'Eschatology.' " *BTB* 19 (1989): 63–69.

———. *Response to the End of History: Eschatology and Situation in Luke–Acts.* SBLDS 92. Atlanta: Scholars Press, 1988.

———. "The Uses of Scripture in Acts." Pages 512–28 in *SBLSP 1990.* Ed. David J. Lull. Atlanta: Scholars Press, 1990.

Carroll, John T., and Joel B. Green, with Joel Marcus, Donald Senior, and Robert Van Voorst. *The Death of Jesus in Early Christianity.* Peabody, Mass.: Hendrickson, 1995.

Chance, J. Bradley. *Jerusalem, the Temple, and the New Age in Luke–Acts.* Macon, Ga.: Mercer University Press, 1988.

Charette, B. *The Theme of Recompense in Matthew's Gospel.* JSNTSup 79. Sheffield: Sheffield Academic Press, 1992.

Charlesworth, James H., ed. *The Messiah: Developments in Earliest Judaism and Christianity.* Minneapolis: Fortress, 1992.

Cohn, Norman. *The Pursuit of the Millennium.* Rev. ed. New York: Oxford University Press, 1970.

Collins, Adela Yarbro. *The Beginning of the Gospel: Probings of Mark in Context.* Minneapolis: Fortress, 1992.

———. "The Book of Revelation." Pages 384–414 in *The Origins of Apocalypticism in Judaism and Christianity.* Vol. 1 of *The Encyclopedia of Apocalypticism.* Ed. John J. Collins. New York: Continuum, 1998.

——. *Crisis and Catharsis: The Power of the Apocalypse.* Philadelphia: Westminster, 1984.

Collins, John J. *The Apocalyptic Imagination: An Introduction to the Jewish Matrix of Christianity.* New York: Crossroad, 1984. 2d ed. Grand Rapids: Eerdmans, 1998.

——. *The Scepter and the Star.* New York: Doubleday, 1995.

——, ed. *The Origins of Apocalypticism in Judaism and Christianity.* Vol. 1 of *The Encyclopedia of Apocalypticism.* New York: Continuum, 1998.

Conzelmann, Hans. *The Theology of St. Luke.* London: Faber & Faber, 1960. Reprint, London: SCM, 1982.

Cook, Stephen L. *Prophecy and Apocalypticism: The Postexilic Social Setting.* Minneapolis: Fortress, 1995.

Crossan, J. Dominic. *The Historical Jesus: The Life of a Mediterranean Jewish Peasant.* San Francisco: Harper, 1991.

Croy, N. Clayton. *Endurance in Suffering: Hebrews 12:1–13 in Its Rhetorical, Religious, and Philosophical Context.* SNTSMS 98. Cambridge: Cambridge University Press, 1998.

Culpepper, R. Alan. *Anatomy of the Fourth Gospel.* FF. Philadelphia: Fortress, 1983.

Culpepper, R. Alan and C. Clifton Black, eds. *Exploring the Gospel of John: In Honor of D. Moody Smith.* Louisville: Westminster John Knox, 1996.

Dahl, Nils A. " 'Do Not Wonder!' John 5:28–29 and Johannine Eschatology Once More." Pages 322–36 in *The Conversation Continues: Studies in Paul and John in Honor of J. Louis Martyn.* Ed. Robert T. Fortna and Beverly R. Gaventa. Nashville: Abingdon, 1994.

Daley, Brian E. "Apocalypticism in Early Christian Theology." Pages 3–47 in *Apocalypticism in Western History and Culture.* Vol. 2 of *The Encyclopedia of Apocalypticism.* Ed. Bernard McGinn. New York: Continuum, 1998.

——. "Eschatology." In *Encyclopedia of Early Christianity.* New York: Garland, 1990.

——. *The Hope of the Early Church: A Handbook of Patristic Eschatology.* Cambridge: Cambridge University Press, 1991.

Darr, John A. *On Character Building: The Reader and the Rhetoric of Characterization in Luke–Acts.* LCBI. Louisville: Westminster/John Knox, 1992.

Davies, W. D., and David Daube, eds. *The Background of the New Testament and Its Eschatology.* Cambridge: Cambridge University Press, 1964.

Deissmann, Adolf. *Light from the Ancient East.* 1927. Repr. Peabody, Mass.: Hendrickson, 1995.

DeSilva, David A. *Despising Shame: Honor Discourse and Community Maintenance in the Epistle to the Hebrews.* SBLDS 152. Atlanta: Scholars Press, 1995.

Dibelius, Martin. *James.* Rev. Helmut Greeven. Trans. Michael A. Williams. Ed. Helmut Koester. Hermeneia. Philadelphia: Fortress, 1975.

Donfried, Karl P. "The Imperial Cults and Political Conflict in 1 Thessalonians." Pages 215–23 in *Paul and Empire: Religion and Power in Roman Imperial Society.* Ed. Richard Horsley. Harrisburg, Pa.: Trinity Press International, 1997.

——. "Paul and Judaism: 1 Thessalonians 2:13–16 as a Test Case." *Int* 38 (1984): 242–53.

Duke, Paul D. *Irony in the Fourth Gospel.* Atlanta: John Knox, 1985.

Dunbar, D. G. "The Delay of the *Parousia* in Hippolytus." *VC* 37 (1983): 313–27.

Dunn, James D. G. *Jesus, Paul and the Law: Studies in Mark and Galatians.* Louisville: Westminster John Knox, 1990.

——. "Messianic Ideas and Their Influence on the Jesus of History." Pages 365–81 in *The Messiah: Developments in Earliest Judaism and Christianity.* Ed. James H. Charlesworth. Minneapolis: Fortress, 1992.

——. "Prolegomena to a Theology of Paul." *NTS* 40 (1994): 407–32.

——. *Romans.* 2 vols. WBC 38A–B. Dallas: Word, 1988.

——. *The Theology of Paul the Apostle.* Grand Rapids: Eerdmans, 1998.

——. *The Theology of Paul's Letter to the Galatians.* NTT. Cambridge: Cambridge University Press, 1993.

Dunnill, John. *Covenant and Sacrifice in the Letter to the Hebrews.* SNTSMS 75. Cambridge: Cambridge University Press, 1992.

Dupont, Jacques. ΣΥΝ ΧΡΙΣΤΩΙ: *L'union avec le Christ suivant saint Paul.* Louvain: Nauwelaerts; Paris: Desclée de Brouwer, 1952.

Eisenbaum, Pamela M. *The Jewish Heroes of Christian History: Hebrews 11 in Literary Context.* SBLDS 156. Atlanta: Scholars Press, 1997.

Eisenman, R. "Eschatological 'Rain' Imagery in the War Scroll from Qumran and in the Letter of James." *JNES* 49 (1990): 173–84.

Ellingworth, Paul. *The Epistle to the Hebrews: A Commentary on the Greek Text.* NIGTC. Grand Rapids: Eerdmans, 1993.

Elliott, J. K., ed. *The Apocryphal New Testament.* Oxford: Oxford University Press, 1993.

Elliott, John H. "1 Peter, Its Situation and Strategy: A Discussion with David Balch." Pages 61–78 in *Perspectives on First Peter*. Ed. Charles H. Talbert. SSS 9. Macon, Ga.: Mercer University Press, 1986.

———. *Home for the Homeless: A Sociological Exegesis of 1 Peter, Its Situation and Strategy*. Philadelphia: Fortress, 1981.

Erlemann, Kurt. *Naherwartung und Parusieverzögerung im Neuen Testament: Ein Beitrag zur Frage religiöser Zeiterfahrung*. TANZ 17. Tübingen: Francke, 1995.

Esler, Philip Francis. *Community and Gospel in Luke–Acts: The Social and Political Motivations of Lucan Theology*. SNTSMS 57. Cambridge: Cambridge University Press, 1987.

Eusebius. *The Ecclesiastical History*. 2 vols. Trans. John Ernest Leonard Oulton. LCL. Cambridge: Harvard University Press, 1932.

Evans, C. F. *Saint Luke*. TPINTC. Philadelphia: Trinity, 1990.

Faierstein, Morris M. "Why Do the Scribes Say That Elijah Must Come First?" *JBL* 100 (1981): 75–86.

Falls, Thomas B., ed. *Writings of Saint Justin Martyr*. Vol. 6 of *The Fathers of the Church*. Washington, D.C.: Catholic University Press of America, 1948.

Farrer, Austin M. *A Rebirth of Images: The Making of St. John's Apocalypse*. Boston: Beacon, 1949.

Feuillet, A. "Le sens du mot parousie dans l'évangile de Matthieu: comparaison entre Matth xxiv et Jac v, 1–11." Pages 261–80 in *The Background of the New Testament and Its Eschatology*. Ed. W. D. Davies and David Daube. Cambridge: Cambridge University Press, 1964.

Fishbane, Michael. *Biblical Interpretation in Ancient Israel*. Oxford: Clarendon, 1985.

Fitzgerald, John T. *Cracks in an Earthen Vessel: An Examination of the Catalogues of Hardships in the Corinthian Correspondence*. SBLDS 99. Atlanta: Scholars Press, 1988.

Fitzmyer, Joseph A. *The Gospel according to Luke: Introduction, Translation, and Notes*. 2 vols. AB 28–28A. Garden City, N.Y.: Doubleday, 1981–85.

———. *Luke the Theologian: Aspects of His Teaching*. New York and Mahwah, N.J.: Paulist, 1989.

Fortna, Robert T., and Beverly R. Gaventa, eds. *The Conversation Continues: Studies in Paul and John in Honor of J. Louis Martyn*. Nashville: Abingdon, 1994.

Fowler, Robert M. *Let the Reader Understand: Reader-Response Criticism and the Gospel of Mark.* Minneapolis: Fortress, 1991.

Frankfurter, David. *Elijah in Upper Egypt.* Minneapolis: Fortress, 1993.

Furnish, Victor P. *Theology and Ethics in Paul.* Nashville: Abingdon, 1968.

García Martínez, Florentino. "Apocalypticism in the Dead Sea Scrolls." Pages 162–92 in *The Origins of Apocalypticism in Judaism and Christianity.* Vol. 1 of *The Encyclopedia of Apocalypticism.* Ed. John J. Collins. New York: Continuum, 1998.

Garrett, Susan R. *The Demise of the Devil: Magic and the Demonic in Luke's Writings.* Minneapolis: Fortress, 1989.

———. *The Temptations of Jesus in Mark's Gospel.* Grand Rapids: Eerdmans, 1998.

Geddert, Timothy J. *Watchwords: Mark 13 in Markan Eschatology.* JSNTSup 26. Sheffield: Sheffield Academic Press, 1989.

Gibbs, Jeffrey. " 'Let the Reader Understand': The Eschatological Discourse of Jesus in Matthew's Gospel." Ph.D. diss., Union Theological Seminary in Virginia, 1995.

Ginzberg, Louis. *Legends of the Jews.* 7 vols. Philadelphia: Jewish Publication Society, 1909–38.

Goldstein, J. "How the Authors of 1 and 2 Maccabees Treated the 'Messianic' Promises." Pages 69–96 in *Judaisms and Their Messiahs at the Turn of the Christian Era.* Ed. J. Neusner, W. S. Green, and E. S. Frerichs. Cambridge: Cambridge University Press, 1987.

Goppelt, Leonhard. *A Commentary on 1 Peter.* Ed. Ferdinand Hahn; trans. John E. Alsup. Grand Rapids: Eerdmans, 1993.

Green, Joel B. *The Gospel of Luke.* NICNT. Grand Rapids: Eerdmans, 1997.

———. " 'Salvation to the End of the Earth' (Acts 13:47): God as Saviour in the Acts of the Apostles." Pages 83–106 in *Witness to the Gospel: The Theology of Acts.* Ed. I. Howard Marshall and David Peterson. Grand Rapids: Eerdmans, 1998.

———. *The Theology of the Gospel of Luke.* NTT 3. Cambridge: Cambridge University Press, 1995.

Green, Joel B., and Max Turner, eds. *Jesus of Nazareth: Lord and Christ: Essays on the Historical Jesus and New Testament Christology.* Grand Rapids: Eerdmans; Carlisle: Paternoster, 1994.

Green, W. S. "Introduction: Messiah in Judaism: Rethinking the Question." Pages 1–13 in *Judaisms and Their Messiahs at the Turn of the Christian Era.* Ed. J. Neusner, W. S. Green, and E. S. Frerichs. Cambridge: Cambridge University Press, 1987.

Haenchen, Ernst. *The Acts of the Apostles: A Commentary.* Philadelphia: Westminster, 1971.

Hagner, Donald. "Apocalyptic Motifs in the Gospel of Matthew: Continuity and Discontinuity." *HBT* 7 (1985): 53–81.

Hamm, Dennis. "Acts 3:1–10: The Healing of the Temple Beggar as Lukan Theology." *Bib* 67 (1986): 305–19.

———. "Acts 3:12–26: Peter's Speech and the Healing of the Man Born Lame." *PRSt* 11 (1984): 199–217.

Hare, Douglas R. A. *Matthew.* IBC. Louisville: John Knox, 1993.

Harrington, Daniel J. *The Gospel of Matthew.* SP 1. Collegeville, Minn.: Liturgical Press, 1991.

Harrington, Wilfrid J. *Revelation.* SP 16. Collegeville, Minn.: Liturgical Press, 1993.

Harris, Stephen. *The New Testament: A Student's Introduction.* 2d ed. Mountain View, Calif.: Mayfield, 1995.

Hartman, Lars. *Prophecy Interpreted: The Formation of Some Jewish Apocalyptic Texts and of the Eschatological Discourse Mark 13 par.* ConBNT 1. Lund: Gleerup, 1966.

Hay, David M. *Glory at the Right Hand: Psalm 110 in Early Christianity.* SBLMS 18. Nashville: Abingdon, 1973.

———, ed. *1 and 2 Corinthians.* Vol. 2 of *Pauline Theology.* Minneapolis: Fortress, 1993.

Hays, Richard B. *The Faith of Jesus Christ: An Investigation of the Narrative Substructure of Galatians 3:1–4:11.* SBLDS 56. Chico, Calif.: Scholars Press, 1983.

———. *The Moral Vision of the New Testament: Community, Cross, New Creation. A Contemporary Introduction to New Testament Ethics.* San Francisco: Harper, 1996.

Hecht, R. "Philo and Messiah." Pages 139–68 in *Judaisms and Their Messiahs at the Turn of the Christian Era.* Ed. J. Neusner, W. S. Green, and E. S. Frerichs. Cambridge: Cambridge University Press, 1987.

Heil, John Paul. "The Double Meaning of the Narrative of Universal Judgment in Matthew 25.31–46." *JSNT* 68 (1998): 3–14.

Hellholm, David, ed. *Apocalypticism in the Ancient Mediterranean World and the Near East.* Tübingen: J.C.B. Mohr, 1983.

Hennecke, Edgar, Wilhelm Schneemelcher, and R. McL. Wilson, eds. *New Testament Apocrypha.* 2 vols. Philadelphia: Westminster, 1963–65. 2d ed. Louisville: Westminster John Knox, 1991.

Herford, R. Travers. *Christianity in Talmud and Midrash.* London: Williams & Norgate, 1903.

Himmelfarb, Martha. "A Report on Enoch in Rabbinic Literature." Pages 259–69 in vol. 1 of *SBLSP 1978*. Ed. Paul J. Achtemeier. Missoula, Mont.: Scholars Press, 1978.

Hock, Ronald F. *The Social Context of Paul's Ministry: Tentmaking and Apostleship*. Philadelphia: Fortress, 1980.

Hoffmann, Paul. *Die Toten in Christus: Eine religionsgeschichtliche und exegetische Untersuchung zur paulinischen Eschatologie*. Münster: Aschendorff, 1966.

Holleman, Joost. *Resurrection and Parousia: A Traditio-Historical Study of Paul's Eschatology in 1 Corinthians*. Leiden: Brill, 1996.

Horsley, Richard A. "Messianic Movements in Judaism." In *ABD* 4:791–97.

———. "Palestinian Jewish Groups and Their Messiahs in Late Second Temple Times." Pages 14–29 in *Judaisms and Their Messiahs at the Turn of the Christian Era*. Ed. J. Neusner, W. S. Green, and E. S. Frerichs. Cambridge: Cambridge University Press, 1987.

———. "Popular Messianic Movements around the Time of Jesus." *CBQ* 46 (1984): 471–95.

———, ed. *Paul and Empire: Religion and Power in Roman Imperial Society*. Harrisburg, Pa.: Trinity Press International, 1997.

Horsley, Richard A., and John S. Hanson. *Bandits, Prophets, and Messiahs*. Minneapolis: Winston, 1985.

Hughes, Graham. *Hebrews and Hermeneutics: The Epistle to the Hebrews as a New Testament Example of Biblical Interpretation*. SNTSMS 36. Cambridge: Cambridge University Press, 1979.

Hurst, L. D. *The Epistle to the Hebrews: Its Background of Thought*. SNTSMS 65. Cambridge: Cambridge University Press, 1990.

———. "Eschatology and 'Platonism' in the Epistle to the Hebrews." Pages 41–74 in *SBLSP 1984*. Ed. Kent Harold Richards. Chico, Calif.: Scholars Press, 1984.

Isaacs, Marie E. *Sacred Space: An Approach to the Theology of the Epistle to the Hebrews*. JSNTSup 73. Sheffield: JSOT Press, 1992.

Johnson, Luke Timothy. *The Acts of the Apostles*. SP 5. Collegeville, Minn.: Liturgical Press, 1992.

———. *The Gospel of Luke*. SP 3. Collegeville, Minn.: Liturgical Press, 1991.

———. *The Letter of James: A New Translation with Introduction and Commentary*. AB 37A. New York: Doubleday, 1995.

———. "The Social Dimensions of *Soteria* in Luke–Acts and Paul." Pages 520–36 in *SBLSP 1993*. Ed. Eugene H. Lovering Jr. Atlanta: Scholars Press, 1993.

Jonge, Marinus de. *Jesus: Stranger from Heaven and Son of God.* SBLSBS 11. Missoula, Mont.: Scholars Press, 1977.

——. "Messiah." In *ABD* 4.777–88.

Juel, Donald H. *A Master of Surprise: Mark Interpreted.* Minneapolis: Fortress, 1994.

——. *Messiah and Temple: The Trial of Jesus in the Gospel of Mark.* SBLDS 31. Missoula, Mont.: Scholars Press, 1973.

——. *Messianic Exegesis: Christological Interpretation of the Old Testament in Early Christianity.* Philadelphia: Fortress, 1988.

——. "Social Dimensions of Exegesis: The Use of Psalm 16 in Acts 2." *CBQ* 43 (1981): 543–56.

Käsemann, Ernst. "An Apologia for Primitive Christian Eschatology." Pages 169–95 in *Essays on New Testament Themes.* Philadelphia: Fortress, 1982.

Keck, Leander E., and J. Louis Martyn, eds. *Studies in Luke–Acts.* Philadelphia: Fortress, 1966.

Kelber, Werner. *The Oral and the Written Gospel: The Hermeneutics of Speaking and Writing in the Synoptic Tradition, Mark, Paul, and Q.* Philadelphia: Fortress, 1983.

Kingsbury, Jack Dean. *The Christology of Mark's Gospel.* Philadelphia: Fortress, 1983.

——. *Conflict in Luke: Jesus, Authorities, Disciples.* Minneapolis: Fortress, 1991.

——. *Matthew as Story.* 2d ed. Philadelphia: Fortress, 1988.

——. *Matthew: Structure, Christology, Kingdom.* Philadelphia: Fortress, 1975.

Klappert, Bertold. *Die Eschatologie des Hebräerbriefs.* Theologische Existenz heute 156. Ed. Karl Gerhard Steck and Georg Eicholz. Munich: Chr. Kaiser, 1969.

Klein, Martin. *"Ein vollkommenes Werk": Vollkommenheit, Gesetz und Gericht als theologische Themen des Jakobusbriefes.* BWANT 139. Stuttgart: Kohlhammer, 1995.

Koester, Helmut. "Imperial Ideology and Paul's Eschatology in 1 Thessalonians." Pages 158–66 in *Paul and Empire: Religion and Power in Roman Imperial Society.* Ed. Richard Horsley. Harrisburg, Pa.: Trinity Press International, 1997.

Krentz, Edgar. "Great Expectations, Great Choices." *The Christian Century* 113 (31, October 30, 1996): 1033.

Kurz, William S. *Reading Luke–Acts: Dynamics of Biblical Narrative.* Louisville: Westminster John Knox, 1993.

Kysar, Robert. *John, the Maverick Gospel.* Atlanta: John Knox, 1976.

Laansma, Jon. *"I Will Give You Rest": The Rest Motif in the New Testament with Special Reference to Mt 11 and Heb 3–4.* WUNT 2.98. Tübingen: J.C.B. Mohr (Paul Siebeck), 1997.

Lane, William L. *Call to Commitment: Responding to the Message of Hebrews.* Nashville: Nelson, 1985.

——. *Hebrews.* 2 vols. WBC 47A–B. Dallas: Word, 1991.

Laws, Sophie. *A Commentary on the Epistle of James.* BNTC. Peabody, Mass.: Hendrickson, 1980.

——. *In the Light of the Lamb: Imagery, Parody, and Theology in the Apocalypse of John.* Wilmington, Del.: Michael Glazier, 1988.

Layton, Bentley, ed. *The Gnostic Scriptures: A New Translation with Annotations and Introductions.* Garden City, N.Y.: Doubleday, 1987.

Lerner, Robert. "Millennialism." Pages 326–60 in *Apocalypticism in Western History and Culture.* Vol. 2 of *The Encyclopedia of Apocalypticism.* Ed. Bernard McGinn. New York: Continuum, 1998.

Lieu, Judith. *The Theology of the Johannine Epistles.* NTT. Cambridge: Cambridge University Press, 1991.

Lindars, Barnabas. *The Theology of the Letter to the Hebrews.* NTT. Cambridge: Cambridge University Press, 1991.

Lindbeck, Kristen H. "Story and Theology: Elijah's Appearances in the Babylonian Talmud." Ph.D. diss., Jewish Theological Seminary of America, 1999.

Lindsey, Hal. *The Late Great Planet Earth.* Grand Rapids: Zondervan, 1971.

Long, Thomas G. *Hebrews.* IBC. Louisville: John Knox, 1997.

Louw, Johannes P. and Eugene A. Nida, eds. *Greek-English Lexicon of the New Testament Based on Semantic Domains.* 2 vols. New York: United Bible Societies, 1988.

Luz, Ulrich. "The Final Judgment (Matt 25:31–46): An Exercise in 'History of Influence' Exegesis." Pages 271–310 in *Treasures New and Old: Contributions to Matthean Studies.* Ed. David R. Bauer and Mark Allan Powell. Atlanta: Scholars Press, 1996.

McGinn, Bernard. *Antichrist: Two Thousand Years of the Human Fascination with Evil.* San Francisco: Harper, 1994.

——. "Apocalypticism and Church Reform: 1100–1500." Pages 74–109 in *Apocalypticism in Western History and Culture.* Vol. 2 of *The Encyclopedia of Apocalypticism.* Ed. Bernard McGinn. New York: Continuum, 1998.

——. *The Calabrian Abbot: Joachim of Fiore in the History of Western Thought.* New York: Macmillan, 1985.

———. "The Last Judgment in Christian Tradition." Pages 361–401 in *Apocalypticism in Western History and Culture.* Vol. 2 of *The Encyclopedia of Apocalypticism.* Ed. Bernard McGinn. New York: Continuum, 1998.

———. *Visions of the End: Apocalyptic Traditions in the Middle Ages.* New York: Columbia University Press, 1979.

———, ed. *Apocalypticism in Western History and Culture.* Vol. 2 of *The Encyclopedia of Apocalypticism.* New York: Continuum, 1998.

Mack, Burton. *A Myth of Innocence: Mark and Christian Origins.* Philadelphia: Fortress, 1988.

MacRae, George W. "Heavenly Temple and Eschatology in the Letter to the Hebrews." *Semeia* 12 (1978): 179–99.

Maier, G., ed. *Zukunftserwartung in biblische Sicht: Beiträge zur Eschatologie.* Giessen: Brunnen, 1984.

Malherbe, Abraham J., and Wayne A. Meeks, eds. *The Future of Christology: Essays in Honor of Leander E. Keck.* Minneapolis: Fortress, 1993.

Malina, Bruce J. *The New Testament World: Insights from Cultural Anthropology.* Atlanta: John Knox, 1981.

Marcus, Joel. "Entering into the Kingly Power of God." *JBL* 107 (1988): 663–75.

———. "The Evil Inclination in the Epistle of James." *CBQ* 44 (1982): 606–21.

———. *The Way of the Lord: Christological Exegesis of the Old Testament in the Gospel of Mark.* Louisville: Westminster John Knox, 1992.

Marcus, Joel, and Marion L. Soards, eds. *Apocalyptic and the New Testament: Essays in Honor of J. Louis Martyn.* JSNTSup 24. Sheffield: JSOT Press, 1989.

Marshall, I. Howard. *The Gospel of Luke: A Commentary on the Greek Text.* NIGTC. Grand Rapids: Eerdmans, 1978.

Marshall, I. Howard, and David Peterson, eds. *Witness to the Gospel: The Theology of Acts.* Grand Rapids: Eerdmans, 1998.

Martin, Ralph P. *Mark: Evangelist and Theologian.* CEP. Grand Rapids: Zondervan, 1972.

———. *Reconciliation: A Study of Paul's Theology.* Rev. ed. Grand Rapids: Zondervan, 1990.

Martyn, J. Louis. "Apocalyptic Antinomies in Paul's Letter to the Galatians." *NTS* 31 (1985): 410–24.

———. "Epistemology at the Turn of the Ages: 2 Corinthians 5:16." Pages 269–87 in *Christian History and Interpretation: Studies Presented* to *John Knox.* Ed. William R. Farmer et al. Cambridge: Cambridge University Press, 1967.

———. *Galatians: A New Translation with Introduction and Commentary.* AB 33A. New York: Doubleday, 1997.

———. *History and Theology in the Fourth Gospel.* 2d ed. Nashville: Abingdon, 1979.

———. *Theological Issues in the Letters of Paul.* Nashville: Abingdon, 1997.

———. "We Have Found Elijah." Pages 181–219 in *Jews, Greeks, and Christians.* Ed. Robert Hamerton-Kelly and Robin Scroggs. Leiden: Brill, 1976.

Marxsen, Willi. *Mark the Evangelist.* Nashville: Abingdon, 1969.

Matera, Frank J. *Passion Narratives and Gospel Theologies: Interpreting the Synoptics Through Their Passion Stories.* TI. New York: Paulist, 1986.

———. *The Kingship of Jesus: Composition and Theology in Mark 15.* Chico, Calif.: Scholars Press, 1982.

Mayordomo-Marin, M. "Jak 5,2.3a: Zukünftiges Gericht oder gegenwärtiger Zustand?" *ZNW* 83 (1992): 132–37.

Meeks, Wayne A. "The Ethics of the Fourth Evangelist." Pages 317–26 in *Exploring the Gospel of John: In Honor of D. Moody Smith.* Ed. R. Alan Culpepper and C. Clifton Black. Louisville: Westminster John Knox, 1996.

———. "The Man from Heaven in Johannine Sectarianism." *JBL* 91 (1972): 44–72.

———. *The Prophet-King: Moses Traditions and the Johannine Christology.* NovTSup 14. Leiden: Brill, 1967.

Meier, John P. *The Roots of the Problem and the Person.* Vol. 1 of *A Marginal Jew: Rethinking the Historical Jesus.* ABRL. New York: Doubleday, 1991.

———. *Mentor, Message, and Miracles.* Vol. 2 of *A Marginal Jew: Rethinking the Historical Jesus.* ABRL. New York: Doubleday, 1994.

———. *The Vision of Matthew: Christ, Church, and Morality in the First Gospel.* New York: Paulist, 1978.

Meier, S. "2 Peter 3:3–7–An Early Jewish and Christian Response to Eschatological Skepticism." *BZ* 32 (1988): 255–57.

Metzger, Bruce M. *A Textual Commentary on the Greek New Testament.* New York: United Bible Societies, 1971.

Meyer, Paul W. " 'The Father': The Presentation of God in the Fourth Gospel." Pages 255–73 in *Exploring the Gospel of John: In Honor of D. Moody Smith.* Ed. R. Alan Culpepper and C. Clifton Black. Louisville: Westminster John Knox, 1996.

Meyers, Carol L., and Eric M. Meyers. *Zechariah 9–14: A New Translation with Introduction and Commentary.* AB 25C. New York: Doubleday, 1993.

Milhou, Alain. "Apocalypticism in Central and South American Colonialism." Pages 3–35 in *Apocalypticism in the Modern Period and the Contemporary Age.* Vol. 3 of *The Encyclopedia of Apocalypticism.* Ed. Stephen J. Stein. New York: Continuum, 1998.

Milligan, George. *St. Paul's Epistles to the Thessalonians.* New York: Macmillan, n.d.

Moessner, David P. *Lord of the Banquet: The Literary and Theological Significance of the Lukan Travel Narrative.* Minneapolis: Fortress, 1989.

Moore, A. L. *The Parousia in the New Testament.* Leiden: Brill, 1966.

Moorhead, James H. "Apocalypticism in Mainstream Protestantism, 1800 to the Present." Pages 72–107 in *Apocalypticism in the Modern Period and the Contemporary Age.* Vol. 3 of *The Encyclopedia of Apocalypticism.* Ed. Stephen J. Stein. New York: Continuum, 1998.

Mounce, R. H. *The Book of Revelation.* NICNT. Rev. ed. Grand Rapids: Eerdmans, 1998.

Mulder, Martin J., ed. *Mikra: Text, Translation, Reading and Interpretation of the Hebrew Bible in Ancient Judaism and Early Christianity.* CRINT 2:1. Minneapolis: Fortress, 1990.

Münchow, C. *Ethik und Eschatologie: Ein Beitrag zum Verständnis der frühjüdischen Apokalyptik mit einem Ausblick auf das Neue Testament.* Göttingen: Vandenhoeck & Ruprecht, 1981.

Neugebauer, J. *Die eschatologische Aussagen in den johanneischen Abschiedsreden: Eine Untersuchung zu Johannes 13–17.* BWANT 140. Stuttgart: Kohlhammer, 1995.

Neusner, Jacob. "Mishnah and Messiah." Pages 265–82 in *Judaisms and Their Messiahs at the Turn of the Christian Era.* Ed. J. Neusner, W. S. Green, and E. S. Frerichs. Cambridge: Cambridge University Press, 1987.

Neusner, J., W. S. Green, and E. S. Frerichs, eds. *Judaisms and Their Messiahs at the Turn of the Christian Era.* Cambridge: Cambridge University Press, 1987.

Neyrey, Jerome H. *2 Jude, Peter: A New Translation with Introduction and Commentary.* AB 37C. New York: Doubleday, 1993.

Ngayihembako, Samuel. *Les Temps de la Fin: Approche exégétique de l'eschatologie du Nouveau Testament.* Le Monde de la Bible 29. Geneva: Labor et Fides, 1994.

Nicholson, Godfrey C. *Death as Departure: The Johannine Descent-Ascent Schema.* SBLDS 63. Chico, Calif.: Scholars Press, 1983.

Nickelsburg, G. W. E. "Resurrection." In *ABD* 5.684–91.

Nolland, J. "Salvation-History and Eschatology." Pages 63–81 in *Witness to the Gospel: The Theology of Acts.* Ed. I. Howard Marshall and David Peterson. Grand Rapids: Eerdmans, 1998.

O'Leary, Stephen D. "Apocalypticism in American Popular Culture: From the Dawn of the Nuclear Age to the End of the American Century." Pages 392–426 in *Apocalypticism in the Modern Period and the Contemporary Age.* Vol. 3 of *The Encyclopedia of Apocalypticism.* Ed. Stephen J. Stein. New York: Continuum, 1998.

——. *Arguing the Apocalypse: A Theory of Millennial Rhetoric.* New York: Oxford University Press, 1994.

Olster, David. "Byzantine Apocalypses." Pages 48–73 in *Apocalypticism in Western History and Culture.* Vol. 2 of *The Encyclopedia of Apocalypticism.* Ed. Bernard McGinn. New York: Continuum, 1998.

Orton, David E. *The Understanding Scribe: Matthew and the Apocalyptic Ideal.* JSNTSup 25. Sheffield: Sheffield Academic Press, 1989.

Osborne, E. *Tertullian: First Theologian of the West.* Cambridge: Cambridge University Press, 1997.

Ottati, Douglas F. *Hopeful Realism: Reclaiming the Poetry of Theology.* Cleveland: Pilgrim, 1999.

Overman, J. Andrew. *Matthew's Gospel and Formative Judaism: The Social World of the Matthean Community.* Minneapolis: Fortress, 1990.

Pearson, Birger. *The Pneumatikos-Psychikos Terminology in 1 Corinthians.* Missoula, Mont.: Scholars Press, 1973.

Penner, Todd C. *The Epistle of James and Eschatology: Re-reading an Ancient Christian Letter.* JSNTSup 121. Sheffield: Sheffield Academic Press, 1996.

Perkins, Pheme. *First and Second Peter, James, and Jude.* IBC. Louisville: John Knox, 1995.

Petersen, Norman R. *Literary Criticism for New Testament Critics.* GBS. Philadelphia: Fortress, 1978.

——. *Rediscovering Paul: Philemon and the Sociology of Paul's Narrative World.* Philadelphia: Fortress, 1985.

Peterson, David. *Hebrews and Perfection: An Examination of the Concept of Perfection in the "Epistle to the Hebrews."* SNTSMS 47. Cambridge: Cambridge University Press, 1982.

Peterson, Erik. "Die Einholung des Kyrios (1 Thess IV, 17)." *ZST* 7 (1930): 682–702.

Plank, Karl A. *Paul and the Irony of Affliction.* SBLSS. Atlanta: Scholars Press, 1987.

Plevnik, Joseph. *Paul and the Parousia: An Exegetical and Theological Investigation.* Peabody, Mass.: Hendrickson, 1997.

Ravitzky, Aviezer. *Messianism, Zionism, and Jewish Religious Radicalism.* Trans. Michael Swirksy and Jonathan Chipman. Chicago: University of Chicago Press, 1996.

Reiser, Marius. *Jesus and Judgment: The Eschatological Proclamation in Its Jewish Context.* Trans. Linda M. Maloney. Minneapolis: Fortress, 1997.

Rensberger, David. *Johannine Faith and Liberating Community.* Philadelphia: Westminster, 1988.

Rhoads, David, and Donald Michie. *Mark as Story: An Introduction to the Narrative of a Gospel.* Philadelphia: Fortress, 1982.

Richardson, Cyril, ed. *Early Christian Fathers.* Philadelphia: Westminster, 1953.

Riesner, R. "Der zweite Petrus-Brief und die Eschatologie." Pages 124–43 in *Zukunftserwartung in biblische Sicht: Beiträge zur Eschatologie.* Ed. G. Maier. Giessen: Brunnen, 1984.

Ringe, Sharon H. *Jesus, Liberation, and the Biblical Jubilee: Images for Ethics and Christology.* OBT. Philadelphia: Fortress, 1985.

Robbins, Vernon K. *Jesus the Teacher: A Socio-Rhetorical Interpretation of Mark.* Philadelphia: Fortress, 1984.

Robinson, James M., ed. *The Nag Hammadi Library in English.* New York: Harper & Row, 1977.

Robinson, William. "The Eschatology of the Epistle to the Hebrews: A Study in the Christian Doctrine of Hope." *Encounter* 22 (1961): 37–51.

Roloff, Jürgen. *The Revelation of John: A Continental Commentary.* Minneapolis: Fortress, 1993.

Rosconi, Roberto. "Antichrist and Antichrists." Pages 287–325 in *Apocalypticism in Western History and Culture.* Vol. 2 of *The Encyclopedia of Apocalypticism.* Ed. Bernard McGinn. New York: Continuum, 1998.

Rudolph, Kurt. *Gnosis: The Nature and History of an Ancient Religion.* Edinburgh: T&T Clark, 1983.

Saldarini, Anthony J. *The Fathers according to Rabbi Nathan.* SJLA 11. Leiden: Brill, 1975.

Sampley, J. Paul. *Walking between the Times: Paul's Moral Reasoning.* Minneapolis: Fortress, 1991.

Sanders, E. P. *The Historical Figure of Jesus.* London: Penguin, 1993.

———. *Jesus and Judaism.* London: SCM, 1985.

———. *Paul and Palestinian Judaism.* Philadelphia: Fortress, 1977.

Schnackenburg, Rudolf. *The Gospel according to St. John.* 3 vols. Vol. 1., New York: Herder & Herder, 1968. Reprint, New York: Crossroad, 1980. Vols. 2 and 3, New York: Crossroad, 1980–82.

Schrage, Wolfgang. *The Ethics of the New Testament.* Trans. David E. Green. Philadelphia: Fortress, 1988.

Schürer, Emil, Geza Vermes, and Fergus Millar. *The History of the Jewish People in the Age of Jesus Christ.* 3 vols. Edinburgh: T&T Clark, 1973–87.

Schüssler Fiorenza, Elisabeth. *The Book of Revelation: Justice and Judgment.* Philadelphia: Fortress, 1985.

Schweitzer, Albert. *The Mystery of the Kingdom of God.* Trans. Walter Lowrie. New York: Dodd, Mead, 1914 (orig. 1901).

———. *The Mysticism of Paul the Apostle.* Trans. William Montgomery. New York: Macmillan, 1955 (ET orig. 1931).

———. *The Quest of the Historical Jesus.* New York: Macmillan, 1968 (ET orig. 1910).

Segal, Alan. *Rebecca's Children: Judaism and Christianity in the Roman World.* Cambridge: Harvard University Press, 1986.

Segal, S. *Elijah: A Study in Jewish Folklore.* New York: Behrman's, 1935.

Sellin, G. *Der Streit um die Auferstehung der Toten: Eine religionsgeschichtliche und exegetische Untersuchung von 1 Korinther 15.* FRLANT 138. Göttingen: Vandenhoeck & Ruprecht, 1986.

Senior, Donald. *The Gospel of Matthew.* ANTC. Nashville: Abingdon, 1998.

———. *Matthew.* IBT. Nashville: Abingdon, 1997.

———. *The Passion of Jesus in the Gospel of Mark.* Wilmington, Del.: Glazier, 1984.

———. *The Passion of Jesus in the Gospel of Matthew.* Wilmington, Del.: Glazier, 1985.

Setzer, Claudia J. *Jewish Responses to Early Christians: History and Polemics, 30–150 C.E.* Minneapolis: Augsburg Fortress, 1994.

———. "You Invent a Christ!" *USQR* 44 (1991): 315–28.

Sharot, Stephen. *Messianism, Mysticism, and Magic.* Chapel Hill: University of North Carolina Press, 1982.

———. "Religious Zionism in Israel–A Return to Messianism." Pages 225–37 in *Messianism, Mysticism, and Magic.* Chapel Hill: University of North Carolina Press, 1982.

Siker, Jeffrey S. *Disinheriting the Jews: Abraham in Early Christian Controversy.* Louisville: Westminster John Knox, 1991.

Silva, Moisés. "Perfection and Eschatology in Hebrews." *WTJ* 38 (1976): 60–71.

Sim, David C. *Apocalyptic Eschatology in the Gospel of Matthew.* SNTSMS 88. Cambridge: Cambridge University Press, 1996.

Smith, D. Moody. *First, Second, and Third John.* IBC. Louisville: John Knox, 1991.

———. *John among the Gospels: The Relationship in Twentieth-Century Research.* Minneapolis: Fortress, 1992.

Smolinski, Reiner. "Apocalypticism in Colonial North America." Pages 36–71 in *Apocalypticism in the Modern Period and the Contemporary Age.* Vol. 3 of *The Encyclopedia of Apocalypticism.* Ed. Stephen J. Stein. New York: Continuum, 1998.

Smylie, James H. "A New Heaven and New Earth: Uses of the Millennium in American Religious History." *Int* 53 (1999): 143–57.

Soards, Marion L. *The Speeches in Luke–Acts: Their Content, Context, and Concerns.* Louisville: Westminster John Knox, 1994.

Spicq, Ceslas. "Le philonisme de l'Épître aux Hébreux." *RB* 56 (1949): 542–72; *RB* 57 (1950): 212–42.

Spivey, Robert A., and D. Moody Smith. *Anatomy of the New Testament.* 4th ed. New York: Macmillan, 1988.

Stanton, Graham N. *A Gospel for a New People: Studies in Matthew.* Edinburgh: T&T Clark, 1992.

Stein, Stephen J. "Apocalypticism Outside the Mainstream in the United States." Pages 108–39 in *Apocalypticism in the Modern Period and the Contemporary Age.* Vol. 3 of *The Encyclopedia of Apocalypticism.* Ed. Stephen J. Stein. New York: Continuum, 1998.

———, ed. *The Encyclopedia of Apocalypticism.* Vol. 3: *Apocalypticism in the Modern Period and the Contemporary Age.* New York: Continuum, 1998.

Stone, Michael E., and John Strugnell. *The Books of Elijah: Parts 1 and 2.* SBL Texts and Translations 18. Pseudepigrapha 8. Missoula, Mont.: Scholars Press, 1979.

Strecker, Georg. *The Johannine Letters: A Commentary on 1, 2, and 3 John.* Hermeneia. Minneapolis: Fortress, 1996.

Talbert, Charles H. "II Peter and the Delay of the Parousia." *VC* 20 (1966): 137–45.

———. *Learning through Suffering: The Educational Value of Suffering in the New Testament and in Its Milieu.* ZSNT. Collegeville, Minn.: Liturgical Press, 1991.

———. ed. *Perspectives on First Peter.* SSS 9. Macon, Ga.: Mercer University Press, 1986.

Tannehill, Robert C. "Israel in Luke–Acts: A Tragic Story." *JBL* 104 (1985): 69–85.

——. *Luke.* ANTC. Nashville: Abingdon, 1996.

——. *The Narrative Unity of Luke–Acts.* 2 vols. FF. Philadelphia and Minneapolis: Fortress, 1986–90.

Thiede, Carsten P. "A Pagan Reader of 2 Peter: Cosmic Conflagration in 2 Peter 3 and the *Octavius* of Minucius Felix." *JSNT* 26 (1986): 79–96.

Thompson, Leonard. *The Book of Revelation: Apocalypse and Empire.* Oxford: Oxford University Press, 1990.

Tolbert, Mary Ann. *Sowing the Gospel: Mark's World in Literary-Historical Perspective.* Minneapolis: Fortress, 1989.

Toussaint, Stanley D. "The Eschatology of the Warning Passages in the Book of Hebrews." *Grace Theological Journal* 3 (1982): 67–80.

Tracy, David. *The Analogical Imagination: Christian Theology and the Culture of Pluralism.* New York: Crossroad, 1981.

Tuckett, Christopher M., ed. *The Messianic Secret.* IRT 1. Philadelphia: Fortress, 1983.

Tyson, Joseph B. *Images of Judaism in Luke–Acts.* Columbia: University of South Carolina Press, 1992.

VanderKam, James C. *Enoch: A Man for All Generations.* SPOT. Columbia: University of South Carolina Press, 1995.

——. "Messianism and Apocalypticism." Pages 193–228 in *The Origins of Apocalypticism in Judaism and Christianity.* Vol. 1 of *The Encyclopedia of Apocalypticism.* Ed. John J. Collins. New York: Continuum, 1998.

Vögtle, Anton. "Die Parusie- und Gerichtsapologetik 2 P 3." Pages 121–42 in *Das Neue Testament und die Zukunft des Kosmos.* Düsseldorf: Patmos, 1970.

Wall, Robert W. "James as Apocalyptic Paraenesis." *RestQ* 32 (1990): 11–22.

Watson, Duane. F. *Invention, Arrangement, and Style: Rhetorical Criticism of Jude and 2 Peter.* SBLDS 104. Atlanta: Scholars Press, 1988.

Weber, Kathleen. "The Events of the End of the Age in Matthew." Ph.D. diss., Catholic University of America, 1994.

Weber, Timothy P. *Living in the Shadow of the Second Coming: American Premillennialism, 1875–1982, With a New Preface.* New York: Oxford University Press, 1987.

Weiss, Johannes. *Jesus' Proclamation of the Kingdom of God.* Philadelphia: Fortress, 1971 (German orig. 1892).

Werner, Martin. *The Formation of Christian Doctrine: An Historical Study of Its Problems.* New York: Harper & Brothers, 1957.

Winokur, J. "The Settlement." *Natural History* 105 (December 1996–January 1997): 38–49.

Wright, N. T. *The Climax of the Covenant: Christ and the Law in Pauline Theology.* Minneapolis: Fortress, 1991.

———. *Jesus and the Victory of God.* Minneapolis: Fortress, 1996.

———. *The New Testament and the People of God.* Minneapolis: Fortress, 1992.

Zager, Werner. *Gottesherrschaft und Endgericht in der Verkündigung Jesu: Eine Untersuchung zur markinischen Jesusüberlieferung einschließlich der Q-Parallelen.* BZNW 82. Berlin: Walter de Gruyter, 1996.

INDEX OF MODERN AUTHORS

INDEX OF ANCIENT SOURCES